First World War
and Army of Occupation
War Diary
France, Belgium and Germany

41 DIVISION
Divisional Troops
Royal Army Service Corps
298 Company ASC
3 May 1916 - 31 October 1919

WO95/2631/5

The Naval & Military Press Ltd
www.nmarchive.com
Published in association with The National Archives

Published by

The Naval & Military Press Ltd

Unit 10 Ridgewood Industrial Park,

Uckfield, East Sussex,

TN22 5QE England

Tel: +44 (0) 1825 749494

www.naval-military-press.com

www.nmarchive.com

This diary has been reprinted in facsimile from the original. Any imperfections are inevitably reproduced and the quality may fall short of modern type and cartographic standards.

© Crown Copyright
Images reproduced by permission of The National Archives, London, England, 2015.

Contents

Document type	Place/Title	Date From	Date To
Heading	WO95/2631/5 298 Coy ASC		
Heading	BEF 41 Div Train 298 Coy ASC 1916 May-1917 Oct 1918 Mar-1919 Oct. Italy 1917 Nov-1918 Feb		
War Diary	Aldershot	03/05/1916	03/05/1916
War Diary	Havre	04/05/1916	05/05/1916
War Diary	Strazeele	06/05/1916	01/06/1916
War Diary	La Creche	02/06/1916	16/08/1916
War Diary	Fontaine	17/08/1916	22/08/1916
War Diary	Long	23/08/1916	05/09/1916
War Diary	Flixecourt	05/09/1916	05/09/1916
War Diary	Longpre	06/09/1916	06/09/1916
War Diary	Bure	07/09/1916	10/09/1916
War Diary	Albert	11/09/1916	17/09/1916
War Diary	Bure	18/09/1916	28/09/1916
War Diary	Becordel	29/09/1916	12/10/1916
War Diary	Bure	13/10/1916	15/10/1916
War Diary	Argoeuves	16/10/1916	16/10/1916
War Diary	Grandsart	17/10/1916	19/10/1916
War Diary	Godewearveldt	20/10/1916	21/10/1916
War Diary	Reninghelst	22/10/1916	06/04/1917
Miscellaneous	On March Route	07/04/1917	08/04/1917
War Diary	Salperwick	09/04/1917	23/04/1917
War Diary	Noordpeene	24/04/1917	24/04/1917
War Diary	Steenvord	25/04/1917	25/04/1917
War Diary	Reninghelst	26/04/1917	12/06/1917
War Diary	R.E. Dump Oudedum	13/06/1917	15/06/1917
War Diary	Outerdum	16/06/1917	21/06/1917
War Diary	C.28. M.3.b.8.8.	22/06/1917	22/06/1917
War Diary	C.28. M.4.c.	23/06/1917	30/06/1917
War Diary	Thieushouk	01/07/1917	21/07/1917
War Diary	M.11.c.35.80	22/07/1917	31/07/1917
War Diary	M.11.c.35.80 Canada Corner	01/08/1917	04/08/1917
War Diary	Canada Corner	05/08/1917	12/08/1917
War Diary	X.4.A.5.6. Thieshouck	13/08/1917	13/08/1917
War Diary	Thieshouck	14/08/1917	20/08/1917
War Diary	E.5.c.6.0. Sheet D N.E. Esquerdes.	20/08/1917	25/08/1917
War Diary	Esquerdes	26/08/1917	13/09/1917
War Diary	Staple	14/09/1917	14/09/1917
War Diary	X.4.A.7.6	15/09/1917	16/09/1917
War Diary	Huron Camp	17/09/1917	19/09/1917
War Diary	Lion Camp	20/09/1917	27/09/1917
War Diary	D.3.c.6.5	28/09/1917	30/09/1917
War Diary	Sheet 19 D.3.C.6.5	01/10/1917	03/10/1917
War Diary	D.3.c.6.5	04/10/1917	04/10/1917
War Diary	W.18.c.5.7.	05/10/1917	31/10/1917
War Diary	Camposampiero	01/03/1918	04/03/1918
War Diary	St. Michel	05/03/1918	08/03/1918
War Diary	Ivergny	09/03/1918	19/03/1918
War Diary	Marieux	20/03/1918	20/03/1918
War Diary	Bouzincourt	21/03/1918	21/03/1918

War Diary	Acuiet-Le-Petit.	22/03/1918	24/03/1918
War Diary	St. Amand	25/03/1918	25/03/1918
War Diary	Nr. Baulleilmont	26/03/1918	27/03/1918
War Diary	Saulty	28/03/1918	28/03/1918
War Diary	Authie	29/03/1918	31/03/1918
War Diary	Thievres.	01/04/1918	02/04/1918
War Diary	(Petit. Houvin)	03/04/1918	03/04/1918
War Diary	Eecke	04/04/1918	07/04/1918
War Diary	Sheet 28. G.4.DA.3.0	08/04/1918	09/04/1918
War Diary	Sheet 28. G.4.A.3.0	10/04/1918	13/04/1918
War Diary	Sheet 28. G.4.A.A.3.0	14/04/1918	25/04/1918
War Diary	A.16.A.8.4.	26/04/1918	26/04/1918
War Diary	F.28.b.4.0	27/04/1918	28/04/1918
War Diary	Sheet 27. F.28.b.4.0.	29/04/1918	30/04/1918
War Diary	Sheet 27. F.21.c.1.1.	01/05/1918	02/06/1918
War Diary	Sheet 27. B.20.B.1.8.	03/06/1918	03/06/1918
War Diary	Sheet 27. G.33.D.0.3.	04/06/1918	09/06/1918
War Diary	St. Martin-Au-Laert.	10/06/1918	24/06/1918
War Diary	Kinderbelk.	25/06/1918	25/06/1918
War Diary	Sheet. 27. H.23.B.5.0	26/06/1918	29/06/1918
War Diary	Sheet. 27. K.21.D.7.4.	30/06/1918	28/08/1918
War Diary	Renescure	29/08/1918	29/08/1918
War Diary	St. Martin Au Leaurt	30/08/1918	31/08/1918
War Diary	Zermezeele	01/09/1918	01/09/1918
War Diary	Sheet 27 K.18.c.9.7.	02/09/1918	02/09/1918
War Diary	Sheet 27. K.17.b.7.1.	03/09/1918	06/09/1918
War Diary	Sheet. 27. L.23.a.5.2	07/09/1918	16/09/1918
War Diary	L.33. Central	17/09/1918	27/09/1918
War Diary	Brandhoek	28/09/1918	30/09/1918
War Diary	H.24.c.3.4.	01/10/1918	13/10/1918
War Diary	Sht. 28. I.9.c. Central	14/10/1918	15/10/1918
War Diary	K.17.B.8.2.	16/10/1918	18/10/1918
War Diary	Sht. 29. G.20.c.	19/10/1918	20/10/1918
War Diary	G.29.b.5.2.	21/10/1918	23/10/1918
War Diary	Sheet. 29. G.29.b.5.2.	24/10/1918	28/10/1918
War Diary	H.32.a.10.2	29/10/1918	31/10/1918
War Diary	Sheet 29. H.32.a.10.2	01/11/1918	01/11/1918
War Diary	Sheet 29 H.34.c.6.0.	02/11/1918	04/11/1918
War Diary	Sheet 29. I.32.c.3.8	05/11/1918	06/11/1918
War Diary	Sheet 29. I.9.a.7.7	07/11/1918	09/11/1918
War Diary	Sheet 29. J.33.a.9.0	10/11/1918	10/11/1918
War Diary	Sheet. 30. M.22.c	11/11/1918	13/11/1918
War Diary	Sheet. 30. N.23.a.9.9.	14/11/1918	17/11/1918
War Diary	Gammerages	18/11/1918	19/11/1918
War Diary	Les. Deux Acren	20/11/1918	11/12/1918
War Diary	St. Pierre Capelle	12/12/1918	12/12/1918
War Diary	Lembecq.	13/12/1918	13/12/1918
War Diary	Mont St. Pont	14/12/1918	15/12/1918
War Diary	Houtain-Le-Val	16/12/1918	16/12/1918
War Diary	Sombreffe.	17/12/1918	17/12/1918
War Diary	Bothey	18/12/1918	18/12/1918
War Diary	Leuze	19/12/1918	19/12/1918
War Diary	Pitet	20/12/1918	21/12/1918
War Diary	Near Huy. on Huy-Ampsin Main Road.	22/12/1918	11/01/1919
War Diary	Wahn Germany	12/01/1919	29/01/1919
War Diary	Heumar. (Germany).	30/01/1919	13/05/1919

War Diary	Heumar Cologne Germany	14/05/1919	17/05/1919
War Diary	Heumar Cologne	18/05/1919	22/05/1919
War Diary	Heumar Germany	23/05/1919	05/06/1919
War Diary	Heumar Cologne	06/06/1919	10/06/1919
War Diary	Heumar Germany	11/06/1919	17/06/1919
War Diary	Engelskirchen.	18/06/1919	29/06/1919
War Diary	Heumar	30/06/1919	30/06/1919
War Diary	Heumar Cologne	01/07/1919	16/08/1919
War Diary	Heumar	17/08/1919	31/08/1919
War Diary	Siegburg	01/09/1919	31/10/1919

WO95/2631/5

298 Coy ASC

BEF

41 DIV TRAIN

298 Coy ASC

1916 MAY — 1917 OCT
1918 MAR — 1919 OCT

~~IN~~ ITALY 1917 NOV — 1918 FEB

Army Form C. 2118.

WAR DIARY
INTELLIGENCE SUMMARY

(Erase heading not required.)

No 398 Coy A.S.C.
4th Div. VCRI

Instructions regarding War Diaries and Intelligence Summaries are contained in F. S. Regs., Part II. and the Staff Manual respectively. Title Pages will be prepared in manuscript.

Place	Date	Hour	Summary of Events and Information	Remarks and references to Appendices
Aldershot	3/5/16	2 p.m.	H.Q'rs of Company marched out of Mytchett Hutments & entrained with HQ'rs 123 Bde. & Signal Section R.E, arriving Southampton at 6 p.m. (Baggage & Supply wagons entrained with respective units.) Embarked on S.S. Archimedes	
HAVRE	4/5/16	2 pm	Arrived & disembarked. No casualties on voyage. Proceeded to No 1 Rest Camp & remained there for night.	
HAVRE	5/5/16	10.30 a.m.	Marched out of No 1 Rest Camp to Gare des Marchandises where unit entrained at 12 noon.	
STRAZEELE	6/5/16		Arrived GODEWAERSVELDE STN. at 12.30 p.m. & detrained. Moved into billets at STRAZEELE village. Lt Ladd (S.O) having proceeded in advance & secured a week in advance of the Company, rejoined on this date.	
" "	7/5/16		Withdrew Baggage & Supply vehicles from units of 123 Bde. In addition Baggage & Supply wagons of 19th Middlesex (Pioneers) & Supply wagons of 233 2nd Coy RE & 138th F. Ambc. were attached. Also trailers as follows joined on 8/5:	
" "	8/5/16		Loaders joined attached :- 5 Infantry Batts - 1 N.C.O. + 4 men each. HQ'rs 123 Bde, 138th F.Amb., 233 2nd Coy. R.E. 1 N.C.O + 1 man each = 31 N.C.O's & men in all. Supply Section refilled at MERRIS at 3 p.m. & delivered Supplies to units.	
" "	9/5/16		Supply Section refilled at MERRIS at 3 pm.	
" "	10/5/16		" " " " " "	

WAR DIARY
or
INTELLIGENCE SUMMARY

(Erase heading not required.)

Army Form C. 2118.

Place	Date	Hour	Summary of Events and Information	Remarks and references to Appendices
STRAZEELE	11/5/16			
"	12/5/16		Supply Section refilled at STRAZEELE at 9 a.m. T/36247 D/Smith G. evacuated 139th F¹ Ambulance.	
"	13/5/16		Supply Section refilled at STRAZEELE at 9 a.m.	
"	14/5/16		"	
"	15.5.16		Supply Section refilled at STRAZEELE at 9 a.m. Supply & equipment of 19th Middlesex (Pioneers) & 233 Field Co. R.E. transferred to 2 Coy. 41 Div. Train.	
"	16.5.16		Supply Section refilled at STRAZEELE at 9 a.m.	
"	17.5.16		Supply Section refilled at STRAZEELE at 9 a.m.	
"	18.5.16		1.30 a.m. Company stood to until gunshell orders by 123 A.T. H.Q. in consequence of gas attack on Ypres/Sart. Dismissed 2.15 a.m. Supply Section refilled at 9 a.m.	
"	19.5.16		Supply Section refilled at STRAZEELE at 9 a.m. a/Sgt Robertson withdrawn from 139th Field Ambulance rejoined this Company on instruction from A.C. Train now sent to Head- Quarters Coy for disposal.	S.M. Rutter Capt OC 3 Coy 41 Div Train

Army Form C. 2118.

WAR DIARY
or
INTELLIGENCE SUMMARY

(Erase heading not required.)

Instructions regarding War Diaries and Intelligence Summaries are contained in F. S. Regs., Part II. and the Staff Manual respectively. Title Pages will be prepared in manuscript.

Place	Date 1916 May.	Hour	Summary of Events and Information	Remarks and references to Appendices
STRAZEELE	20th		Supply Section refilled at STRAZEELE at 10 a.m. 1 Rtg Horse + Mule returned to the Coy by 139th Fd Ambulance. Sent mk HdQrs Coy for disposal. Also 1 set N.C.O. harness + set mule harness.	
"	21st		Supply Section refilled at STRAZEELE at 10 a.m.	
"	22nd		" "	
"	23rd		" "	
"	25 "		" "	
"	26 "		Supply Section refilled at STRAZEELE at 10 a.m. Supply wagons as follows attached from HQrs Coy:- Signal Coy 1. Motor Ref. Sec. 1. Sanitary Sect. 1. Lth. Cyclist Coy 1. F.S.wagon with 4 Gns. 2 G.S. wgns. D.A.C. 9 wgns. Also 10 RCO's + new fittgs Coy (which some Coy moved in the same to BRUSLE at LA CRECHE?). Baggage wgns of 10 R.W.Kents + 2 DoT D.L.I. sent to unit.	
"	27 "		Supply Section refilled at STRAZEELE at 10 a.m. Remainder of Baggage wagons Sent to units. 4 Supply wagons of D.A.C. Sent to unit. Also supply wagon & 1 Frwk Cart, the D.S.Syce, wagon & 1 Rider returned from unit. Kit & Sec.n for Dept. Coy & 2 HD horses. Supply wagon of Machine Gun Coy sent to 123 BDE HQrs.	
"	28 "		Remainder of Supply wagons & 1 wagon of D.T. 5 DAC. Supply Section refilled at STRAZEELE at 10 a.m. Remainder of Supply wagons & escort to their units.	

2449 Wt. W14957/Mg0 750,000 1/16 J.B.C. & A. Forms/C.2118/12.

Army Form C. 2118.

WAR DIARY
or
INTELLIGENCE SUMMARY
(Erase heading not required.)

Instructions regarding War Diaries and Intelligence Summaries are contained in F. S. Regs., Part II. and the Staff Manual respectively. Title Pages will be prepared in manuscript.

Place	Date	Hour	Summary of Events and Information	Remarks and references to Appendices
STRAZEELE	May 1918 29th		Remainder of Supply Section refilled at STRAZEELE at 10 a.m. Supply wagon of 23rd Middlesex & 11th R.W. Surrey delivered Supplies & then were attacked to N? 2 Coy. The six Supply wagons of Divisional Troops which were attached to this Coy. on 26th went to N?5 & 7th Coy. after delivering Supplies. Capt Lead (S.O.) & Lt Andrew (Transport Offr) proceeded to LA CRÈCHE together with Supply Section.	
	30.		Supply Section refilled at LA CRÈCHE. @ H.Q? of Coy at STRAZEELE.	
	31.		" " " " " STRAZEELE. Hq? of Coy at STRAZEELE.	

E. M. Ruttle Capt
o/c 3 Coy. Train
41st Divl. Train

Army Form C. 2118.

WAR DIARY
or
INTELLIGENCE SUMMARY

(Erase heading not required.)

Instructions regarding War Diaries and Intelligence Summaries are contained in F. S. Regs., Part II. and the Staff Manual respectively. Title Pages will be prepared in manuscript.

Place	Date 1916	Hour	Summary of Events and Information	Remarks and references to Appendices
	June			
STRAZELLE	1st		Headquarters of Company with Capt. Rule & Lt. Pulleyne moved to billets vacated by No 2 Coy at LA CRÈCHE. Supply Section army supplies in billet at STEENWERCK Station direct from railway truck & made a detailed issue at dumps near by. Baggage wagons of 17.3 Inf. Bde. & 4 Baggage wagons of 18.7 A. Bde. joined the Coy.	
LA CRECHE	2nd		Whole Coy moved into billets vacated by No 2 Coy, 5th Divisional Train at LA CRECHE. Supply Section refilled at STEENWERCK.	
"	3rd		Supply Section refilled at STEENWERCK. One baggage wagon without horse sent to 10th R.W.Kent, 21st D.L.I., 23rd Middlesex for fatigue work, horses to take supplies by regiment.	
"	4th		Supply Section refilled at STEENWERCK. 1 baggage wagon without horse sent to 11th R.W. Surrey.	
"	5th		Supply Section refilled at STEENWERCK. 2 baggage wagons without horse sent to Hd. Bde. R.F.A.	

Sm. Rulin Capt
O.C. 3 Coy. Train,
4th. Div. Train.

Army Form C. 2118.

WAR DIARY
—or—
INTELLIGENCE SUMMARY

(Erase heading not required.)

Instructions regarding War Diaries and Intelligence Summaries are contained in F. S. Regs., Part II. and the Staff Manual respectively. Title Pages will be prepared in manuscript.

Place	Date 1916	Hour	Summary of Events and Information	Remarks and references to Appendices
LA CRECHE	June 6th		Supply Section refilled at STEENWERCK.	
"	7th		"	
"	8th		"	
"	9th		"	
"	10th		"	
"	11th		"	
"	12		"	
"	13		"	
"	14		"	
"	15		"	

E. W. Poulton Capt.
O. C. 3 Cor{n} Train
4th Aug{.} 20

Army Form C. 2118.

WAR DIARY
or
INTELLIGENCE SUMMARY

(Erase heading not required.)

Instructions regarding War Diaries and Intelligence Summaries are contained in F. S. Regs., Part II. and the Staff Manual respectively. Title Pages will be prepared in manuscript.

Place	Date 1916	Hour	Summary of Events and Information	Remarks and references to Appendices
LA CRECHE E.16.a.	June 17th		Supply Section refilled at STEENWERCK.	
" "	18th		Supply Section refilled at STEENWERCK. Baggage louden returns to unit as follows:— 1st BDE RFA. 5 Bow.t 1 Gun.; 2 D.L.I. 23rd Midd.x: 1 L.Cpl & 2 Ptes.; 115 Rn. Surrey. 3 Ptes. 1 Cpl & 2 Ptes.; Rn. Kents. 3 Ptes.	
" "	19th		Supply Section refilled at STEENWERCK.	
" "	20th		" " " "	
" "	21st		" " " " Company inspected in full marching order by O.C. Train at 6 p.m.	

Sgn. Ruben Cuttle
Capt.
O/C 3Coy 5th Div. Train

Army Form C. 2118.

WAR DIARY
INTELLIGENCE SUMMARY
(Erase heading not required.)

Instructions regarding War Diaries and Intelligence Summaries are contained in F. S. Regs., Part II. and the Staff Manual respectively. Title Pages will be prepared in manuscript.

Place	Date	Hour	Summary of Events and Information	Remarks and references to Appendices
LA CRÈCHE	June 22nd		Supply Section refilled at STEENWERCK.	
"	23rd		"	
"	24th		N°T/4/057,660 D.r Howell T. evacuated to hospital N°T/2276 A/ce Cpl. Leatheale S.S. shock off his strength.	
"	25th		Supply Section refilled at STEENWERCK.	
"	26th		"	
"	27th		"	
"	28th		"	
"	29th		Supply Section refilled at STEENWERCK in morning at 8.45 am & & forward to units. Second refilling at 3pm, supplies being afterwards delivered to units.	
"	30th		Supply Section drew supplies from Rail head at 7.20 am & delivered to 41st Divisional Supply Column at FLETRE	
NOTE.			During this month the Baggage Section was employed daily in delivering G.M. Rations Canteen stores & & refreshments to units.	

G.M. Butler Capt.
O.C. 3 Coy 41[?] D[?]

2449 Wt. W14957/M90 750,000 1/16 J.B.C. & A. (Forms/C.2118/2.

Army Form C. 2118.

WAR DIARY
or
INTELLIGENCE SUMMARY
(Erase heading not required.)

Instructions regarding War Diaries and Intelligence Summaries are contained in F.S. Regs., Part II. and the Staff Manual respectively. Title Pages will be prepared in manuscript.

Place	Date 1916	Hour	Summary of Events and Information	Remarks and references to Appendices
La Clide	July 1		Supply section rifilled at Steenwerck, a Farrier Drawn & Wheeler Drawn attached for Horses.	
"	2		Supply section refilled at Steenwerck.	
"	3		" " " "	
"	4		" " " "	
"	5		A.D.M.S. reconfirms to 139th Field Ambt.	
"	6		reflour carnels.	
"	7		Supply section refilled at Steenwerck. Our Drawn & Pr Saddle drawn formed from Pr Box Horse transport dept. Captain Rutter temporarily attached to Div. Hosp.	
"	8		as veterinary to D.A.Q.M.G.	
"	9		Supply section refilled at Steenwerck	
"	10		" " " "	
"	11		" " " "	
"	12		" " " "	
"	13		" " " " at 6 am marched 7 am as usual.	
"	14		" " " " to Sarril & evacuated.	
"	15		" " " "	
"	16		Officer " Inspection of camp and horse lines by Commanding	

J.V. Fleming Capt.
3rd Wessex FA

WAR DIARY
or
INTELLIGENCE SUMMARY

Army Form C. 2118.

Place	Date 1916	Hour	Summary of Events and Information	Remarks and references to Appendices
La Clef	Feb 17		Supply section of coy refilled at Steenwerck.	
	18		One S.S. wagon & double set of harness received from 123rd Bde Machine Gun coy. Coy been under letter attachment.	
	19		Supply section refilled at Steenwerck.	
	20		" " " "	
	21		" " " "	
	22		" " " "	
	23		" " " "	
	24		Captain T.V. Fleming, A.S.C. taken command. 3 Coy to replace Captain Ruttan temporarily attached to Bn H.qrs. Captain E.B. Ladd A.S.C. transferred to 4 Coy as Supply Officer to 124th Bde. to W.S. Hale transferred from H.qrs Coy to 3 Coy as Supply Officer to 123rd Bde. Supply section refilled at Ballieul. Stewart. Dr ambulance transferred to 4 Coy for shell transferred from 4 Coy.	
	25		Supply section refilled at Steenwerck.	
	26		" " " "	
	27		" " " " Marching order inspection, ammunition by Company Officer. Pte S. Hea evacuated.	

T.V. Fleming Capt.
OC 3 Coy. 41st Div'l Train

Army Form C. 2118.

WAR DIARY
or
INTELLIGENCE SUMMARY

(Erase heading not required.)

Place	Date	Hour	Summary of Events and Information	Remarks and references to Appendices
La Creche	29		Supply section refilled at the Steenwerck	
"	30		"	
"	31		"	
			Note. During the month the baggage sections have been employed on fatigues.	

T.V. Flemming Capt.
O.C. 3 Coy. 41st Div Train

WAR DIARY
or
INTELLIGENCE SUMMARY

(Erase heading not required.)

Army Form C. 2118.

Instructions regarding War Diaries and Intelligence Summaries are contained in F.S. Regs., Part II. and the Staff Manual respectively. Title Pages will be prepared in manuscript.

Place	Date Aug	Hour	Summary of Events and Information	Remarks and references to Appendices
LA CRÈCHE	1st	18 o'clock	Daily Routine:— Reveille 4:15 AM. Stables 4:45 & 5:55. Non Stable 11:15 & 12:30. Evening Stables 3:45 & 6 pm. Brigadiers duties and Men alternate days by the Baggage & Supply Sections. Remainder of day horses not on duty are turned out in field All arming states, harness, lists & linen disinfected 3 times weekly. Turns of meals Breakfast 6 am. Dinner 12:30. Tea 5 pm. Hot first always kept for men out on duty. Quality of rations good & quantity ample. GAS HELMETS & respirators receiving inspection. Maj for S.T.V. LAWFORD C.B. accompanied by Lt Col W.W. WOLONY, A.S.C. C.O. 41st Div Train paid a surprise visit to No. 3 Coy 41st Div Train at noon & inspected the camp. Maj General S.T.Y. LAWFORD C.B. expressed himself satisfied with the condition of camp & horses. Weather hot & dry. Supply Section refilled at STEENWERCK. Wagons despatched for green forage.	
	2nd	18 o'clock	Usual Daily Routine. Weather HOT & DRY. 2/Capt V. FLEMING A.S.C. posted to Pulget Transport of the 123rd Bde. Supply Section refilled at STEENWERCK. Hostile aircraft passed over camp at 10.15 o'clock. T/2nd Lt G.C. HOLMAN A.S.C. left 6 report for duty with R.F.C. Horse sun & grooming this afternoon. Horses legs arrested. Wagons despatched for green forage.	
	3rd	18 o'clock	USUAL DAILY ROUTINE. WEATHER HOT & DRY. No.3 Coy. paid 30 Francs per man. "LAST PAY JULY 6". The A.D.V.S paid a visit and expressed himself satisfied with condition of horses. Supply Section refilled at STEENWERCK. Wagons supplied for green forage.	
	4th	18 o'clock	USUAL DAILY ROUTINE. WEATHER Bright & Windy. One H.D. horse sent to Mob. Vet. Sec. Companies exchanged CH7/266 DRIVER SAWDON T A.S.C. granted 1 month leave from 4th inst. to 1st Sept. on re-engagement. Proceeds to England. Rum of 7.70. Supply Section refilled at STEENWERCK. Wagons supplied for green forage.	
	5th	18 o'clock	USUAL DAILY ROUTINE. DULL IN Forenoon. Bright later. 3 H.D. of No. 3 wg + 3 H.D. attached from Hd. Qrs. Exchanged for 3 pairs of mules Oc H.A.T. including these stock of through No. 58, + 8. All horses legs washed down with disinfectant. 5 pairs trousers out for green forage. Supply Sec. refilled at STEENWERCK	
	6th	15 o'clock	USUAL DAILY & SUNDAY Routine WEATHER FINE. CHURCH PARADE Company at Battn & prisoners with Clean underclothes. Numerous enemy Aircraft Over camp during day. Supply Section refilled at STEENWERCK	

Army Form C. 2118.

WAR DIARY
or
INTELLIGENCE SUMMARY
(Erase heading not required.)

Instructions regarding War Diaries and Intelligence Summaries are contained in F. S. Regs., Part II. and the Staff Manual respectively. Title Pages will be prepared in manuscript.

Place	Date	Hour	Summary of Events and Information	Remarks and references to Appendices
LACRECHE	Aug. 7	18 o'clock	Usual Daily Routine. Hot dry weather. Following DRIVERS joined No 3 Coy 41st Div Train from 1st Base Horse Transport Depot. T27831 CASSIDY.B, T15R/764 GORTON.W, T11859 LIMB.L. One H.D horse withdrawn from Hd.Qrs. No 213 evacuated to No1 Vet Sec. Inspected swings. Horse lines, stands, chandeliers. The G.O.C 41st Division expressed himself as being pleased with the general turnout of No 3. Coy & O.C. 41st Div Train. Horses currycombed - mens camp 4.30 am. Supply sec returns at St Omarch.	
	9"	18 o'clock	Usual Daily Routine. Weather fine. Six mules received in exchange for Sick H.D horses. Horses curried or camp at dawn. Wagons provided for pres forage. Supply section see ret. fields St Omarch.	
	9"	"	Usual daily Routine. Weather very hot. Rifle Eye helmet & Iron Ration inspection. Horses legs washed. Wagons provided for forage. Italian Aircraft [illeg] over camp 4 & 5 a.m. Supply section 2 filled at St Omarch.	
	10"	18 o'clock	Manual Daily Routine. Mules lw harrowing. Hot baths. Drivers foot exam of 5 teams. Wagons provided for pres + forage R.E's. Supply sec re-filled St Omarch.	
	11"	18 o'clock	Usual Daily Routine. Weather fine. Hot baths. Wagons provided for divise curry & R.E's. Mansfield horse line. Grooming Kits issued. Supply sec. re-filled St Omarch.	
	12"	18 o'clock	Usual Daily Routine. Weather overcast, some rain during night. Horses legs washed. Wagons provided Corps curry, straw + R.E's. Supply sec re-filled St Omarch.	
	13"	18 o'clock	Sunday & Usual Daily Routine. Cloudy forenoon. fine later. Church parade. Men rifles & clean clothes issues. Divise curry. Supply sec. re-filled St Omarch.	
	14"	18 o'clock	Usual Daily Routine. Cloudy weather. some rain. C.O. 41st Div Train inspected supply curry at 7 A.M. system forage curry provided. Ex No 3 Coy. Inspected Regt Transport 1/25 J Batty. Supply sec re-filled Regt St Omarch.	

WAR DIARY or INTELLIGENCE SUMMARY

Army Form C. 2118.

Place	Date Aug	Hour	Summary of Events and Information	Remarks and references to Appendices
La CRECHE	15	18.00	Usual Routine. Weather cloudy in forenoon. 233 F Coy RE supply wagon re-joined unit. Baggage Column re-joined unit. 1/2 Bde. Supplies re-filled at Steenwerck. Convoy provided.	
"	16th	18.00	Usual daily routine. Weather squally. 7 Supply & baggage wagons with for 18 y Bde RFA returned by H.Q. Co. 1 Lt & 6 OR wagon Uniforms attached to CRE 41st Division. Above convoys. Horses lys washed. Gas helmets inspection. Supplies re-filled at Steenwerck.	
FONTAINE	17"	18.00	3 Company Steamers trekked to FONTAINE HOUCK handing vacated camp at La Creche over to No 3. 233 Dr. Train. Trains 2½ hrs. Weather wet. NEW Camp. Clean not clean & in food order. Supplies re-fillers at Steenwerck.	
"	18"	18.00	Usual daily Routine. Weather fine. Baggage wagons re-joined company. Supplies re-fillers at CROIX. Camp inspected by C.O. 4/STAM TRAIN.	
"	19"	18.00	Usual daily Routine. Weather fine. Horse lys washed. Supplies re-fillers at CASTRE.	
"	20"	18.00	Usual daily Routine. Weather fine. Supply wagons 233 F Coy R.E. re-joined. Supplies Division returns at CASTRE. NCOs & men paid. 5405f g 2 3 d. Cpl. Reid RWM. re-joined off special leave.	
"	21"	18.00	Usual drill. Routine. Weather fine. Rifle Inspection. I.H.D. horses taken in strength of Coy. Tu. 172 Que Pte AUNFORD Dc. Joined from 1st H.T. Base Dep.t Supplies 2 action re-filled at CASTRE.	
"	22	18.00	Usual daily Routine. Weather fine. Supplies & Baggage re-filled at CASTRE (Gaston issue) Pte Jones unit.	
LONG	23	2.4 noon	3 Company Hays entrained at BAILEUL for LONG. Journey 9 hrs. No casualties. Weather. Some rain.	
"	24	16 cm	Men in camp marquees in laying out Camp & Horse lines. Supplies re-filled at AILLY. Supplies Baggage actn. Re-joined. Weather - rain.	

Army Form C. 2118.

WAR DIARY
or
INTELLIGENCE SUMMARY
(Erase heading not required.)

Instructions regarding War Diaries and Intelligence Summaries are contained in F. S. Regs., Part II. and the Staff Manual respectively. Title Pages will be prepared in manuscript.

Place	Date	Hour	Summary of Events and Information	Remarks and references to Appendices
LONG	25"	16 o'clk	Usual Daily Routine. One Bitter horse struck off strength of company. Inspection of Camp by O.C. 41st Div Train. Supples as before at AILLY. Weather wet. Horse Lines washed.	
"	26"	18 o'clk	Usual Daily Routine. Supply at Lines at AILLY. Weather - some rain. Horses legs washed Rifles Inspection.	
"	27"	18 o'clk	Inspection of Harness Saddlery Machines. Weather - some rain. One missing horse taken on strength from Hop Coys. Supples as before at AILLY.	
"	28"	18 o'clk	Usual Daily Routine. Weather - wet. O.C. 41st Div Train supervise Inspection of horse lines and departures. Harness and Saddlery Rifles etc. Kitmus inspection. Supply as before at AILLY. Clear unusy provisions.	
"	29"	18 o'clk	Usual Daily Routine. Weather - wet. Supples arrive as before at AILLY.	
"	30"	18 o'clk	Usual Daily routine. Weather very wet. Horse Lines Shifted. O.C. 41st Div Train inspected lines. Clear Unusy provisions. Supples as before at AILLY.	
"	31"	16 o'clk	Usual Daily Routine. Weather finer. I.H.D. horse destroyed for pneumonia. Supples as before at AILLY.	

T.V. Fleming Capt.
O.C. No 3 Coy 41st Div Train
for Lt Col

WAR DIARY
or
INTELLIGENCE SUMMARY
(Erase heading not required.)

Army Form C. 2118.

No 2 Coy

Instructions regarding War Diaries and Intelligence Summaries are contained in F. S. Regs., Part II. and the Staff Manual respectively. Title Pages will be prepared in manuscript.

Place	Date 1916	Hour	Summary of Events and Information	Remarks and references to Appendices
LONG	1st Sep.	18.00.00	DAILY ROUTINE Reveille 4.15am. Shaves 4.45am to 5.55 Noon stables 11.15 to 12.30 Evening stables 3.45 & 5 pm. Supply duties varied in attempts from baggage & supply dets of Cos. Runners & horses out in dark fringes of woods grooming lads their Chinfields 2 lines wide. Times of meals Breakfast 6 am Dinner 12.30 Tea 5 pm. Hot food always kept for men out on duty. Quality of rations very good & quantity ample. OC 4 1st Div Train inspected No 3 Coy full marching order and expressed himself as very satisfied. HD horses off strength Weather - some rain. Heavyrain in afternoon orders for re-fix at AILLY.	
"	2nd Sep	18	Usual Daily Routine Weather hot. Supply dets re-filled AILLY. Clare convoy provided. 5.45am.	
"	3"	18	Usual & Sunday Routine. Weather Squally. Divisional Sports. Supplys refixes at AILLY. 1 HD horse struck off.	
"	4"	18	Usual Daily Routine. Weather wet. 4 CSM Matthews transferred to 138th TA. to relieve 4/c.SM. Mac Kenzie for duty as 4 CSM No 3 Coy. 1 mule struck off strength. Horse lines severed & moved to met. Supplys refixes AILLY. until 10 am.	
FLIXECOURT	5"	10am	Mtrs returns to forward by column of route FLIXECOURT to join 123" JB camp for night at LONGPRE. Left LONG at 10 am arr LONGPRE 8 pm into supply section. No Casualties Weather fair	
LONGPRE	6	2.14am	Left LONGPRE at 8 am arr BURE. 6pm leaving supplys wagon to re-fix. Supply wagon proceeded to units & delayed overnight. Drowning parts. Entrainment from LONG & arr BURE 5 pm.	
BURE	7	8/	Usual Daily Routine. Supply re-filled at BURE. Wagons formed up for CRE 1 mule drawn from Hqq Coy.	
"	8	8/	Usual Daily Routine. Receipt that Supplys re-filled at BURE at 1.30 pm. Baggage parties returned from	

Army Form C. 2118.

WAR DIARY
or
INTELLIGENCE SUMMARY

(Erase heading not required.)

Instructions regarding War Diaries and Intelligence Summaries are contained in F. S. Regs., Part II. and the Staff Manual respectively. Title Pages will be prepared in manuscript.

Place	Date	Hour	Summary of Events and Information	Remarks and references to Appendices
BURE	9th	10am	Usual Saturday routine. Weather fine. Supplies &c refilled at BURE. Baggage wagon on front line Convoy. Farriers Sgt C.R.E. L/cpl Air. 1 Cpl & 2 Sappers R.E. posted as orderlies for C in C (MAJORS) on refilling party. 123rd I.Bay. Bearers of baggage held on T/B6873 Driver PASSMORE G - Struck off strength Aug 31st	
"	10th	10 o'clock	Usual Sunday routine. Weather fine. No supplies drawn. 2 H.D. horses Trekkers on strength from 17th Coy. Training parade for men & Orthern wheelers in afternoon	
ALBERT	11th	18"	3 Coy March to new company ground. 1 mile SE ALBERT. Supplies drawn by 123rd I.B. first line transport. Baggage wagons returned from units. Weather fine	
"	12th	18"	7am march with wagons to ?? Attached to 233rd F.C. R.E. 2 ??? ??? for ??? 123rd I.B. Supplies drawn by first line transport. 4 pr horses for Ren Salvage dump inspection drafted types referred. Small ram weather crew	
"	13th	16"	Usual daily practice. Supplies drawn by first line transport. 4 pr HD wagon for drug unit DAC. 1 C.S. wagon sent to MERICOURT for Officers kits for 123 J.B. 4 form 1st line wagon forwarded for CRE weather wet	
"	14th	16"	Supplies drawn by 1st Line Transport. 3pm Ry on provisions for 123 J.B. for Hay. 3 ditto for R.E. dump. 1 ditto for salvage. Baggage prs re green units. 1 H.D. horse died from shell shock. Weather cooler	

Army Form C. 2118.

WAR DIARY
or
INTELLIGENCE SUMMARY

(Erase heading not required.)

Instructions regarding War Diaries and Intelligence Summaries are contained in F. S. Regs., Part II. and the Staff Manual respectively. Title Pages will be prepared in manuscript.

Place	Date	Hour	Summary of Events and Information	Remarks and references to Appendices
ALBERT	15th	18 —	3 Coy. Standing to starting to move. Supplies carried by Supply Sec. at BRICOURT. 4 drivers promoted for Pioneer Duties. Weather cold. Supply wagon stayed with units.	
"	16th	18 —	3 Coy standing by ready to move. Supplies carried by Supply Sec. Weather wet.	
"	17th	18	3 Coy standing by ready to move. Supplies carried by Supply Sec. 1 for + OR promoted for Am. Subways dump. Weather cold.	
BURE	18th	18	3 Coy moved to BURE arr. 11AM. Supplies drawn on ALBERT Road by Supply See Baggage wagons. Alterations to Coy Vehicles very well met.	
"	19th	18	Usual Daily Routine. Supplies drawn by Supply Sec. at BURE. Weather very wet. No TS/911.5 Sent AT N wagram R.N. received to BASE. Hrs ref. HARVE + Strain of Strength of 17 not inclusive.	
"	20th	18	Usual Daily routine. Supplies drawn by Baggage Sec. at BURE. Supply See promoted in relief for Hvy Coy. 1 HR. Sent to 62 -M dr Vet. Sec. Horse Inspection as taken by the ADVS. 11+D struck off strength. breaths. her.	
"	21st	18	Usual Daily Routine. Supplies drawn by Baggage Sect. Inspection of Rifles. From ration for relief. Weather improves.	
"	22nd	18	Usual Daily Routine. 5 Baggage Pers. supplied for Hvy. Coy. Supplies. 1 wagon hauled to return convoy to Base. Hospital admit. Transport Horses inspection by D. Col. Waldworth. Ret. at H 20 fm. Baggage wagon link to unit. Weather fine.	

Army Form C. 2118.

WAR DIARY
or
INTELLIGENCE SUMMARY
(Erase heading not required.)

Instructions regarding War Diaries and Intelligence Summaries are contained in F.S. Regs., Part II. and the Staff Manual respectively. Title Pages will be prepared in manuscript.

Place	Date	Hour	Summary of Events and Information	Remarks and references to Appendices
BURE	23rd	18	Usual details. Routine Supplies on Supply See. Capt T.V. FLEMING takes 131 Recruits for Division from MERICOURT. Weather fine.	
"	24"	18	Sunday. Usual Routine. Church parade 9 am. Supply See. for Supplies. Weather fine. Men's musketry washed. Weather fine. Sort wagon received from 3rd Supply Bat. B.G.A.	
"	25"	18	Usual details. Routine Supplies by Supply See. 9/c Bulletin brew newsmin for division from MERICOURT (Mn's.J.). Company training at Divisional trainer under C.O of 3 Company. Weather fine.	
"	26"	18	Usual details. Routine. Supply See. for Supplies. Company fours out. Weather very fine. Still attends news to All Ranks Qtrs.	
"	27"	18	Usual details. Routine. Supply See. for Supplies. Inspection of gun equipment guns & wheels. 3 pm 4 prs. proceed to Mons Engine. Weather very wet.	
"	28"	18	Usual details. Routine. Supply See. for Supplies. Returning at RECORDEL. Weather wet.	
BECORDEL	29"	18	Company change to BECORDEL. Supply by Supply See. Weather wet. Baggage horse & wagons returned 1 GS wagon att. for Nº 2 by Nº 2 Er R.E. return. 1 GS from att by to 227 R.E.S.	
"	30"	15	Usual details. Routine. Supply wgn Supply See. & language wngs in lead army & issue of train. Bv.1 om motorlies Pgm & transport. 1 GS. Sup Reg. Weather fine.	

T.V. Fleming
O i/c, Yc 3 Coy
1st Aux Japan

Army Form C. 2118.

WAR DIARY
or
INTELLIGENCE SUMMARY

(Erase heading not required.)

Instructions regarding War Diaries and Intelligence Summaries are contained in F. S. Regs., Part II. and the Staff Manual respectively. Title Pages will be prepared in manuscript.

Place	Date Oct	Hour	Summary of Events and Information	Remarks and references to Appendices
BELGRADE	1st	18	Usual Sunday routine. Stable 6am to 7. Muster 11-12.15. Evening 4-5.15. Alteration from "Summer" to "Winter" time. Church parade 5.45. Supplies by Supply Sec. with Baggage pairs as usual. Fine	
"	2nd	18	Usual daily routine. Supplies by Sup. Sec. Remainder of Baggage wagons returned to Coy 1 ad H.Q. in from at 10 pm to Brigade Run under Major MAIR. Weather wet. Qr. M. 11th Div Train inspected horses, harness & equipment - better alteration of harness wire. Fitting straps effected condition.	
"	3rd	18	Usual daily routine. Supplies by Sup. Sec. with Baggage pairs as usual - roads very heavy. 3 S.M. 3 p/m A.D. Att. to 283rd T Coy R.E. weather wet.	
"	4th	18	Usual daily routine. Supplies by Sup Sec. with Baggage pairs as usual. 1 Dr. 2 HD & Cpl (Extra Forage) Wagon returned from H.Q. Train to Coy. Weather wet S4/060516 Cpl Cork admitted to 139 F.A. weather well.	
"	5th	18	Usual daily routine. Supplies by Sup Sec. with Baggage for as usual. 2 Dr + 2 p/r HD + 2 GS wagons forwarded under "B" Lieut Inskeen for green forage S4/060516 Cpl Cook + T35695 Dr WALDON A. returned to Coy. Weather wet. Issue of Rum to Coy.	
"	6th	18	Usual daily routine. Supplies by Sup Sec with Baggage pairs as usual. Weather very bad.	
"	7th	18	Usual daily routine. Supplies by Sup. Sec. re filling from railhead at ALBERT. Enemy Shells dropping on route. Roads no condition. Weather very bad.	

Army Form C. 2118.

WAR DIARY
or
INTELLIGENCE SUMMARY
(Erase heading not required.)

Instructions regarding War Diaries and Intelligence Summaries are contained in F. S. Regs., Part II. and the Staff Manual respectively. Title Pages will be prepared in manuscript.

Place	Date	Hour	Summary of Events and Information	Remarks and references to Appendices
BECORDEL	8th	18	Usual & Sunday Routine. Baggage Sec on Supplies re-fill ALBERT. 30th G.H.A. & 3 gds woggs returned to Itly by lorry. Reinforcemt attached to 2/2, 2/3, 2/33, & 237 F.C. R.E's. Weather wet.	
"	9th	18	Usual Daily Routine. Baggage sec on Supplies refilled ALBERT. Weather very wet. Issue of Rum made to bty.	
"	10th	18	Usual Daily Routine. Supplies drawn by Sup. Sec. from ALBERT. Taken to unit by Baggage Secs who returned with unit. 31 Bummis to Division drawn by 2/L: Dueline from ALBERT. Coal: T.V. TURNING on Traffic control. 3 pns NCO & 10 dvts with 233 F.Coy R.E. re Junr Coy. Weather fair.	
"	11th	18	Usual Daily Routine. Supplies drawn by Sup. Sec from ALBERT. Baggage pes returned to Coy. Weather fair.	
"	12th	16	Usual Daily Routine. Supplies drawn by Sup. Sec. from ALBERT. Baggage pts re-joined units. Weather fine.	
BURE	13th	18	Supply Sec. refills at ALBERT. re-fills at BURE. Coy moved to BURE am. 11am. Bag: pts returned to Coy. Weather dull.	
"	14th	18	Usual Daily Routine. Supplies fileed at EDGE HILL re-fills at BURE. Weather fair.	

Army Form C. 2118.

WAR DIARY
or
INTELLIGENCE SUMMARY

(Erase heading not required.)

Instructions regarding War Diaries and Intelligence Summaries are contained in F.S. Regs., Part II. and the Staff Manual respectively. Title Pages will be prepared in manuscript.

Place	Date	Hour	Summary of Events and Information	Remarks and references to Appendices
BURE	15th	18	Sunday. Though Rough rations. Suffolk to sup to 1HD No 82. Sent to 23rd Mentiers Lou. Baggage for 20 Brish units. 1 for HQ, 1 G.S. wagon for. Joined from Hay. C/y for duty with 233rd C.R.E. Weather wet.	
ARGOEUVES	16th	20.45	Monday. Company moved by route march camping the night at St. SAUVEUR arriving there 6 p.m. Capt. T.V. Fleming left on 7 days leave. Command of Company being taken over by Lieut. W.S. Maile. No Casualties. Weather fine.	
GRANDSART	17th	22	Tuesday. Route March Continued at refilling at LONGPRE – 5.45; Company arrived at GRANDSART ROAD at 21.30 – Weather wet – No Casualties.	
GRANDSART	18th	18	Refill at 5 A.M. Ants again at 10.30 p.m. Lieut H. P. Merin went to VENACOURT to draw 30 Remounts stayed there the night – Weather showery –	
GRANDSART	19th	18	Refill at 3.30 A.M. Supply Wagon stayed with unit. Remounts arrived at 2 P.M. Company left at 7 p.m. Entrained at PONT REMY at 11.30 p.m.	

Army Form C. 2118.

WAR DIARY
or
INTELLIGENCE SUMMARY

(Erase heading not required.)

Instructions regarding War Diaries and Intelligence Summaries are contained in F. S. Regs., Part II. and the Staff Manual respectively. Title Pages will be prepared in manuscript.

Place	Date	Hour	Summary of Events and Information	Remarks and references to Appendices
GODEWAERSVELDT	20	18	Friday. Company moved at 12 noon with exception of Supply Wgn, 1 Motor, 2 drivers from H.T. Depot. No Refill. Millioner & Queens joined. HAVRE Dr Moore & Minnes. Weather full frosty	
"	21	18	Saturday. Refill at 6 am at MONT DE CATS & again at 2 P.M. Br Jones. J. admitted to 139 field Ambulance. Weather fine frosty	
RENINGHELST	22	18	Sunday. Company moved off at 9 AM arriving at Noon. Supply Section filled in detail at WIPPENHOEK siding - 1 HD Grey Gelding No 211 Dent Mobile & Mitchry Section. Capt T.N. Fleming returned from leave. Weather fine	
"	23	18	Monday. Supply drew Supplies for Reinhears at WIPPENHOEK. 1st line transport on filling at RENINGHELST. Baggage &c re youd Lry T30.26896 D/Pickersgill E.A & T374.01 D Lloyd G admitted to hospital. 4 GS wags promised for COAL. Walker, Inst	
"	24	18	Supplies drawn from Reinhears on Monday 5pm & 4 S wags promised for COAL 820 lthnday to 60 ANERSVELT Vlet YPRE for hides. Weather fine	

Army Form C. 2118.

WAR DIARY
or
INTELLIGENCE SUMMARY

(Erase heading not required.)

Instructions regarding War Diaries and Intelligence Summaries are contained in F.S. Regs., Part II. and the Staff Manual respectively. Title Pages will be prepared in manuscript.

Place	Date	Hour	Summary of Events and Information	Remarks and references to Appendices
RENINGHELST	25	18	Wednesday. Supplies as on Tuesday. 3 for foreman for Cmdt. Weather wet. Inspection of Rifles 9001hrs. 1 train rations	
"	26	18	Thursday. Supplies as on Wed. Capt T.V. FLEMING on TRAFFIC control. 4/ors for Cmdt at 7am. 9 lors for Strars at 9am. 5 lors at 4.15pm to draw smokes from YPRES. weather wet.	
"	27	18	Friday. Supplies as on Thursday. 9 L/c PULLINE drew remnts for 41st Divn. The 2/c O.C. 41st Divn came a visit to Camp & hurd him & reported himself as relation such condition of horses to O.C. 3 Coy. Weather wet.	
"	28	18	Saturday. Supplies as on Friday. 111059 Dr LIMB L rejoind coy from train troops. 2/ors for strars at 9 am. 165 wagp provided for mule conwy to YPRES 5 pm. weather wet.	
"	29	18	Sunday. Supplies as on Sat. Capt T.V. FLEMING on Traffic control. weather wet.	
"	30	18	Monday. Supplies as on Sunday. 4 lors + 2 wagp + N.C.O provided for 225 F.C. RE workshp. No 211. H.A. horses returned from 57th Mort. Use. weather wet.	
"	31	18	Tuesday. Supplies as on Monday. 5 lors 4 gs + N.C.O provided for Cmdt. 226 F.C. Q.E workshp. LIEUT. B. LEM ANDREW left on leave for England. 1 HA hurce No 9 arul 's 52nd amb.ltt. Final clipping of horses commenced. T.V. Fleming lely. OC 3 Coy. 4 lors Divn TRAIN	

249 Wt. W4957/M90 750,000 1/16 J.B.C. & A. Forms/C.2118/12.

Army Form C. 2118.

WAR DIARY
or
INTELLIGENCE SUMMARY
(Erase heading not required.)

Instructions regarding War Diaries and Intelligence Summaries are contained in F. S. Regs., Part II. and the Staff Manual respectively. Title Pages will be prepared in manuscript.

Place	Date Nov.	Hour	Summary of Events and Information	Remarks and references to Appendices
REMINGHELST	1.	18	Wed. DAILY ROUTINE as follows – Reveille 5 am Morning Stables 5.30 to 6.30. Midday Stables 11–12.15. Evening Stables 3.30–4.30 (taking advantage of daylight) Horses all fed with out straw as forage at 8 pm nights. Supplies by Supply Sec. from railhead. 7/3 6,778 F/M (Dartington) MAXWORTHY K. admitted h. 13 g. 7 ams 2 prs for lorries 2.30 pm for YPRES for 1 G.T. H.q. daily detail. 3 prs. fly's waggs to DICKEBUSCH for duck boards. Company used hot baths + were provided with clean clothes. Weather fair.	
"	2.	18	Thursday. Supplies by Supply Sec. 4 prs. & fs wags for duty's ruin. 2287 Cy. R.E. OUDERDOM. 2 prs. + 12 ps wags. for lorries at YPRES. 1 Pte. Chestnut arrd. 15 huts. Ser. 20.5 on strength of 3 cy. lost in duty's. One admitted in DIVN ORDERS. Weather – wind + rain. Men rolling rifles + gas helmets inspected.	
"	3.	18	Friday. Supplies by Supply Sec. 2 prs + fly's wags. parade at 8 am for duck boards. + prs for duty's ride 2287 C. y RE. as amn. 2 prs. + ys. wags at 3.30 for lorries at YPRES. Weather showery.	
"	4.	18	Sat. Supplies by Supply Sec. Oc. 3 Cy + Cmg Sgt Major attended at Div'n Gas School at 9.20 am for instruction. H.R.H. The Duke of CONNAUGHT passed Camp at 2.30 pm. 2/prs. for lorries at 3.30 pm YPRES. Weather fine.	
"	5.	18	Sunday + Ordinary routine. Supply by Supply Sec. + Pt 4 G.S. for RE's at Eqn (22 TF Cy) 2 prs + 1 N.C.O. to YPRES for lorries. 10 prs. fly S wags. 1.30 pr straw 2 prs. fly S. to DICKEBUSCH for duck-boards". Inspection + instruction in new pattern boyo's helmets. Weather very windy.	

Army Form C. 2118.

WAR DIARY
or
INTELLIGENCE SUMMARY
(Erase heading not required.)

Instructions regarding War Diaries and Intelligence Summaries are contained in F. S. Regs., Part II. and the Staff Manual respectively. Title Pages will be prepared in manuscript.

Place	Date	Hour	Summary of Events and Information	Remarks and references to Appendices
RENINGHELST	6th	18	Thursday. Supplies to Supply Sec. The D.M.S. 2nd Army inspected camp at 10.30am. 10 hrs Fly maggots Straw covers. 4 hrs fatigue to 226 F.Cy. R.E. 2 hrs for YPRES for straw Strides. S4060466 L/Cpl ROSSER T.O. Reported for duty from 2nd Army HdQrs. Weather windy & wet.	
"	7	18	Tuesday. Supplies to Supply Sec. 10 hrs flys maggots for Straw. 2 hrs for strides at YPRES. Chestnut mare 15 hnds No 2 in charge of company advertises in Rur Orders as last week of mule at WATOU. Rum issued to Coy. Weather very well. Inspection of rifles.	
"	8	18	Wed. Supplies to Supply Sec. 4 hrs for 228 F.Cy. R.E. 2 hrs for YPRES for strides. 10 hrs for Straw at 2pm. Weather well.	
"	9	18	Thursday. Supplies to Supply Sec. 4 hrs fatigue N.C.O. to 226 F.Cy. R.E. 2 hrs for Straw covers. Brigade H.Q. army returns to Cy. T4057401 Pt MIDDLETON W Grenadier Gds chgo leave to proceed to England. G.O.C. 41st Divn visited camp. Weather fine.	
"	10	18	Friday. Supplies to Supply Sec. Capt. TUCKERING on Influenza. 6 hrs Fly maggots Straw covers. 1 hr flys for Duckboards. Any Natives three change of clothes. TNR. att. for rations. Pte. SAMSON J. returns from Bgde. HdQrs. 2/Lieut ANDREW B. L. returns off leave.	

WAR DIARY or INTELLIGENCE SUMMARY

Army Form C. 2118.

Place	Date	Hour	Summary of Events and Information	Remarks and references to Appendices
RENINGHELST	11th	18	Sat. Baggage Gds on lupfrs. 4 prs on R.E 228 dump. 4 prs. tp to Stores camp. Gas helmet instruction for Coy. Weather fine.	
"	12	18	Sunday. Baggage Gds. on Lupfrs. 7 prs tps warg. Parades at 6 am for H.Q. & Coy Lupfrs. Q.O.R. inspected & awarded medals to 1.2.2. J.B. & 3 Cy R.S.C. provision 1 Offr 1 M.C.O. & 8 NCOs. Weather fine. 4 prs at P.O. for R.E. 228 Coy. Church Parade at Divine Cy to school 3 pm for Cleaning.	
"	13	18	Monday. Supplies by supply Col - 7 prs L.T. Gp drays to recover Hors. Cy. H.Cy. Coming 1pm Sprs. Weather Foggy	
"	14	18	Tuesday. Supplies by supply Col. Following drivers transferred to Bugl Hdqrs: 1.2.3. T36235 Dr. MUNDEN E.J. T/1651 Dr LIMBY T35595 Dr WALDEN A T35638 Dr WOODCOCK W.J. T36598 Dr COLLINS. G.C. 4 prs. trnsp. provide for R.E workshp. Following drivers returned to Cy from R.E. Wksps T36348 Dr. STONEAGE A T/405738 Dr. EVANS W T36548 Dr. MITCHELL J. 40557-75 Dr. GENDERS. C.S. Whole company paraded daily with rifles for O.C. Cy. at 2 pm. Weather fine	
"	15	18	Wed. Supplies by supply Col, 4 prs trnsp for R.E. wrkshps. 3 prs on Stores camp. T56933 Sgt TAILOR W Co. O. leave to England. Weather frosty.	

2449 Wt. W14957/M90 750,000 1/16 J.B.C. & A. Forms/C.2118/12.

Army Form C. 2118.

WAR DIARY
or
INTELLIGENCE SUMMARY
(Erase heading not required.)

Instructions regarding War Diaries and Intelligence Summaries are contained in F. S. Regs., Part II. and the Staff Manual respectively. Title Pages will be prepared in manscript.

Place	Date	Hour	Summary of Events and Information	Remarks and references to Appendices
RENINGHELST	16	18	Thursday. Supplies by supply sec. Supply sec. inspected by Adjutant. 8prs. trsps. provided for the 6 Coys. supplies. Whole company (except fatigue) changed. 5pr. trsp. on Straw convoy. Weather fine.	
"	17	3.15	Friday. Company inspected all transport Clerks. 2nay. outfit to drills & inspections by OC 41st Div. train. Reinforcement. T4057781 Dr ARKLE W.H. sent to 140.7 A. Weather fine.	
"	18	18	Sat. Supplies by supply sec. Straw convoy. 5pr. 15psrcsp. T302700 Dr NAYLOR W.S. proceeded on leave to England. Weather well.	
"	19	18	Sunday. Usual ground. Supplies by supply sec. 4 prs. trsps. to RE. wagons. 3 prs. trsps. for straw convoy. T4057634 Dr HOPE W.T., T4057367 EVANS W. T36651 Dr APPLEBY H. T4065285 Dr JONES A.L. admitted to 140.7 A. 2pr. trsps. Straw convoy. New corn rations & 9 pr. gs. arrived to company. Weather well.	
"	20	18	Monday. Supplies by supply sec. 16.00 PTE CARTER 27th MX. admitted 6140.7A. 34065285 Dr JONES A.L. discharged from hospital. Weather well.	
"	21	18	Tuesday. Rationing began at WIPPENHOECK Station. 6.30 am. Supplies delivered to troops. T4057901 Dr MIDDLETON W. returned off leave. T4057634 Dr HOPE W.T. T36651 Dr APPLEBY H. discharged from hospital. Weather sunny.	

WAR DIARY
or
INTELLIGENCE SUMMARY

(Erase heading not required.)

Army Form C. 2118.

Place	Date	Hour	Summary of Events and Information	Remarks and references to Appendices
RENINGHELST	22nd	18	Wednesday. Refit as yesterday at WIPPENHOECK. 4 pm 485 Wagon IWC 0 to 229 Coy R.E. Antwerton. 8 am. Weather fine	
"	23rd	18	Thursday. Refit by Baggage Section as usual. Company Dis Batu RENINGHELS Change of undercloths. Lieut Maile returned from leave. Gas helmet-goggles and iron rations inspected 2 pm. Weather fine	
"	24	18	Friday. Weather fine. Refit as usual. 3 hours on their lorries 8 a.m. Commenced supplying Brigade School. Weather fine	
"	25	18	Saturday. Wet. Refit as usual. Supply details under Lieut Meade went to WIPPENHOECK. 4 pm 4 GS IWCO. 228 F Coy. Workshops. 8 a.m. Private Carter 1607 discharged from hospital. Sergt Sterry went on leave. Stopped supplying to Funck Mn Fu 84. Weather wet.	
"	26	18	Sunday. Refit as usual. Capt T V Fleming resumed command of company's routine activity.	
"	27	18	Monday. Supplies to supply See. T.9. Lieut PAULINE ASC on leave to England T566933 A/Cpl TAYLOR WE. Command of Leave Annu feijupment inspected by OC Cy. Weather wet.	
"	28	18	Tuesday. Supplies to Supply See. 4 tr. rcago. to R.E. workshops. S4060516 A/Cpl COLE H.M. rejoined to personnel. Privates IWC Coy men [officers] for TANKS rangers. Recommend by NO Weather fine thro'5.	
"	29	16	Wednesday. Supplies to Supply Sec. Capt N FLEMING ASC on traffic control. 3 Priv. Corps Ammu T4065205 DS MELLER JH 14 T. Lieut to England. Weather wet & foggy.	
"	30	15	Thursday. Supplies to Supply See. Lieut MAILE ASC on Special duty to BOULOGNE. T302718 DS NAYLOR WS returned ft Leave. Annu for fight Country 980 Noon rather inspected. Weather rain. T.V. Fleming Capt OC 3 Coy 1st 10 D Train	

WAR DIARY or INTELLIGENCE SUMMARY

Army Form C. 2118.

Place	Date	Hour	Summary of Events and Information	Remarks and references to Appendices
RENINGHELST	1916 Dec 1	18	Friday. Daily routine as follows. Reveille for Supps Sec 3.15 am, First Shift 5.30 to 7.30 am. Midday, 11–12 noon. Evening 3.30 to 4.30. Wagons washed in turn. Cleanly. Remounts. Dinners. Horses cleaning during afternoon. Dr. 3 boys parade immediately. Doubts at 1.30 pm. Supplies. Lce Supps Arshire TS8697 Cpl ARTHUR A. proceeds to Scotland on leave. T40S7367 R. EVANS sen. discharged from hospital. Pte. BELLAMY details to 233 R.F.G. Weather dry + frosty.	T/A
	2	19	Sat. Supplies by Supps Sec T40652S9 A/T HOOPER A.H. to England on leave. S404397 Cpl REEF.W transferred to M.G.G. Corps. S406046 Cpl ROSSER J.O.G. Mil Cy. S4055576 Pte KEER.G. L/Lce Cpl S4O704 Pte (?) JOHNSTON W. to M.2 Coy. SGT JENKINS transferred to M.G. from 301. 5/Cpl ASHWORTH from 3031 & Pte 3 Gs, Pte's BARBER & BARRABURN from No. L.C. M.3.G. Company (scout.) Weather dry + frosty	T/O
	3	81	Sunday. Supplies to Supps Sec. Rate Train 7 am. Cold. Wet weather with frosts.	
	4	18	Monday. Supplies to Supps Sec. Cpl TV FLEMING on traffic control. Afpt r'cay for R.E.1 Company takers weather, frosty	T/O
	5	18	Tuesday. Supplies by Supps Sec T37640 L/Cpl NEWMB A.F. to England on 10 days leave. T40S3634 R HOPE W.G. transferred to C.B. Weather raw + cold.	T/O
	6	31	Wed. Supplies by Supps Sec. 4 pm for R.E.S. Wellington.	TD

WAR DIARY
or
INTELLIGENCE SUMMARY

(Erase heading not required.)

Army Form C. 2118.

Place	Date	Hour	Summary of Events and Information	Remarks and references to Appendices
RENINGHELST	7	18.	Thursday. Supplies by Supply Sec. T20456 Sgt SARRUP J. returned off leave. S4624911 Cpl JOHNSTON E. proceeded to England on leave. T37401 Dr LLOYD G.A. struck off strength S405023 2/Lt REED R.W.M. posted. Reinforcements prev. on attainment of military age. Weather foggy	TJ
"	8	18	Friday. Nos 3 Cy. Off on duties. Pay Parade to Company personnel recovering. Supplies to follow by Nos 2 + 4 Coy train. Weather mild. T12568 Sgt Phillips. A transferred from No 1 Coy. No 3 Coy. Sgt. WELFORD W transferred from No 1 Coy. No 3. S40 19670 Cpl. MURTON S. proceeded to England on leave.	TJ
"	9	18	Sat. Supplies by Supply Sec. Nos 7 and Ifpersstop. paraded at 10.45 am for No 2 Coy Supplies. Capt TUFLEMING on traffic control. Afters swap. for R.E. Weather cold. 2/Lt PULLEINE 70 joined.	TJ
"	10	18	Sunday. Supplies by Supply Sec. Church parade at 3 p.m. T36554 Dr JONES J. struck off strength. T58697 Sadr. Cpl ARTHUR appointed A/Sgt. transferred to No 4 Coy. T71155 Dr Sibbs CABROL R.F.S. transferred from No 4 to No 3 Coy. Weather mild.	TJ
"	15	18	Monday. Supplies by Supply Sec. Afters sf.s. swap. for R.E. Fatigue details renewing cover for R.E. in village. Weather fine.	TJ

WAR DIARY or INTELLIGENCE SUMMARY

Army Form C. 2118.

Place	Date	Hour	Summary of Events and Information	Remarks and references to Appendices
RENINGHELST	12th	18	Tuesday. Supplies to Suffolks. T406.5205 Pte NELLIS A. returned off leave from England. Weather — some snow.	TVG
"	13th	18	Wed. Supplies to Suffolks &c. 4 pts. Hqrs. the way for RE's. T4160283 Dr WEBSTER admitted to Hospital. T4065705 Pte JONES A.L. awarded 7 days C.C. by OC 3 Coy for having dirty harness. Weather cold.	TVG
"	14th	18	Thursday. Supplies to Suffolks &c. Sec. Hqrs. Hqs way for RE's. Capt. TUFF LEDING on Traffic control at Rue Haus. T386927 Cpl ARTHUR prisoner off leave & reported to Post Adj. Weather milk frost.	TVG
"	15th	18	Friday. Supplies as yesterday. T/A 065259 Dr Hopper A.H. returned off leave from England. Damf. Capt. FLEMING left on leave for England. Lt. HAILE appointed acting adjutant at Tram H. Qrs.	TVG

Army Form C. 2118.

WAR DIARY
or
INTELLIGENCE SUMMARY
(Erase heading not required.)

Instructions regarding War Diaries and Intelligence Summaries are contained in F.S. Regs., Part II. and the Staff Manual respectively. Title Pages will be prepared in manuscript.

Place	Date	Hour	Summary of Events and Information	Remarks and references to Appendices
RENINGHELST	16.	18.	Saturday: Supplies as usual. 4 pairs (fur) R.E's at Outtersdom 5.30. Wheeler West G.E. remanded for summary evidence. Fine.	TS/5125
	17.	18.	Sunday: Supplies as usual. 4 p.m. one N.C.O. & a.m. R.E. T4/094242. Dr Kelbrick T. T/091843 Dr Bailey F. sent to Brigade Qrs to review duties. T/1659 Dr Lamb L.L. and T/35595 Dr Walden A. returned to Company duties. Foppy.	TS
	18.	18.	Monday: Supplies as usual. TS/7649 Lt. Corpl Munt A.J. returned off pass from England. 4 pairs (fur) N.C.O. for R.E. at Outterdom 8.30 a.m. Loy Paid at 1.30 p.m. Soldiers inspected at 3 p.m. TS/8125 Wheeler West G.E. awarded 14 days No.1 F.P. by C.O. Rainfand Hay Convoy. Chickens	TVS
	19.	18.	Tuesday: Supplies as usual. 3 pairs. N.C.O. Rainfand Hay Convoy. Weather fine and fresh. Cards issued.	TVS
	20.	18.	Wednesday: Rfts charged from 6.30 to 9.30 a.m. for 1 month. 4 p.m. R.E. OUTERDOM E.G.H. Gas helmets - iron rations. Steel helmets inspected. Caps handed in to DADOS. T/9 037435. Dr Dale H. awarded 4 days C.C. Entol Frost. Snow.	TVS
	21.	18.	Thursday: Supplies as yesterday; 4 prs. I.N.C.O. OUTERDOM R.a.m. T/1659 D. Lamb L. T/35595 D. Walden A. awarded 14 days No1. F.P. awarded to A.P.M. 5 p.m. Windy x rain.	TVS

2449 Wt. W14957/M90 750,000 1/16 J.B.C. & A. Forms/C.2118/12.

Army Form C. 2118.

WAR DIARY
or
INTELLIGENCE SUMMARY
(Erase heading not required.)

Instructions regarding War Diaries and Intelligence Summaries are contained in F.S. Regs., Part II. and the Staff Manual respectively. Title Pages will be prepared in manuscript.

Place	Date	Hour	Summary of Events and Information	Remarks and references to Appendices
RENINGHELST	22.	18.	Friday. Supplies as usual. S4/065673 Corporal Gordon S. returned off leave from England. T9/027709 Sgt Nourse G. went on leave to Scotland.	TV3
	23	18.	Saturday. Supplies as usual. A/for R.E. OUTERDOM. Intraining – Heavy gale	TV3
	24	18.	Sunday. Christmas Eve. Supplies as usual. Water cart inspected 10 a.m. 3 pairs. N.C.O. Hay convoy 12.30 WIPPENHOECK. T4/056714 Q. M. Sgt Smith C. reported for duty with 3 Coy. Cold day.	TV3
	25.	18.	Monday. Christmas. Supplies as usual. C.O. visited dinners at 5.45. Windy Celebrated 2.45.	TV3
	26.	18.	Tuesday. Supplies as usual. Horses inspected by General Lanford. Weather fair's.	TV3
	27.	18.	Wednesday. Supplies as usual. 4 pairs for R.E.'s OUTERDOM. 8 a.m. 5 p.m. 1 S/Sgt 3 p.m. to Ypres to Guido. Fine afternoon.	TV3
	28.	18.	Thursday. Supplies as usual. Just Pulleine 5 drivers 1 G.S. wagon to draw rations from WIPPENHOECK. 8 a.m. for R.E.'s 8 a.m. All available men on field. Captain T. F. Herring returned from England.	TV3
	29.	18	Friday. Supplies by Supply Sec. S/for turnip. to YPRE for trichr. 9037. HQ Ambulance gell. destroyen Capt. TV FLEMING on traffic control at Radlone. T/406147 Dr MORRIS Hammers G. 1407A Weather wet.	TV3

Army Form C. 2118.

WAR DIARY
or
INTELLIGENCE SUMMARY
(Erase heading not required.)

Instructions regarding War Diaries and Intelligence Summaries are contained in F. S. Regs., Part II. and the Staff Manual respectively. Title Pages will be prepared in manuscript.

Place	Date	Hour	Summary of Events and Information	Remarks and references to Appendices
RENINGHELST	30th	18	Sgt Supplies to Supply Sec. S/4043918 Corpl. JOHNSON. E returned off leave. Weather wet. Company [illegible].	IV.j
"	31"	15	Sunday & usual routine. Supplies to Supply Sec. TS/8125 Driver West G.E. returned to duty. Pte. Roberson Camp. C.S.M. MACKENZIE. E and Sgt HOOKS. H. interviewed by O.C. on application for infantry commission. Weather very [illegible].	IV.j

T.D. [signature] Capt
O.C. 3 Coy A.S.C.
H/1st Divn Train

In the Field. 31·12·16

Army Form C. 2118.

WAR DIARY
or
INTELLIGENCE SUMMARY
(Erase heading not required.)

Instructions regarding War Diaries and Intelligence Summaries are contained in F. S. Regs., Part II. and the Staff Manual respectively. Title Pages will be prepared in manuscript.

Place	Date	Hour	Summary of Events and Information	Remarks and references to Appendices
RENINGHELST	1 Jan 1917	18	Supplies by Supply Sec. Daily Routine Reveille 5tr. running orders 5.30. 6.30 mon Shift 11-12. Evening Shift 3.30 - 4.30. OC Coys parade clerks with Rifles 1.30. Picket mounted 6 pm. Weather fair.	TO
"	2/18		Tuesday. Supplies by Supply Sec. 4 pmt tps ways. for R.E. 8 am. Reinf. detail for 2 hours for duis Stores dump. Weather fine rides.	TO
"	3	18	Supplies by Supply Sec. Capt T.V. Fleming on Traffic Control at Raidhaus. 2/65 tfs. for R.E's 8 am. T355 Sgt. D. WALKER. A T11659B Limb & chailingen from Kind. Reliem Camp. T.30271 P.R. NAIRN returned off pass from Scotland. Weather cold & windy.	TO
"	4 18		Supplies & Baggage Sec. Hdqrs 1/p for R.E's 8 am. Weather wet rode. Men Resting & the kilarks inspected.	TO
"	5 18		Supplies by Supply Sec. Usual scrubbing. and Rifle inspection in afternoon. Weather fine.	TO

Army Form C. 2118.

WAR DIARY
or
INTELLIGENCE SUMMARY

(Erase heading not required.)

Instructions regarding War Diaries and Intelligence Summaries are contained in F. S. Regs., Part II. and the Staff Manual respectively. Title Pages will be prepared in manuscript.

Place	Date	Hour	Summary of Events and Information	Remarks and references to Appendices
RENINGHELST	6	18	Supplies by supply sec. Push from Cdis Repair on Wagon. Emergency Ration by APM to Posts on wagon on SOCRE Road, under picket, & for furage for REG. Weather cold raw.	TVJ
"	7	18	Supplies by supply sec. Inspection by Adjt. MVO of camps & quarters. 10967 Pte T V FLEMING on Smith's arrival at Railhead. 10967 PTE A. POOLE Cadmitted to 144 TA Evacuated Bcc... Ann Stone. 1btd 12.10 on fire at Windmills at 1.30am. Cap. T V FLEMING to fire picket on duty. Weather wet raw	TVJ
"	8	18	Supplies by supply sec. 3 mn 3 pa wagn for Corps BELGE. 9.30 pm to convey Muel Poten Paris to CHIPPENca camp. Weather wet.	TVJ
"	9	18	Supplies by supply sec. Capt T V FLEMING inspecting observe rations for 123 I.B. in Trenches 3 mn 3 pa wagns for coal dump 6am. 1NC + 2 NCO munitie reported to 7th Cop. for reinforcements T3/02 6953. C.S.M. MACKENZIE proceeded to England being detailed for Temp. Infantry Commissn. Army Commander inspected Camps in area. Weather dull mild.	TVJ
"	10	18	Supplies by supply sec. Inspection WOffcant Tram Adjt. T406 5247 Sgt. MORRIS F. detained to C US a shuck off Strength. W21/1 HD taken on Strenyh. APM. 11th Coy. Lyle DOHERTY. 1 PTE TAYLOR.J wounded accid. Major Bright MC . Hellie marshall	TVJ

2449 Wt. W14957/M90 750,000 1/16 J.B.C. & A.; Forms/C.2118/12.

WAR DIARY
or
INTELLIGENCE SUMMARY
(Erase heading not required.)

Army Form C. 2118.

Place	Date	Hour	Summary of Events and Information	Remarks and references to Appendices
RENINGHELST	1917 Jan 11		Supplies by Supply Sec. Pack train full — 26 full wagons. Weather blowing gale.	TV3
"	12		Supplies by Supply Sec. Inspection of Baggage Sec. by Adjt. & Q.M. Weather rain & snow.	TV3
"	13		Supplies by Supply Sec. Capt T/Lieutine on traffic control. Hostilmay for R.E. Pte MENZERGROUCH 96332 & Lt Sa Hess. In place Pte RUSETTE. B.E.F. returned to duty. 96332 Dr MEARS. R.14672.A. came on duty. Rain & snow.	TV3
"	14		Sunday. Several routines. Supplies by Supply Sec. 4/m many parades 2.30 pm for duty men. Pte A.S.R. 1 Black mule died. 57106 Spr W. Allport A. proceeded to England on leave. Weather cold.	TV3
"	15		Supplies by Supply Sec. Brass Band held 12 pm to 3.30 am Quadrille Western 114 Rumba C.518.A. Weather mild rain.	TV3
"	16		Supplies by Supply Sec. Pack train held 10.30 am. 4 pt Thing In R.E. 1521 Pte L.N. E. Jones on Bardon from 125 T.M.B. In is place Pte N. Pearson Joined. 36378 N. H. ARY returned from the D.A.C. Blow frost.	TV3
"	17		Supplies by Supply Sec. 1 MCO + 44 Pts. proceeded at Vinack hut to attend lecture on Censorship.	TV3

Army Form C. 2118.

WAR DIARY
or
INTELLIGENCE SUMMARY
(Erase heading not required.)

Place	Date	Hour	Summary of Events and Information	Remarks and references to Appendices
FENNING HEATH	18	18	Supplies to Supply Sec. Capt. T.V. FLEMING on traffic control. 4 p.o. men. to R.E.'s. stellar Cpl.	T/8
"	19	18	Supplies to Supply Sec. 4 p.o. men. for R.E.'s. 7401547 Sgt. MORRIS. Properties from Qm. i/c H of S. learn etc.	T/8
"	20	18	Supplies to Supply Sec. Early return again. Park-train W.S. 15 ton. 2 N.S. SMITH proceeded to H.Q. ERROL on arm of Pump, unfortunately returns same night. S4044263 Sgt HOOKS G.H. proceeds to Eng. to sent. w. 4 of Tempy. J.Commission. T4160263 D. WEBSTER drawings for D.R.S. weather wet.	T/8
"	21	18	Supplies to Supply Sec. Q.M.G q.4.5 a.m. 4 p.o. men. to 4 p.o. N.C.O. E.G. Smith interned. 4 p.o. in w/ same men of H.W. Quarter 11 team. Dismissed 3 ill. 5 p.o. men. intering forage in canps. Officers- W. Lunn w.e.f. Delopment as milling Supply Lionel - weekly daily reports to Army Officer.	T/8
"	22	18	Supplies to Supply Sec. T5164947 L/p Prevost Reported to Hdq. for duty (temp) 2 H.A. 2nr 111, 112, inoculated to identity. Weather bright frosty.	T/8

2449 Wt. W14957/M90 750,000 1/16 J.B.C. & A. Forms/C.2118/12.

WAR DIARY or INTELLIGENCE SUMMARY

Army Form C. 2118.

Place	Date	Hour	Summary of Events and Information	Remarks and references to Appendices
RENINGHELST	23	18	Supplies by Supply Sec. Inspection of Water Cart 10 am. Draw Hqrs. Capt. T.V.Fleming. Traffic Control. Weather very frosty.	TVF
"	24	18	Supplies by Supply Sec. Pack Trans Thur Calls. 1 NCO & 18 OR returning for Leave. Weather colder.	TVF
"	25	18	Supplies by Supply Sec. Pack Drawn. Orders re fire 11 am. 5 pm change for extra forage. Sgt. Horton transf from 10 R.W.K. returned to unit to proceed to England. Duty Comm. Weather colder.	TVF
"	26	18	Supplies by Supply Sec. Pack Drawn. Inst. re fire 2.15 pm. 5 pr t/o for Extra forage. Weather very cold.	TVF
"	27	18	Supplies by Supply Sec. Pack Drawn. Wa. 10. fire 2.40 pm. 1 NCO & 14 pr. R.E's. T2SR206 Spl. Welford A.J returned off leave. Weather very cold.	TVF
"	28	18	Sunday. Travel provisions. Supply by Supply Sec. Pack Drawn. Insn. re fire 2.15 pm. Capt. T.V.Fleming Traffic Control. weather very cold.	TVF

Army Form C. 2118.

WAR DIARY
or
INTELLIGENCE SUMMARY

(Erase heading not required.)

Place	Date	Hour	Summary of Events and Information	Remarks and references to Appendices
REMINGHELST	29	18	Supplies by Supply Sec. Reqn 8 60mm. INCO Reqn for RE's. Inspection of gr returns 5. OC workshop. Weather cold	TVS
"	30	18	Supplies by Supply Sec. Inspection Vet & Cart Drawn Office 10mm. Weather very cold. 1763 Pte TAYLOR 23 MOT att. as transp. from Bdy School absented himself from 3 pm reported to OC Bdy School.	TVS
"	31	18	Supplies by Supply sec. Parade 8mm 4/os RE's. Weather cold, some snow	TVS

T Browning Capt.
OC 3 Coy. 41st Divl Train.

In the field 31/1/17

WAR DIARY
or
INTELLIGENCE SUMMARY
(Erase heading not required.)

Army Form C. 2118.

Place	Date	Hour	Summary of Events and Information	Remarks and references to Appendices
RENINGHELST	Feb 17 1st	18	Daily routine - Reveille 4.45am. Stables 5.15 – 6.15. Breakfast. Carrying arms off at 6.45am. Room Stables 11-12. OC Coy's parade with rifles 11.30 daily. Harness cleaning 2 – 3 pm daily. Evening Stables 3.20-4.30. Sundries amount & Impicted 6 pm. — Stores fed with hay 8pm — Supplies by Supps Sec. Coy parade Stow Suburne by Major Procter RSC on Wanderson team. Vehjager. Supplies by Supps Sec. re fill 2.30pm. Capt V Fleming on Traffic Control 1 NCO 4 hrs RE6. Weather very cold.	Minor
"	2	18		Minor
"	3	18	Supplies by Supps Sec re-fill 1pm. 1 NCO 13 yrs for Straw. Weather very cold.	Minor Staton
"	4	18	Supplies by Supps Sec re-fill 1pm. Vet by Church Parade 5+5. Weather very cold.	Minor
"	5	18	Supplies by Supps Sec. re-fill 2pm. 1 NCO 4 hrs RE's Weather very cold	Minor
"	6	18	Supplies by Supps Sec. re-fill 7am. Capt V Fleming Traffic Control T406 1247 & Morris Road G 138" J.A. weather very cold. —	Minor

Army Form C. 2118.

WAR DIARY
or
INTELLIGENCE SUMMARY

(Erase heading not required.)

Instructions regarding War Diaries and Intelligence Summaries are contained in F. S. Regs., Part II. and the Staff Manual respectively. Title Pages will be prepared in manuscript.

Place	Date	Hour	Summary of Events and Information	Remarks and references to Appendices
RENMILHEIST	FEB 1917 7	16	Supplies by Suffolks Sec. X fell 12 noon. Coy parade 1.30 km of adolluit inspection NCO 4.4 pm. "RE5 21/2/25 Opl. MEYERS W.H 1.0" RWK found as limbers T57913 WH Sgt SHUTTLEWORTH 79.46 S.A. Sgt NICHOLS 6933 7am Sgt TAYLOR A Hannus at Staff Sgts. Weather cold.	Meyers [illegible]
"	8	16	Supplies by Suffolks Sec. X fell 11.30 am. Coy training parade. Weather cold	[illegible]
"	9	18	Supplies by Suffolks Sec. X fell 1.30 pm. NCO reps RE5 1HD + Munz Tween on Strength of Coy. Weather cold.	Meyers
"	10	18	Supplies by Suffolks Sec. re fur 3.30 pm. NCO 4p/m Straw. Coy parade 1.20. inspection of kit Capt TV FLEMING traffic control. Weather cold.	Meyers
"	11	18	Supplies by Suffolks Sec. re fill 1.30 pm p Coy parade Aug 5km. Weather mild	[illegible]
"	12	18	Supplies by Suffolks Sec. X fell 11.30 am NCO 4pm RE5. Weather mild	[illegible]

WAR DIARY
or
INTELLIGENCE SUMMARY
(Erase heading not required.)

Army Form C. 2118.

Instructions regarding War Diaries and Intelligence Summaries are contained in F.S. Regs., Part II. and the Staff Manual respectively. Title pages will be prepared in manuscript.

Place	Date	Hour	Summary of Events and Information	Remarks and references to Appendices
RENINGHELST	13	18	Supplies by Supply Co. ut fus 11 a.m. NCO + 1ps Straw Convoy. Walk out inspection 10 a.m. T2536 Cpl CHIDGEI. H joined from No 2 Coy. 1540145 Pte BAILEY E rejoined from 123 I.B. Italy. T36728 Dr MAXWORTHY C. transferred to 128 I.B. Italy. S4059673 Cpl GORDON A. F/F/Sgt. Rifle inspection 1.30. Weather mild.	Mercer
"	14	18	Supplies by Supply Co. re fus 8.30am. NCO + 1ps for R.E's. TS3700 Far/Cpl. ENTWISTLE to 138 F.A. Conference 1.30. Inspection of turnouts + steel helmets. CAPT V.FLEMING. Coy truck control. Weather cold.	Mercer
"	15	18	Supplies by Supply Co. re fus 9.30 am. NCO + 1ps R.E's. TS3835? D'ARLEIGH H. to 138 F.A. Coy truck parade 1.30. Clean clothes provided. Weather cold.	Mercer
"	16	18	Supplies by Supply Co. re fus 10.30 am. TH057367 D'EVANS S. proceeded on special leave to England. T4065705 Dr MORRIS H. from 138 F.A. CAPT V.FLEMING I/c coal convoy (27 m) Weather mild.	Mercer

Army Form C. 2118.

WAR DIARY
or
INTELLIGENCE SUMMARY.
(Erase heading not required.)

Instructions regarding War Diaries and Intelligence Summaries are contained in F. S. Regs., Part II. and the Staff Manual respectively. Title pages will be prepared in manuscript.

Place	Date	Hour	Summary of Events and Information	Remarks and references to Appendices
RENINGHELST	17	16	Supplies & Supply Coy at the 8am, 1 NCO 2hrs REJ. The Company Clerk thro' Orrs injured by HOC 4.10 Am, sharp springs himself a highly intelligent to company commander. Thunderstorm in force. Weather mild.	(Sgd?)
	18	18	Supplies as usual, returned 7.30am 2hrs reported 6 SSO 7am. TL 004933 & Smith proceed on Sanitary Course. 3 hrs provided for coal unning. Cpl T V FLEMING Yr. TOS 17 81 & A DKL 6 CG 138 7.A. Weather milder.	(Sgd?)
	19	18	Supplies as usual, returned 4.30am. CAPT N FLEMING traffic control T 356570T APPLEBY returned from 138 JA. 1 NCO 3 prs. for RASOS T 27125 & Sodn CARROL J. reported for tempy duty at Div HQ, weather milder.	(Sgd?)
	20	18	Supplies as usual, returned 10.15. 1 NCO & 3 prs. Or June cunning, weather cool.	(Sgd?)
	21	16	Supplies as usual, returned 10 am. Weather cold, mild.	(Sgd?)

WAR DIARY
or
INTELLIGENCE SUMMARY

(Erase heading not required.)

Army Form C. 2118.

Place	Date	Hour	Summary of Events and Information	Remarks and references to Appendices
RENINGHELST	22	18	Supplies by suppl. See return thru NCO hfs for REs. Coy parade for Bathing & Inspection of Sunday dress. 1 H.O. Taken on strength from 2 Hl. Inspection of Cook Houses by OC Cookery School. Satisfactory expressed. Weather wet.	
"	23	18	Supplies as usual. Return 15 Hm. NCO hfs Straw away. Some hut of Coy. to Bathed, Spare clothes provided. Weather wet.	
"	24	18	Supplies as usual. Return 7 am. NCO tps to YMCA at BAISVILLE Coys. T. J. FLEMING on Traffic control. Coy parades Brunsmeles marching order. Up from Hut. foreward. Weather cold.	
"	25	18	Supplies as usual. Refil 10 a.m. 6 pair to Supplies 122 Bry see. T.9/64493. 3t Smith 3.10 am from Sanatrium Course. Boeschepe. Cold.	
"	26	18	Supplies as usual. Refil 10 a.m. N.C.O. 4 pain. R.E. OUTERDOM. T/1/6605 Pte Lamb Supplies as usual. 4pr. Halladash Dumb (working parts.) to RENINGHELST 4pr. Halladash Dumb (working parts.) from detention camp. Coy parade 1.30. Rifle inspection Mild.	
"	27	18	Supplies as usual. Refil 10 a.m. 1 Sgt 4 pairs Poperinghe — RENINGHELST. Bombardier Henry for O.C. 3 Coy 4th R.E. Signs to 4 pm.	
"	28	18	Supplies as usual. Refil 10 a.m. Mild. Lieut Pallé rejoins from 2 C.C.S. NIPPENHOEK	

WAR DIARY or INTELLIGENCE SUMMARY

Army Form C. 2118.

Place	Date	Hour	Summary of Events and Information	Remarks and references to Appendices
RENINGHELST	MAR 1917	1	Daily Routine Reveille 5:30am. Stables 6-7. Confirm Ok. & Exam. Supplyp. pr. parade & materials 8:45. Camp Inspection by Lt. Bury 10am. Stables 11-12. Cut parade 1:30 ahrs. for inspection of equipment as per detail. Harness cleaning 1:30-3. Evening Stables 3:30 & 4:20. Lights out at 6pm. Lights out 9pm. Supplies by Supply &c. T27175 Pte Sadd. Carrol opp. Sad. Cpl. Ames transferred 6 to Coy. T22087 A/Lsgt Bull W. transferred 202 Coy. S405963 A/S. Sgt Gordon transferred to Brown Hay. T14027487 Pte Matthews J " T5998 " Lada Dickerson J.B. joined from 1 Coy. T55087 Dr. Higham 5/38 7.A. LIEUT. NAY. W.S. returned from Dunkirk. 1:30 Coy parade. Inspection of gas helmets drum ration water etc.	TM
"	2	"	" re fill 170mm. 1/or 1/or Rev. Reun. 1 N.O. dyps fr. N.E. Weather etc.	TM

WAR DIARY
or
INTELLIGENCE SUMMARY.

Army Form C. 2118.

Place	Date	Hour	Summary of Events and Information	Remarks and references to Appendices
RENINGHELST	3	16	Supplies by lorries. See return T406/205 Dr MELLISH, H.L. dilution weather fine stormy.	TVS
"	4	"	Sunday routine. T405/367 Dr EVANS R. returns off leave. 1 NCO R. Evans from VOORMEZEELE to NIEPPEBOSCH. Weather fine + hot.	TVS
"	5	"	refill 10am 1pm tp WNCA RENNINGHELST CAPTU FLEMING traffic control. weather showery.	TVS
"	6	"	refill 10am 1pm 1 NCO R's eqpt up for stay. Coy parade 1.30 for cycle inspection. T4/6650 1 Dr MOORE H.G.C.G.S. weather mild.	JM
"	7	"	refill 1pm. Coy parade 1.30 inspection 4/0 Lt/C HELMISH + J R. 1HO 9061 1 Rider W no E.S.2 Hub Vet weather cold + windy	JM

WAR DIARY
or
INTELLIGENCE SUMMARY.
(Erase heading not required.)

Army Form C. 2118.

Place	Date	Hour	Summary of Events and Information	Remarks and references to Appendices
REMINGHELST	7	18	Supplies by supply col. 10 fill 11am. 1 NCO & 4 WS to R.E. Ord. Depôt purchase. no Church of England available. Undestroke. snow.. 1 fr. 6 APMS office. S40403 S/Sgt Jackson transferred to No 1 Coy. S 405?0 Sgt BARKER joined from No1 Coy. weather showing.	TO
"	8	18	to fill 10am. 1 NCO + 4 fts to Stores. 735659 S/Hermans C.A. Mallory joined 1.30. T40 65205 A. MELLISH 11 from attention. Clean cases (minor) weather cold.	TO
"	9	18	1 NCO 4 fr to Stores. Capt VElBDING in traffic control. sup plies mroA	TO
"	10	18	1 efill 10am. Coy church parade 5.45 10SR fr inoculation. weather cold.	TO
"	11	18	sup. 10am 1NCO 4 fr R.E.O. 1 fr to YMCA. 1 fr to functional. weather cold	TO
"	12	18	stkell MAIL by DvS	TO

WAR DIARY
or
INTELLIGENCE SUMMARY.
(Erase heading not required.)

Army Form C. 2118.

Place	Date	Hour	Summary of Events and Information	Remarks and references to Appendices
REMNGHELD	13	18	Supplies by Supply Col 99 PM 100m 10 OR for inoculation. Weather cloudy.	TVO
"	14	18	" " " " " S4 04 3902 Pte COLLARA HC to detention, etc.	TVO
"	15	18	" " " " " Coy rifle range practice. No cloth practices. 10 OR inoculation 5.30 pm Weather misty	TVO
"	16	18	Company officer H AL Butler to prepare for inspection by O.C. L⁴ D.N Train. Futenas, misty.	TVO
"	17	18	Company inspected by O.C. L⁴ D.N Train. Full marching order. Supplies as usual. Refus 1.00am 1 NCO + Pte REA 1 for escort POIRIENCE 1 pr GS + limber for MT Coy. 1 NCO 3 Pts for straw. Weather cooler.	TVO
"	18	18	Sunday rothing eating Refus 1.00am. 1 NCO 4 PteS for straw Escort U.F. FLEMING. Fatigue continues. 10 OR for inoculation. Weather milk.	TVO

Army Form C. 2118.

WAR DIARY
or
INTELLIGENCE SUMMARY.
(Erase heading not required.)

Instructions regarding War Diaries and Intelligence Summaries are contained in F.S. Regs., Part II. and the Staff Manual respectively. Title pages will be prepared in manuscript.

Place	Date	Hour	Summary of Events and Information	Remarks and references to Appendices
RENINGHELST	19	18	Supplies by Supply Col. refill 10am. Coy parade 1:30pm. inspection rifles Armourers 72/27 H. Pulline left on Paris Leave. Weather like Thursday.	TNA
"	20	18	" " " refill. 8am. Stables 11:30am. Inc. 74 ptes R.E. Coy parade 1:30 equipment inspection. T112 4/S 1st Fry C. T406832 1st Kent At. 115737 1st Manley PA. 1 own from Base. Weather cold.	TNA
"	21	18	" " " refill 8am. ptes for Rstrongl. 4 ptes for Canteen. Coy parade 1:30 for inspection fire helmets, Iron rations, steel helmets. 9 for 38th RWR. 1 NCO 3 ptes for Liverpool Rgt. weather upto river.	TNA
"	22	18	" " " refill 8am. 1 NCO 4 ptes to R.E.'s. 1 pte to Liverpool Rgt. Coy Bath parade 1:30. complete change of underclothing. Coy office T406 205 1st Mellish H. awarded 7 days C.B. Coy pay parade. Weather weather.	TNA
"	23	18	" " " refill 8am. 1 pte to 3 E Kents. Coy bath parade 1:30. Weather warm & very cold.	TNA

Army Form C. 2118.

WAR DIARY
or
INTELLIGENCE SUMMARY.
(Erase heading not required.)

Instructions regarding War Diaries and Intelligence Summaries are contained in F. S. Regs., Part II. and the Staff Manual respectively. Title pages will be prepared in manuscript.

Place	Date	Hour	Summary of Events and Information	Remarks and references to Appendices
RENAICHELLI	24	18	Supplies by lorries, see orders from 1NCO H/qrs RE's. Weather cold, sunny.	TWO
"	25	18	Pack Train late, re filled 9 am. 1NCO H/qrs for stores. Summer Time dinner at 2 o'clock. Capt. J.V.Fleming Traffic control. Weather cold sunny.	TWO
"	26	18	Pack Train late, refill 12.30. 1NCO H/qrs RE's. Capt H.Pulliene Wheeler off Paris leave. Weather wet, warm.	TWO
"	27	18	refill 2.30pm. 1NCO H/qrs RE's. Conference Inspector Rifles Revolvers. Weather fine wet.	TWO
"	28	18	refill 3 pm. Capt. J.V.Fleming Traffic control. 3 prs p horses for bricks. Weather fine sunny.	TWO
"	29	18	refill 11 am. 1pm Rifle Inspn. off Rev. Weather fine.	TWO

Army Form C. 2118.

WAR DIARY
or
INTELLIGENCE SUMMARY.
(Erase heading not required.)

Instructions regarding War Diaries and Intelligence Summaries are contained in F. S. Regs., Part II. and the Staff Manual respectively. Title pages will be prepared in manuscript.

Place	Date	Hour	Summary of Events and Information	Remarks and references to Appendices
RENINGHELST	30	18	Supplying Dropping Area w/m 4 am. 1 NCO 4 pvs BORED. 1 from 2/1 R.W.S. Congratulations parade cancelled. Weather ack.	2/0
"	31.	15		WY

10 Oman. 1 NCO 3 pts to camp for Coy. wounds return.

T. Manning
Capt
O.C. 3 Coy.
Hst Aux Brown.

In the field.
31/3/17.

A5834 Wt. W4973/M687 750,000 8/16 D. D. & L. Ltd. Forms/C.2118/13.

WAR DIARY
or
INTELLIGENCE SUMMARY.
(Erase heading not required.)

Army Form C. 2118.

Place	Date	Hour	Summary of Events and Information	Remarks and references to Appendices
RENINGHELST	1st April 1917	1 P	DAILY Routine as follows. Reville 5.45am. Stables 6.15 & 30 & 30. Grooms Rooms 5.30. Stables 6-7. Fatigue fatigue 8.30am. Inspection of Camp. Stables the room by O.C. Company. Stables 11-12. Company paraded for Inspection as ordered by O.C. Company. 1.30 pm Stables Divisions tea 3/o. Stables 3.30 - 4.30. Picket mounted by C.S.M. 6.30 night. Signals mr 9 pm	TO
	2		Supplies, Supplies &c as per 8am S.W.G. 4p/c Res 1 for 26 Reur R.W.S.	
			Site, S. Hale S O.O. (Brigade in Trenches) Administrations in Trenches. Weather wet.	
		18	4th 9am. 1 N.C.O. 2/c Res: T D.S. 126 Sgt WELFORD A. T/405 7759 Cpl FISHER. on course of gas Instruction. Weather cold & wet.	TO

WAR DIARY
or
INTELLIGENCE SUMMARY.
(Erase heading not required.)

Army Form C. 2118.

Place	Date	Hour	Summary of Events and Information	Remarks and references to Appendices
PENNINGHEUK	Apl 3	18	Supplies to Potyte 10 fn 9 am. 1 NCO. Apr. RE 5. Capt T.V Fleming on Traffic Control. weather Sunny.	M
"	4	18	" " " " ne fri 8am. 1 NCO 14 frs RE 5. Ony provate Muncher order inspection to be Capt. 8 am. Weather wet.	M
"	5	18	" " " " ne fri 8am. Ampere paces. Baggage wagon and to units. 12.00 Lt T.W.Elford's A. Tr OS 7707 4p FISHER S. discharged (MD) Cmmdt of the Institution withdrew find	(1)
"	6	18	No 3. Coy. 1 yt 7 am. Train loads command. Capt T.V FLEMING proceeded by Emmstomale to STEENPOORDE halting for night. Supplies ne fries at WYPENHOEK at 8 am. Aux forwarded to units and return. weather not good. Horses picketed int.	M

WAR DIARY
or
INTELLIGENCE SUMMARY.
(Erase heading not required.)

Army Form C. 2118.

Place	Date	Hour	Summary of Events and Information	Remarks and references to Appendices
ON MARCH ROUTE	Apr. 7	18	Company continues trek to NOORDREEN arr. 1.30 clock. 1 River No 6. Left at previous night (Einne) killed MAERSHEG 3 A.F. No 1 being duty handed to Companies and A.O.s of Div. Artillery. Supplies refuelled at STEENFORD and proceeded to units return that night. Three returns out. S4072280 4/Gdr ASHWORTH app. act/cpl with pay S4044337 A/Sgt BARKER G.A. transferred to R.A.S.C. T/4172944 Pte DUNFOR G.R. " " S4043990 A/S.S. KEEFE W. " " from " C 3 Coy S4070721 Cpl SATHENNATE G. " " from " C 3 Coy Weather fine T4057781 Pte ARKLEE W.H. reported from Hospital to Co 2 Coy	
"	8	8.15	Coy continues trek at 8am to SALPERWICK arr. noon. Billets drier under own arrangements. O.C. 4th Train visited Coy. Weather very fine.	

A5834 Wt.W4973/M687 750,000 8/16 D. D. & L. Ltd. Forms/C.218/13.

WAR DIARY
or
INTELLIGENCE SUMMARY.
(Erase heading not required.)

Army Form C. 2118.

Instructions regarding War Diaries and Intelligence Summaries are contained in F. S. Regs., Part II. and the Staff Manual respectively. Title pages will be prepared in manuscript.

Place	Date	Hour	Summary of Events and Information	Remarks and references to Appendices
SALPERWICK	Sept. 9	18	Supplies by Supply Co. ex-file 9 am. Rail way. withdrawn from limits. condition fair. S.S.O. visited camp. weather very bad - heavy showers in various forms.	
"	10	18	" " " " " Weather bad - snow storm	
"	11	18	" " " 9 am. 3 prs FYS for forage. weather rain + snow.	
"	12	18	" " " 9 am. 2 prs FYS on forage " rain + snow	
"	13	18	" " " 9 am. Weather fine, cold + snow	
"	14	18	Supplies &c. India St. B. Lieut ANDREW. 10 prs. Vys wago 140 Rs. Pursuance emanated to RENINGHELST. Coy Supply wago + Bdy Limber (empty) retained. Bdy S.O. & details moved to WATTOU. Tho S 7781 D'ARKLE. W.H. reported R 3 Coy. B.C. H/S Div Train visited Camp. Weather fine - cold wind.	

Army Form C. 2118.

WAR DIARY
or
INTELLIGENCE SUMMARY.
(Erase heading not required.)

Instructions regarding War Diaries and Intelligence Summaries are contained in F. S. Regs., Part II. and the Staff Manual respectively. Title pages will be prepared in manuscript.

Place	Date	Hour	Summary of Events and Information	Remarks and references to Appendices
SALPERWICK	Apr 15	18	Supplies by M.T. Any supply Hug. In WATTON for Supplies. Horses exercised. Weather wet.	T.O.
"	16	18	Capt. T.V. FLEMING visits 1st Line transport. Horses exercised — duties — windy.	T.O.
"	17	18	" " duties — rain much	T.O.
"	18	18	" " duties — Any parade 11.30 a.m.	
			Lectures by Lt. B. Ing on dumps of ammunition. Capt. T.V.FLEMING lectures all Officers NCOs of party on A.S.C. weather wet.	T.S.
"	19	18	Horse exercise. Any for move for inspection of equipment SCO & SO of Bde. Modern Camp. weather wet.	T.S.

WAR DIARY
or
INTELLIGENCE SUMMARY.
(Erase heading not required.)

Army Form C. 2118.

Place	Date	Hour	Summary of Events and Information	Remarks and references to Appendices
SALPEARNICK	20	18	Supplies by M.T. Bay had Sports there afternoon. Bdy. D.O. visited camp. Weather fair	
"	21	18	" " " Oc. 41st Divn visited Camp. Inspection of rifles elsewhere. Weather fair	
"	22	18	" " Bay see the French trenches with units. Weather fair	
"	23	18	" " Moved to Bay See trenches with units. Hdqtrs of Coy by route march to NOORPEENE. am 3 pm. Horses picketed in weather fair	
NOORPEENE	24	18	" " by Bay. See. Bay. regs. re Xmas Coy. after re-fit and delivery this day. Hdqtrs Coy by route march to STEENVORDE. Bde 41st Divn visited Camp. Horses picketed. Weather fair.	
STEENVORDE	25	18	" " " Hdqtrs Coy marched with Bdy. to RENINGHELST. am 1 pm O.C. 41st D.N. inspected horses, yeltons, & Ft. Andrew and Surfer. See horse drivers before Ft. detachment R.E.a	

St. B. Lieut. Andrew R.E.a.

WAR DIARY
or
INTELLIGENCE SUMMARY.
(Erase heading not required.)

Army Form C. 2118.

Place	Date	Hour	Summary of Events and Information	Remarks and references to Appendices
RENINGHELST	26	18	Supplies to Supply Co. Refill 10am. 1 NCO & prs. 6 g/ds ways to REO Capt. T/Fleming on traffic control, weather fine. Coy brushing & wash 1130 am - Clean clothes previous.	910
"	27	16	" " " " " " "	910
"	28	16	Refill 10am. 1 NCO + pr. Flying REs. 1 Sgt 10 prs Fatigue for REs. Brushing parade 1130. Complete change heads fine.	910
"	29	16	Refill 10am. 1 NCO to REO Capt T/Fleming for traffic control. Also NCO + pr. for gen. duties.	910
"	30	16	Refill 10am. Conference 11.30. Inspection of MLU and Trouble D 111A. Walked on gas.	910

WAR DIARY
INTELLIGENCE SUMMARY

Army Form C. 2118.

Place	Date	Hour	Summary of Events and Information	Remarks and references to Appendices
RENINGHELST	MAY 1917 1.		DAILY ROUTINE. Reveille 5.30 am. Starts 6–7. Breakfast 7 am. Starts 6–7. Advanced supply fans parade 7.45. Unit supply wagon parade 8.45 am. Coy Parade for fatigue etc 8.30 am. Coy Office 9.30 am. Inspection of Camp Shirts etc by O.C. Coy 10 am. Starts 11–12 noon. Coy Parade 1.30 pm for Inspection of Gymkhana etc. on Division. Humber Drago returning via 8 pm Evening starts 2.30–4.30. Picket mounts 6 pm Lights out 9 pm. G.O.C. 123 Ib trained Camp & watered demonstration of Lewis & Stokes guns carried out by O.R.nos J.r BLEM ANDREW to No 1 Coy (temporary measure) 2/Lt LUFF from Drew Hedge to Camp Duty.	
			Supplies by Supply Sec. re hire 10 am. 1 NCO 6 prs RE's 7.3 pm. Coy Parade to join Fr Helenis. What Nor West T/SB 125 in arrest for shunning. weather fine.	
"	2	"	Reg. Sec. 10 Feb 10 am. 1 MO 8 prs RE's 7.30 am. 1 NCO + for RE's 8.15 am. Cap.t T.V. FLENING Traffic Control. 2 w.o allowm 10.20 pm necessary action taken weather fine	

WAR DIARY
or
INTELLIGENCE SUMMARY.

Army Form C. 2118.

Place	Date	Hour	Summary of Events and Information	Remarks and references to Appendices
RENINGHELST	May 3 1917	18 100am	Supplies by bay. See re fuel 100am. Hqrs RE's 8.15am. INCO 6pm. RE's Dickiebusch 8.30pm. T4.2571/6 C.S.M. IRVING A join from 50 Div. Fire in 20' DH Camp 1.30am. Fire Piquet turned to. O.C. 41st Div. TRAIN Inspected camp. Weather fine.	
"	4 18		INCO 8pm EQs to RE Dump DICKIEBUSCH 7.20pm. Q.O.C. 41st Div. visited camp and inspected attachment to Army Machine Guns on Pack Saddles. Coy B. Army Parade 1.30pm. Weather fine	
"	5 18	10am	INCO 8/15 to Hqrs RE 7.30pm. Capt T.V. FLEMING in Traffic control. Rifle Bandolier Inspected. Weather fine.	
"	6 18	10am	INCO 4pm to RE OUDEZEELE 7.30am. TS7727 W/L Cpl. PIMFEELM, fr RE. DICKIEBUSCH 7.30pm. T4056719 A/A/M/L Cpl. ATA HAIRE 45 GF proceeded to Rest Camp WATTEN with T16611 A/KELLY J. returned to Unit from course of Instruction	

WAR DIARY
INTELLIGENCE SUMMARY

Army Form C. 2118.

Place	Date	Hour	Summary of Events and Information	Remarks and references to Appendices
RENINGHELST	1917 MAY 7	18	Supplies by Day. Div. @ Jn. 10 a.m. 1 NCO 6 hrs type wago for R.E. Ackiebusch 7.30. TSgt & SStWKR West GE tried by F.C.C. charges drunkenness. Capt. V. Fleming demonstrates methods of carrying LEWIS & STOKES guns on pack saddle at D.H.Q. noon. Weather fine.	
"	8	18	1 NCO 4 pts 4 gps RE Ouréadine 6.30 am 1 NCO 6pts 6 ps. to R.E. Ackiebusch 7.30 pm. To 5702E Dr Nule G in arrest. Cavy of this charged by A.P.M with leaving horses unattended 3 days CB. Y go lectures 3pm OC bs + 2 gun NCO ostsiners. Weather rain	
"	9	18	1 NCO 6 pts & Gs wago for R.E. Ackiebusch 7.30 pm. Capt. T. V. Fleming draft conference. Weather fine.	

WAR DIARY
or
INTELLIGENCE SUMMARY.
(Erase heading not required.)

Army Form C. 2118.

Place	Date	Hour	Summary of Events and Information	Remarks and references to Appendices
RENINGHELST	MAY 10	18	Supplies by A.S.C. See re fin 10am. 1 NCO 4 prs H/wap for work until 2 3 7 by R.E.'s NICHIE BUSCH 7 am. 1 NCO 8 prs Eqpt wap R.E. dump NICHIE BUSCH 7.30 [text] 1 NCO 5 prs 5 gp wap for Strom. Parkhurst drill 3 pm and fitting of Picksteam on box weather fine	
"	11	18	1 NCO 4 prs Hywap for R.E.'s 8 am. 1 NCO 10 prs Eqpt wap NICHIE BUSCH 7.30 pm weather fine	
"	12	18	1 NCO 4 prs Equip wap for R.E.'s 7 am. 1 NCO 1 pm 11 go for APM 1.30 pm. 1 NCO 10 prs Eqp wap for NICHIE BUSCH 7.30 pm. weather fine	
"	13	18	1 NCO 4 prs 4 gp wap R.E.'s 8 am. 1 NCO 10 prs Pwap R.E. 8.15 pm weather fine	
"	14	18	2 prs G/S wap for R.E.'s 7.15 am. 2 prs 2 gp wap R.E. 11.30 pm 1 NCO 10 prs 10 gp wap clowaps R.E.'s 4.5 pm weather wet.	

Place	Date	Hour	Summary of Events and Information	Remarks and references to Appendices
RENINGHELST	15	18	Difficulty supplies. 1 OR wn ret fr. 4 for 5 tps mag. NCO's Off Hutting 7.30am 1 NCO 10 tps mag for R.E. 8.45 from. Weather fine.	
"	16	18	" " " 1 for 1 dap on mag. Weather fine. Querer Commander BROCHEPE 16 + T4057634/B" HOPE WI. 1/m Hq 1 tp mag. For unls + lower dietures fr movement with TW School 1/cop T36248 N THOMAS 94 + B Fn. 814 1 N SAWDON T. Cont 1/m Hd. Rgo mag. dietures for movl with Roulers School, POPERINGHE. 2 for 42 tp mags to R.E. 11.30 am. 1 NCO 3 for 3 groups to 1st Ammunition dump Cog 7.15/am 2pm 2 gp mags to R.E. NICKIE BUSCH. 8.45 from. 4 hrs mls to C.R.O. OUDERDOM. 9.30 am. Weather fine.	

WAR DIARY
or
INTELLIGENCE SUMMARY.

Army Form C. 2118.

Place	Date	Hour	Summary of Events and Information	Remarks and references to Appendices
RENINGHELST	17.18		Supplies to Dragouflin rtn fm Dom 2 prs 2/1 wago RE's DICKIEBUSCH 11.30 p.m.	
		8.45 a.m.	"	
		7.15 p.m.		
			1 NCO 3 " 3 " 1st Canadian Div.	
			T/4/135528 R MINNIST + 2 LHR + 9 A.way. returned from 1st Div.	
			RMRE. S/Sgt KEEFE.N transferred att. he + Cy	
			S/4/04573 S/Sgt BARKER G.A. " 3 key.	
			Weather wet. horses under cover.	

Army Form C. 2118.

WAR DIARY
or
INTELLIGENCE SUMMARY.
(Erase heading not required.)

Instructions regarding War Diaries and Intelligence Summaries are contained in F. S. Regs., Part II. and the Staff Manual respectively. Title pages will be prepared in manuscript.

Place	Date	Hour	Summary of Events and Information	Remarks and references to Appendices
RENINGHELST	18	16	Supply by Bag. Section 2e H.A. 10am. 4/ors Hars for CRO. 12 pm. 2/ors H9. 2 gs wag RE's 8.45 pm. 2 pm. H9 2 Army. REs. 11.30 pm. 1 NCO 3 prs. + 2 gs wag 6 pm. 7 O/R's temporary attached to 103 Cy # H.A. Hars + 2 gs wag returned to Hq 2 Cy. 2/Lieut PULLEYE 6 O.R's proceeded to CALAIS on re-mount duty. Tu'orquies N° BRIGGS, E. in Crust on Gunnear Charge (A.P.M.) — deal with by C.O. Train. weather fine.	
"	19	18	4/ors H.A. CRO midnight. 1 NCO 5 prs Hars Hq Army 1st Canadian Tunnel Cy 6 pm. 2 pr HA 2 Gs wag RE's 8.45 pm. 2 prs. Hrs 2 gs wag RE's 11.30 pm. weather fine	
"	20	18	Hq. 2 pr 2 gs wag RE's 6.45 am. 1 NCO 5 prs Hrs 4 wag 1st Canadian Tunn Cy 6 pm. 4 prs H.A. 12 pm. weather fine	

WAR DIARY
or
INTELLIGENCE SUMMARY.

Army Form C. 2118.

Place	Date	Hour	Summary of Events and Information	Remarks and references to Appendices
RENINGHELST	21	18	Supply to Baggage Sec. 20 Jul 10am. 2 ors HS & Gs wag. RE. 11am. 1 NCO Sports HS Gs wag. 1st Can Tunby 2/15pm. 4 ors HS. CRO. 12 midnight. S406056 PTE COLE. AW proceeded to Rest Camp. TS7717 D. Whr Pum FREI.W T405(5)0'S D'ANDREW GF returned from Rest Camp. Sgt. BLE.M ANDREW, 1SY & horse attached to No 1 Coy. 2/LT LUFF temporary att. in Sig. To No 1 Coy. O.C. LI?Div Train & ADVS 41st Div. Works inspected horses of No 3 Coy. NCO i/c Night Guard reported hostile aircrafts over camp. No bombs dropped. Weather fine.	
"	22	18	2 ors 2 Gs wag. RE. 11.30am. 1 NCO ors HS 5 Gs wag. 1st Can Tun Coy. 6pm. 4 ors HS CRO. 12 midnight. 2/LT PULLING & party returned from CALAIS. Weather well.	
"	23	18	22 April 11 am. 2 ors HS 2 Gs wag. RE. 11.30pm. 1 NCO Sports HS 5 Gs wag. 1st C.T. Coy. 9 am. 4 ors CRO. 12 midnight. Weather fine.	

WAR DIARY
or
INTELLIGENCE SUMMARY.
(Erase heading not required.)

Army Form C. 2118.

Place	Date	Hour	Summary of Events and Information	Remarks and references to Appendices
RENINGHELST	24.18		Supplies to Supply Sec. on fill 10 am. 2 for 2.90 maps RE's 11.30 pm. 1000 Spr. 5 Yo 1st Can Tun Cy. 6 pm. 4 fors. HQ CRO 12 midnight. Welsh Line	
"	25.18		7 AM. 2 fors 240 maps. RE's 11.30 pm. 1000 Spr. SYs map. 10" Canadian Tun. Cy. 6 pm. 4 fors CRO. 6 pm "Welshline". 123 fors Div. Iron Ams.	
"	26.18		7 AM. 1000 Spr. SYs maps "Winter Dim Cy. 6 pm. HT 1 Rider No. 6 Dismounted to 52nd Tnch Vet Ser SHS evacuated to 52nd Mov Vet. for Special Intelmus No. 9, 93, 99, 211, 81. Rule No. 1 any detachments w/o T.M.S. reported Capt. Parade 2.30. Inspection Qm Helmets by Lt. T. Evans. Traffic control O. C. 441st 453rd Dn in inspection from fire wellsh line.	

WAR DIARY
or
INTELLIGENCE SUMMARY.

(Erase heading not required.)

Army Form C. 2118.

Place	Date	Hour	Summary of Events and Information	Remarks and references to Appendices
RENINGHELST	May 27	1P	Supplies by lorries. See return. 11am 4 P.CRO. 12 from 1 NCO 5/prs. 5/ps magr. 1st Can. Inn G/plan. 11.40 SD OS D'ANDREWS Q.F. Ceremonial B 126 DA. Parade for Divine Service 6pm. weather fine.	
	28	11	7am 2 P 246 May RES. 7.15pm. 1 WO 9/prs 1st Can Inn G. 6pm 4 Prs CRO 12 midnight. 2 & 3 B" ANDERSON v OLLEREAN 4 P. mostly off no 2 wg. Gas Alarm 1.45am. Necessary action taken. Phoned regt Officer for new WATER Es. above numbers. Shell fire 736548 R" M1 NISBET. wounded + evacuated to CCS. 2 waggon wheels to Abanbour, T.S.S.S.G & L/Cpls. SMITH JE V/c & Shower clothing & great. Uniforms. 2 HR was Cpr & 261 & 1 Ryder No 109 Promoted. weather fine.	

WAR DIARY
or
INTELLIGENCE SUMMARY
(Erase heading not required.)

Army Form C. 2118.

Place	Date	Hour	Summary of Events and Information	Remarks and references to Appendices
RENINGHELST	29	18	Supplies by lorry as per Army A/m #CRO. 12 midnight 1 NCO 5 prs & grooms for 1st Army Train lorry 6 pm. 1 pm 2 grooms for RE. 1356.— 3 ors 3 grooms for Reginald Farm 10 am. 2 ors the for Water at ROZENHIL Camp. 9 am. C/offs T/Plumb firstfield arrived weather fine.	
	20	16	7 am. 5/ors 5 grooms. 1st Am. Train lorry 6 pm. 14/ors CRO midnight. Weather fine.	
	21	15	Trigging his up with 8/ors am draw son. 1/W.M.M.M. Yellow Mules Attacked. Returned to Farm under 2 hour this day. 11068 Corpl Leaver A. 18345 Corpl Wilson G. 11676 L/Corpl Doughty D. 33983 Pt Watts L.T.G. 023630 Pt Hayward M G 16007 Carter A 15371 Pt Lucey H 109650 Pt Redding G. 55900 Rars L 36679 Lancto L Wn131005 Pioneer Heming F.P.C. 201502 Pt Bolsover C 201504 Pt Bruce J. Mirn from Ranks to act as Nurses. 201506 Pt Cassidy J. 201670 Pt Jones J. 2014 99 Pt Brondreta J. 2014 79 Pt Entkins H 201501 Barrow C 2014 89 Blake F 20154 6 Neill H. 201555 Geoghan Wm 201598 Honworth G. 66786 Pte Chapman T admitted into 138 Fld Amb	

Army Form C. 2118.

WAR DIARY
or
INTELLIGENCE SUMMARY.
(Erase heading not required.)

Instructions regarding War Diaries and Intelligence Summaries are contained in F.S. Regs., Part II. and the Staff Manual respectively. Title pages will be prepared in manuscript.

Place	Date	Hour	Summary of Events and Information	Remarks and references to Appendices
RENINGHELST	1 JUNE 1917	8	Daily Routine. Reveille 5.30 am. Shave 6-7. Supple Sr. Parade 7.30 am. Coy Parade 8.30. Muster Statis 11-12. Coy Parade 1.30 pm. Evening Statis 3.30-4.30. Eatra duties for parties of fatiguing mentioning at 8.30 daylight 9 p.m. Supple by Bugling &c. at pm. 2pm. Bath trains times D/I TV Flemming seaplane/airk. 4 or HQ. CRO. 12 midnight. 2 pm HQ. 2 pm reg. 4° Aly 7.30 pm 1 pm 1 go reg Pokers turn by 6 am 3 HQ No's 9, 12, 13, 211. Returned from Junt Vet Lee. Weather fine.	Volume
"	2	12	"	
"	9	12	" 1 pm. Organ Rate. 1 NCO + prs 1/0 + 9 men/pl from prog. 4/aw. Sw Force Shot hills. Weather fine	Verna
"	3	18	" 12 noon " 4 pm. HQ CRO. 12 midnight W.O.C. 1/1st Div Dram. m usn horn Lunch. Weather fine	Volume

A 5834. Wt. W4973/M687 750,000 8/16 D. D. & L. Ltd. Forms/C.2118/13.

Army Form C. 2118.

WAR DIARY
or
INTELLIGENCE SUMMARY.
(Erase heading not required.)

Place	Date	Hour	Summary of Events and Information	Remarks and references to Appendices
RENINGHELST	4	10	Supplies by Rail/Pack Ade 90 NCH 10.30. NCH 4 for 11th CRO, Reninghelst. Return 11th Inf. returns to 57 Div in ref to France. Nor in stream from Infantry. T. +16691 Sgt Mooney EF (malaria) to 1st Army. 11th 2nd returns to duty from St Omer. B.IX 11th punitive roman animals under 9200 lbs. T.305 ACP T.H.M.A. CA 1845 A/Fry H. Humes from T.M.S. 51 RV HS M.O.) 14,156 & 1hr mares 10. SS4 Animal to duty with A.O.S. 93 Poulaining.	Blue
			Sick ,, ,, 1 Killed. 1 NCO 4 pte HS to 1st CRO midnight. 11th A. & 1. 6 hn Vet for special treatment. 1100 approxmps Reynolds Glen. 1 BSG 4e EHP 7 VI Ca. A.S. treated control admin park	Blue

WAR DIARY
or
INTELLIGENCE SUMMARY.
(Erase heading not required.)

Army Form C. 2118.

Place	Date	Hour	Summary of Events and Information	Remarks and references to Appendices
RENINGHELST	June 6	18	Supplies by lorry as per program. 4 p.m. the C.R.O. rendezvous. 1 NCO + 1 man + 2 pairs wgs CRE 8.30 p.m. 1 Russ. no transfers from No 16 hosp'l, October fire.	Returns
"	7	18	Supplies as per program. 8.30 a.m. 1 NCO 6 p.r.s. lHs transp't for CRE. 8.30 a.m. 1 NCO + 4 p.r.s. lHs transp't for Rly Officer 1 p.m. 1 NCO 6 p.r.s. lHs fy duty motor work until 9.30 p.m. T.40862 SS MELLERS H.L. + 2 H.A. hours no 62 + 63 slightly wounded. Urethra not being much care.	Returns

Army Form C. 2118.

WAR DIARY
or
INTELLIGENCE SUMMARY.
(Erase heading not required.)

Place	Date	Hour	Summary of Events and Information	Remarks and references to Appendices
RENINGHELST	8	18	Supplies by lorries - see no hill 10 am. 1 NCO 5 prs HQ R/s wags REs 7.30 am. 1 NCO 5 prs HQ HQ wag for Area Commandant 4 am. OC HQ Res Irani inspected camp. S404970 S/Sgt REEF W. proceeded to England on leave. weather fine.	[sig]
"	9	18	10.30 am. 1 NCO 5 prs HQ Ryowag REs 7.30 am. 1 NCO 6 prs HQ wag for CRE. 1.30 pm. weather fine.	[sig]
"	10	18	10.30 am. 1 NCO 16 prs HQ for work with road cars. 2 prs HQ wag for Ouderdom club 8 am. 1 Hd No 81 returned from MD etc SC. Capt TWEEDIE on Traffic control. Church Parade 6 am. weather fine	[sig]
"	11	18	1 NCO 6 pro HQ wag CRE 7.30 am. 1 pr HQ wag for A.P.N. 1 pm. 1 NCO 6 prs HQ wag for Regt Officer from 1 Hd & 1 mule pulled to No 2 Co. 2 pro + wag left Camp 36. weather fine	[sig]

WAR DIARY
or
INTELLIGENCE SUMMARY.

Army Form C. 2118.

Place	Date	Hour	Summary of Events and Information	Remarks and references to Appendices
PENINGHURST	June 12/18		Inspection by Supply Sec. refuse 10am. NCO 6 prs HQ to Guway. CRE 8.15am. 1 pr HQ to guay for reinforcement drafts. 1 Rider 116 transferred from M25 to 3 Coy. weather - heavy rain.	Blank
R.E. Dump OUDEZUM	13/18	10 am	2/pr HQ + 2 gp to guay. CRE 7am. No 3 Coy march from Camp 36. 12am am Camp 15. 1pm weather fine	Blank
"	14/18	10.30am	2/pr HQ + 2 gp to guay for Reg. Office 2/am. NCO 2/prs HQ to guay. RE. 6am. 1 NCO 6 prs HQ to guay. CRE 7.45am. weather fine	Blank
"	15/18	" Baggage Sec "	1 NCO 6 prs HQ to range. 1 pr CRE 2.30am. 2/pr HQ for rails. Cav. 7.3am. 2/prs 2 gps wag for Reg office 1.30am. T.4.05.70.23 B. Dale H proceeds to England on leave. weather fine.	Blank

WAR DIARY
or
INTELLIGENCE SUMMARY.
(Erase heading not required.)

Army Form C. 2118.

Place	Date	Hour	Summary of Events and Information	Remarks and references to Appendices
OUDEZOOM	July 17 16	18	Supplies by Baggage Sec. 98-fill 8. am. 2 prs the ego wag. for Div. Salvage 6.6am. 1000 S hrs to Sp hrs. CRE 5 30am. 1 pm Hrs truy for APM 9am. 2 hrs 2 Gp. wag. for Rev. Office. 12:20am. Capt T V FLEMING untd. 1p & Enemy shelled Railhead. Casualties all in 24th Div. Tram. 41st Div. Tram. Run. cleared. weather fine.	Bourne
"	17	18	" " 9am. O.C. 41st Div. Train inspected horsestand at 2.30pm. Church parade 6 pm. During the Enemy shelling Railhead OUDEDOM refilling returned to WIPEN HOEK. weather fine	Bourne

WAR DIARY
or
INTELLIGENCE SUMMARY.

(Erase heading not required.)

Army Form C. 2118.

Place	Date	Hour	Summary of Events and Information	Remarks and references to Appendices
OUTERDOM	June 18 Monday		Supplies by Supply Section. Refil 4.15 a.m. 1 N.C.O. 4 pair A.S.S. wagon for R.E. Workshops OUTERDOM 7.30 a.m. 1 N.C.O. 3 drivers for train H.Q. to bring Remounts for Requisitioning 2 p.m. 1 N.C.O. 3 pair 3 wagon for Requisitioning 1.30 p.m. T/4/186501 Dr Moore E.F. Officer returned to duty from Rest Camp T/05 8705 Dr Andrews S.F. returned to duty from Hospital. Capt FLEMING proceeded on leave to England.	(Signed)
"	19 Tuesday		Refil 4.15 a.m. 1 N.C.O. 4 pain 4 S.S. wagon for R.E. Workshops OUTERDOM. 2 pair 2 S.S. wagon for R.O. 1 p.m. RAIN	(Signed)
"	20 Wednesday		Refil 4.15 a.m. 1 N.C.O. 4 pain A.S.S. wagon for C.R.E. OUTERDOM 7.30 a.m. 1 N.C.O. 2 pair 2 S.S. wagon for R.O. 1 p.m. Capt MAINE proceeded on leave to PARIS. No 3 Coy men from Camp 9.30 a 7.15 p.m. arrive camp in Square M.4 (Zevecoten N.E.) 5.10 a.m. RAIN	(Signed)
"	21 Thursday		Refil 4.15 a.m. 1 N.C.O. 4 pain 4 S.S. wagon for 253 Coy R.E. Yoorzeele 7 a.m. 4 pain A.S.S. wagon for R.O. 10 a.m. RAIN	(Signed)

Army Form C. 2118.

WAR DIARY
or
INTELLIGENCE SUMMARY.
(Erase heading not required.)

Instructions regarding War Diaries and Intelligence Summaries are contained in F. S. Regs., Part II. and the Staff Manual respectively. Title pages will be prepared in manuscript.

Place	Date	Hour	Summary of Events and Information	Remarks and references to Appendices
C.28. M.3.6.8.8.	June 22.	18.	Supplies to Supply Return. Refil 4.15 a.m. Wippenhoek. 1 N.C.O. 4 pair. 4 G.S. wagon to 233 Coy. Voormezeele 7 a.m. 1 pair 1 G.S. wagon for R.O. 1.30 a.m. Staff Sgt Keep W. returned to duty from leave to U.K. No 3 Coy move from Zevecote to O.K. 9.15. a.m. M.3.6.3.8. 9.15.	30/04/3976 [illegible]
C.28.	23	"	Supplies. Refil 4.15 a.m. 1 N.C.O. 4 pair. 4 S.S. wagon to R.E. dump Voormezeele 6.45 a.m. 2 pair 2 S.S. wagon for R.O. 3.30 a.m. 2 pair for duty with water carts 6 a.m. to Voormezeele 2 p.m. No 3 Coy move camp to C.28. M.4.C. 2 p.m.	None
M.4.C.	24	"	FINE. Refil 4.15 a.m. 1 N.C.O. 4 pair. 4 S.S. wagon 6.45 a.m. 2 pair for duty for Voormezeele. 1 N.C.O. 4 pair 2 pair for duty with water carts to Voormezeele 11.15 a.m. for R.E.S. Voormezeele went under Rain's working duty owing to hostile shell fire to complete.	Returned
"	25	"	FINE. Refil 4.15 a.m. 1 N.C.O. 4 pair. 4 S.S. wagon 6.45 a.m. 2 pair FINE R.E dump Voormezeele 6.45 a.m. 2 pair. 2 S.S. wagon for R.O. 1.30 p.m. 1 pm 1 S.S. wagon for Area Commandant BOESCHEPE 1.30 p.m.	[illegible]

Army Form C. 2118.

WAR DIARY
or
INTELLIGENCE SUMMARY.
(Erase heading not required.)

Instructions regarding War Diaries and Intelligence Summaries are contained in F. S. Regs., Part II. and the Staff Manual respectively. Title pages will be prepared in manuscript.

Place	Date	Hour	Summary of Events and Information	Remarks and references to Appendices
C 28 П.4.C.	June 25	18	1.H.D. No 81 belonging No 1 Coy attached No 3 Coy sent to Mobile Veterinary Hospital. Pairs working for R.E. 1 Voormezeele were unable to complete owing to Hostile shell fire.	Fine
C 28 M.4.C	26	18	Supplies by Supply Section Ref U 6.30 a.m. 1 NCO 4 prs 4 GS Wagons 6.45 a.m. 1 pr 1 GS Wagon 2 Special Coy RE met us here 2 prs 2 GS Wagons for Repairs R.7 b.13 7 a.m. Requisitioning Officer 1.30 pm Fine.	Fine
C 28 M.4.C	27		Supplies by Supply Section Ref U 6.30 a.m. 1 NCO 4 prs 4 GS Wagons for 233 Field Coy RE Ridgewood 6.45 a.m. 3 prs 3 GS Wagons for Requisitioning Officer 1.30 pm. T/4/057023 Dr Dale H returned to duty from leave. T/15737 Dr Mowley PA proceeded on leave. Fine	Fine

Army Form C. 2118.

WAR DIARY
or
INTELLIGENCE SUMMARY.
(Erase heading not required.)

Instructions regarding War Diaries and Intelligence
Summaries are contained in F. S. Regs., Part II.
and the Staff Manual respectively. Title pages
will be prepared in manuscript.

Place	Date	Hour	Summary of Events and Information	Remarks and references to Appendices
C.2.8 M4.e	June 28	18	Supplies by Supply Section. Refill 6.30 am. 3 prs for duty with water carts 6.30 am. 1 pr 1 G.S. Wagon for duty with 1/R.W. Kents Ridge Wood. 6.30am. 2 prs 2 G.S. Wagons Requisitioning Officer 1.36 pm. Rain.	Strong
C.28 M4.e	29	18	Supplies by Supply Section. Refill 6.30 am. Rain	Strong
C.28 M4.e	30	18	Supplies by Supply Section. Refill 2 pm "Ea Cyte" NCO 2 prs mtd + drive from Reinforcement Camp to DADOS 1pm. Baggage Wagons sent to units 11.30 am 2/Lt Pillains in charge 1 by 1 GS Wagon for SSO 3.30 pm. Rain	J H Williams 2/Lt A/1st Brit for O.C. Coy gone 3 RS

Army Form C. 2118.

WAR DIARY
or
INTELLIGENCE SUMMARY.
(Erase heading not required.)

Instructions regarding War Diaries and Intelligence Summaries are contained in F. S. Regs., Part II. and the Staff Manual respectively. Title pages will be prepared in manuscript.

Place	Date	Hour	Summary of Events and Information	Remarks and references to Appendices
THIEUSHOUK	July 18.		Breakfast 7 a.m.	
		5.30 a.m.	Reveille. Stables 6 a.m. Company parade fatigues 8.30 a.m. Co. Office 9 a.m.	
			Inspection of Camp by O.C. 10 a.m. Stables 11 a.m. Harness cleaning 1.30 p.m. Stables 3.30 p.m.	
		5 p.m.	Picket mounts 6.p.m. Lights out 9.p.m.	
			Tea 5 p.m.	
		2 p.m.	Supplies by Supply Section Refill. No 3 Coy B.S.C. moves from Camp Sheet 27 M.9.c.	
		8 a.m.	Ammunition in camp Sheet 27. P 34 d 5.4	
		12 noon	Captain Male returned to duty from leave. T5/9369 Cpl Coates R L. T/057751 Dr	Absens
			A. L L W.H. proceeded to Cairo for remounts.	
	2.	"	FINE.	
			1 pair. 1 G.S. wagon for R.O. 3.30 p.m.	
			Baggage trains return to Company.	Absens
			O.C. 41 Dist Train inspected Camp 3 p.m.	
	3	"	FINE. 1 pair . 1 G.S. wagon for R.O. 3 p.m.	Absens
	4.	"	FINE. 1 pair 1 G.S. wagon for R.O. 3 p.m.	
			1 M.C.O. 1 pair 1 G.S. wagon for S.S.O. 1 p.m. T/9369 Cpl. Coates R.L. T/057761 Dr Addle W.H. returned to duty from Calais.	Absens

Army Form C. 2118.

WAR DIARY
or
INTELLIGENCE SUMMARY.
(Erase heading not required.)

Instructions regarding War Diaries and Intelligence Summaries are contained in F. S. Regs., Part II. and the Staff Manual respectively. Title pages will be prepared in manuscript.

Place	Date	Hour	Summary of Events and Information	Remarks and references to Appendices
THIEUSHOUK	Jul. 5	18.	Supplies by Supply Section. Refil 2 p.m. 2 p.r. 2 G.S. Wagons for R.O. 3 p.m. 1 loader, 1 driver, 1 G.S. wagon 1 p.r. H.D. detatched to No 1 Coy. T4/057996 Dr Dickson A-201698 Pr Howartt G. Horses No 1043 attatched from No 1 Coy 8 & 2 1 N.C.O. 1 Dr Turner 1 loader 8 G.S. wagons. 8 p.r. H.D. 1 Rdr.	Blank
	6	18	" " " FINE. 2 p.r. 2 G.S. Wagon for R.O. 7.15 p.m. 8.30 a.m. Coy parade for inspection of accoutrements	Blank
	7	"	" " " 2 p.r. 2 G.S. Wagon for R.O. 3.15 p.m.	Blank
	8	"	" baggage " FINE. 1 p.r. 1 G.S. wagon for S.S.O. 1.30 p.m. 1 p.r. 1 G.S. wagon for R.O. 2.30 p.m. Church parade 3 p.m. T4/058231 Pr Sadcliffe A. proceeded on leave to U.K.	Blank
	9	"	" supply " RAIN.	Blank
			" baggage " FINE. 2 p.r. 2 G.S. wagon for R.O. 2.45 p.m.	Blank

2353 Wt. W2544/1454 700,000 5/15 D. D. & L. A.D.S.S./Forms/C. 2118.

Army Form C. 2118.

WAR DIARY
or
INTELLIGENCE SUMMARY.
(Erase heading not required.)

Instructions regarding War Diaries and Intelligence Summaries are contained in F. S. Regs., Part II. and the Staff Manual respectively. Title pages will be prepared in manuscript.

Place	Date	Hour	Summary of Events and Information	Remarks and references to Appendices
THIEUSHOEK	June '19 10th	18	Supplies by Dag. Lee. re fill 2 pm. Coy Batting Parade 8:30 a.m. 1 pr HA + 9 O.Rs. for Repair Office 2:45 pm. 1 NCO 6 ORs to Bgde waggons. 6 SSO 1 pm. weather fine	TVS
"	11	18	" Supplies " " 2 pm. CAPT. IV. FLEMING returned from Special Leave. T/4 041105 Dr BRIGGS E. 201555 PTE GARGHAN W. 2 Hrs O.Nr. 83 d. + 1 2 p. hrs a.g. discharges from hosp. att 223 Coy RE. weather fine.	TVS
"	12	18	S Coy H duds for Coy Sports. 4 prs & Go to Hqrs for Races heads. Numerous Enemy aircraft over camp during the morning hours. weather fine.	TVS
"	13	18	Supplies by Duff. Lee. re fill 11:00 am. 1 NCO 6 pers Fatigue for Suffolk Drive had by 8:00 a.m. 1 Pnr No 117 dirt to Medical for weather fine.	TVS
"	14	18	" " " 11 am. " weather rain.	TVS
"	15	19	" " " 11 am. 1 23 Inf Bde Sports weather fine.	TVS

Army Form C. 2118.

WAR DIARY
or
INTELLIGENCE SUMMARY.
(Erase heading not required.)

Instructions regarding War Diaries and Intelligence Summaries are contained in F. S. Regs., Part II. and the Staff Manual respectively. Title pages will be prepared in manuscript.

Place	Date	Hour	Summary of Events and Information	Remarks and references to Appendices
THIEUSHOCK	July 16	16	Supplies by Suffly See Return 11am. 1 NCO 6 ors 1st Glos. for Suffly Duties No 2 Coy. 4.30 pm. No 3 Coy inspected by G.O.C. 24th Div. 1HA. No 106 Sentr. G. Punts see weather fine	TV2
	17	18	" 11am. Coy Bathing Parade 2.30 pm. T 40577 H NARKLEWT proceeded to Settlements Camp weather fine	TV
	18	18	" 11am. 1 NCO 3 for HQ tramsfer to Suffly Aries No 4 Coy. 3 pors. 3 enlisted 3 for HQ att. G 3 Coy from A.S.C anges att G no 4 Cory weather fine	TH
	19	18	" 11am. " weather fine	
	20	31	" 11am. Bag. " T 4058235 LS/Cpl SLIFA returns from leave. T LIEUT'S LE MANDREW transfer from No 3 to No 4 Coy. weather fine	TV
	21	18	" 11am. Suffly " Bag. Ser. Hamlin at unit. 1 am. QAC 6th Frepost cerange att. no 2 Coy. No 5 Coy moved from Camp Q 3 + 8.85 from to M11C 3580. Coy 6 pm weather fine	TV

WAR DIARY
or
INTELLIGENCE SUMMARY.
(Erase heading not required.)

Army Form C. 2118.

Place	Date	Hour	Summary of Events and Information	Remarks and references to Appendices
MU.CCS 80	July 22nd	18	Supplies to Supps bec 26th 11.30 pm. Bdy Hqrs returned to Hd 3 Coy. Weather fine	TVS
"	23	"	T.292.326 to Nunn M Porter L.Cpl 3 Coy. OC 122nd Infants Bdy and Bdy Sergt killed. Weather fine	TVS
"	24	"	11 am. Bdy Hqrs reported 6 units furnace point under Capt. TV Fleming present & mother. T.576/3 S/Sgt. Sittleworth H. proceeded home to England. Weather fine.	TVS
"	25	"	11 am. 1100 HH to proceed 08.30 am Capt. T.V. Fleming Traffic Control. Weather rich.	TVS
"	26	"	9 hr 10 am. 2/Lt LHD for relief of service 15 P.A. 10 am. Bdy Hqrs returned to Hd S Coy - H2 MCC 10" Howitzer 1 per H.A. 79 S wag. OTE Weather fine.	TVS

WAR DIARY
or
INTELLIGENCE SUMMARY.

Army Form C. 2118.

(Erase heading not required.)

Place	Date	Hour	Summary of Events and Information	Remarks and references to Appendices
M11 C3380	Jan 27th	18	Atmospheric sulphide no fire. 11am BAR proceed to Ballas below 2 mins. Brass dropped too hard - enough movement of camps 10pm. No enemies reaction.	TO
"	28	16	" 11am. 20 H 58 SP. Q 32 NQ Parted 8023 " for 238 Employment Coy. 20.4. OPE. ATP with defensive fire. Supply to Ormu Hugn. return here.	TO
"	29	16	Very dull 2 11am	TO
			for JH+Q, MAPh. 11am. To 72 B Munnij Ra returned Leine and proc. to B33 + jon to 9 left. Q/c Pom fu + T 20 25' to B36 Q.R proven. G.S Par camp 2 pm weather rain.	
"	30	18	" Supp. L.C. Tea........ for mist Safe Alfred Mar + 200 & ZY for 202-9a : to Tel ozB Nothynced 1583 B A 25 Truck H engaged by enemy as ready	TO

WAR DIARY
or
INTELLIGENCE SUMMARY.

Army Form C. 2118.

Place	Date	Hour	Summary of Events and Information	Remarks and references to Appendices
M11c2580	Aug 31	14	Supplies to Bgy. the 24 hrs 11am 1/pr 1kg May 11am. Lieut B L McAndrew & transport from 9am to 4g 6 ors 2 g, 74,057781 D. Arkle & H. returned off leave.	PG

T Browning Capt
OC 3 Coy H⁴ Div Train

WAR DIARY or INTELLIGENCE SUMMARY

Army Form C. 2118.

Place	Date	Hour	Summary of Events and Information	Remarks and references to Appendices
M11.63580 Canada Camp	1st Jan 1917		Daily Routine Reveille 5:30, Stables 6:45, Breakfast 7:45, Cpy parade 8:30, Cpy of the Army Inspection Carry 9:30 a.m. Stables 11:30. Dinner 12 noon. Parade for Runner Delivery Room Stables 4 pm. Tea 5:15. Roll Call. Parade and Hay up for horses 8:30. Supplies by Bugling. Lights fires 11 p.m.	T/A
	2		,, ,, ,, ,, ,, 11 am Cpy Pay Parade.	T/A
	3		,, ,, ,, ,, ,, 11 am to 3pm, 2 gunners of T N Lewis 118th IB received new guns.	T/A
	4		,, ,, ,, ,, ,, 11 am 1 NCO 1 pte Sto Div Cav Dep, Dpm 1 NCO 2 Drivers 1 HO dep transferred dismounted pm. Arrived 2 Wires & 4pm. 1 NCO 4 Wires on lys 3:30 2 pm supervision for AH"	J.M.A
			11 am 1 NCO 3 ptes tpt to regimental Hos 1:30 pm 4 Drivers 1 pte HA Remount Officer to 133 RE- T.97365 N Drummer E, joins this Coy. THIRZAN Br DRIVER A- to transferred 6149 DA W Walker Whs hack.	T/A

2353 Wt. W2544/1454 700,000 5/15 D. D. & L. A.D.S.S./Forms/C. 2118.

Army Form C. 2118.

WAR DIARY
or
INTELLIGENCE SUMMARY.
(Erase heading not required.)

Place	Date	Hour	Summary of Events and Information	Remarks and references to Appendices
CANADA CORNER	Aug 5	18	Supplies to Bay Sec. 9.30 a.m. 11 a.m. 1 NCO 4 prs HS Forage for Rey Officer 9.30 a.m. 1 NCO 8 prs HS Brown A transferred to 139 7.A. T4925 26 B Nunn N - 2B J.B. Irey weather fine. CHURCH PARADE 6.15 p.m.	TVB
"	6	18	Supplies Sec " 1.45 p.m. Tpr HS for water cart 139 7A. 2 prs HS & 9 wags for In An 2 Field Remount Depot 7.30 a.m. 2 prs HS away for Rey Officer. 1 Rider On 10 cent (?) No 2 Div Remount Depot weather showery	TVB
"	7	18	" 1.45 p.m. 1 NCO 3 prs 3 g-wags for res Officer batting parade 9.30 a.m. weather fine.	TVB
"	8	18	Bay Sec " 12.30 p.m. 1 NCO 3 prs HS & wags for Res Officer Ing batten parade 9.30 a.m. weather fine	TVB
"	9	18	Supplies Sec re-fill 2 p.m. 1 NCO 1pr 2 g-wags for Rey Officer 2 p.m. 1 pr HS Cart for Bn 1935S Pte P_NE W.D. 2238H Pte CUTLER t taken to hosp by Co Orderlies 23E Emp (m with me fine	TVB

Army Form C. 2118.

WAR DIARY
or
INTELLIGENCE SUMMARY.
(Erase heading not required.)

Instructions regarding War Diaries and Intelligence Summaries are contained in F. S. Regs., Part II. and the Staff Manual respectively. Title pages will be prepared in manuscript.

Place	Date	Hour	Summary of Events and Information	Remarks and references to Appendices
CANARA CORNER	10/2	16	Supplies by supply sec re fur 1.30 pm 1 pm HQ meds sent for Bath R am 1 motor lorry & 1 cargo for Bay Othr 1pm. Weather fine.	TVS
"	11th	16	12.30am - 4 prs HQ & attd. water carts return to camp 9am. Bay. Jr. reported sounds 7 pm. weather wet.	TVS
"	12	18	2a.m 2pm. Coy moved from MHC 25.F.O. at 11pm to K4 A56 T4.065.2.F.S at June 1L 2am HQ no 122 sent Mt vel sec forwarded to post camp. weather fine.	TVS
XMAS 6. THIESHOUCK	12	18	"affd 1pm 13.07.69 & Cpl Panty S4.0577 3) Pte Cast L Re attached to dut from Post Camp. 7/2 Lieut. J.B. Aston ASC att. no 3 coy. Bay Prs returned to ho. 3 coy. Weather showers	TVS

WAR DIARY or INTELLIGENCE SUMMARY.

Army Form C. 2118.

Place	Date	Hour	Summary of Events and Information	Remarks and references to Appendices
THIEPVAL WOOD	Aug. 14	18	Supplies to Supply Sec. at tin. 2pm. Inspection of Camp & horse lines by OC. 4:15. Din. 3pm. weather wet.	TVS
"	15	"	Baggage See. Ret pu 12 noon. Railhead BAIEULLE 7 A.M. 1/Cr HA rejoiny. to divar. 2e. mints from Ino 2 Train Re mount deput 2.20 pm. Gry Battery Parade 1.45 pm. 1 NCO. 1 pr HA 1 Driver re-joining. attached from 139 TA. 1 NCO 1 Leader 1 pr HA 1 Driver rejoin. att 122 TA (3q A Div) 1 SI 1 Leader, 1 pr HA rejy way att. 133 RE. 2 SI 2 Leaders 2 pr HA + 2 GS Waga. att. 1Qr Mech Pioneers. weather wet.	TVS
"	16	"	Supply Sec. rejoin 1 pm. 1 NCO 6 pt. 1 Farrier 2 Drivers. to remounts from Ino 2 Remt Dep 1.30 pm. Gry Battery Parade 4.45 pm. Pay Parade 6 pm. weather fine.	TVS
"	17	"	Baggage Sec " 1 pm. 1 NCO 3 Drivers 1 pr HA 1 GS waga to Army re mounts from Ino 2 R Dept T 405 T + SSN. A.A.E. H detached from Ino 3 by Att. E. 122 JB. Hague Hostile aircraft over Camp 9.30 pm. Port Lanterns Taken. weather fine.	TVS

WAR DIARY or INTELLIGENCE SUMMARY

Army Form C. 2118.

Place	Date	Hour	Summary of Events and Information	Remarks and references to Appendices
THIESHOUCK	18	18	Supplies by Supply Coln. ae. hrs. 1p.m. T40565203 L/Cpl LONGHURST. E.G.A. pronounced HAZEBROUCK On Reference Ordnance Corps. T2 92526 R. NUNN N. from 12 S.J.B. Hops. K hrs 3 G. Hostile air craft over Camp Very low. North of by ground fire. Bombs dropped On No 4 Cy. 1 other killed 1 other wounded. Usual precautions taken. weather fine	TVO
	19	18	" Coy. Acc. re. hrs. 1 p.m. T36698 Pte COLLINS C. returns to duty from 125th J. Bty. Wksly. Baggage Pan returned to units taken S40 80 516 PTE COLE. H.N returns of Class from Employment. T3 5651 Pte APPLEBY. H.F.W transferred to 12S J.B. Hops. Hostile aircraft over Camp Q.45 Necessary action taken. 1 AA Bender to up for this Purpose. 138 Ind. Coy. an Pro 3 Coy. weather fine.	TVO

2353 Wt. W2544/1454 700,000 5/15 D.D. & L. A.D.S.S./Forms/C. 2118.

Army Form C. 2118.

WAR DIARY
or
INTELLIGENCE SUMMARY.
(Erase heading not required.)

Instructions regarding War Diaries and Intelligence Summaries are contained in F. S. Regs., Part II. and the Staff Manual respectively. Title pages will be prepared in manuscript.

Place	Date	Hour	Summary of Events and Information	Remarks and references to Appendices
THIESHOUCQ	20	18	Supplies by Supply Col re-fill Bfore at MALIN-CAPPEL. 2 & 3 Coy by road march to Billets at STAPLE. (V.2877) arriv 1.30 pm weather fine	T/8
ESCOBECQUES ME				
ESQUEDES	21	"	re-fill 4 pm. 2 & 3 Coy continues route march Gen. in Camp ESCOB. 4.20 pm weather fine.	T/8
"	22	"	" 1.30 pm - Baggage wagg. re-join 3Coys. T. & 5.76 Pte SV RENAT proceeds on leave to U.K. OC 4th "A" Train inspiers camp. 1 S.O Hour 1 pr H.a CO pm 2.2.8 F. Coy R.E.S weather fine.	T/8
"	23	"	Bagg- re-fill 1 pm. weather fine.	T/8
"	24	"	Supply Col re-fill 1 pm. 4 Pte HA to camp for Chuklera 1.30 pm. OC 4th "A" Train reports Caust 11am weather fine.	CV
"	25	"	" re-fill 1 pm. 1 NCO 2 pte to Hospanys for Cambrai 6.30am weather fine	T/8

Army Form C. 2118.

WAR DIARY
or
INTELLIGENCE SUMMARY.
(Erase heading not required.)

Instructions regarding War Diaries and Intelligence Summaries are contained in F. S. Regs., Part II. and the Staff Manual respectively. Title pages will be prepared in manuscript.

Place	Date Aug/15	Hour	Summary of Events and Information	Remarks and references to Appendices
ESQUERDES	26	18	Supplies by Bay. Lee. retn 1 pm. Church parade 5.45 pm. Weather fine	TV3
"	27	18	Supplies Lee. retn 1 pm. T406528 Dr JONES A.L. returned to duty from R.t.. Lieut T406523 HOPE LONGHORSE E.G.H. returned from Ryhkin Castleway Course. weather wet.	TV3
"	28	18	Bay. Sec. retn 2.30 pm. Inspection of LA Boneta Nurse by Director of Veterinary Services. 2.45 pm Q.G. L 1st Div. Train inspected Ryb Inventions Div 123rd JB. weather wet.	TV3
"	29	18	Supplies Sec. retn 9 am. T29604 Pr NEILL J.J. proceeds on leave 6 to U.K. 1 Sgt. 2 horses 2 OR ways EHQS 19th Div. 1 Driver 1 horses River topeway of 226 3 Uys RES returned " " 233 Fly. RES returned to base. weather wet.	TV3
"	30	18	Bay. Sec. retn 9 am. weather wet. Cup Pay Parade 2 pm.	TV3
"	31	noon	Supplies Sec. retn. 10 am. Q.M. QM. same weather wet. TVG lunch 10.45 Oc. 3 Cy. 4th An. TRAIN	TV3

WAR DIARY
INTELLIGENCE SUMMARY.
(Erase heading not required.)

Army Form C. 2118.

Place	Date	Hour	Summary of Events and Information	Remarks and references to Appendices
ESQUERDES	Sept 1st	18	Daily Routine Reveille 5.30. Stables Groom Prepare for Parade fatigues & emp duties 9 a.m. midday Stables 1-2. Coy. Parade 1.30 pm. Evening Stables 4 pm. Roll call + evening feeds 8.30. Lights out 9 pm. Supplies by Baggery Sec. 8 p.m. 8.30 a.m. OC 4th Div Train Horse Amb'ce 10.30 a.m. Coy Both Parades 1.30 pm Supply Stores Incidents Inspected. Weather wet.	T/3
"	2	18	" Supply Sec. " 8.30 a.m. Motor Ambulance on Circuit 11.45 a.m. Necessary action taken. Weather wet.	T/3
"	3	18	" " 8.30 pm. ditto ditto 11 pm. ditto	T/3
"	4	18	" " 8.30 pm. T.292440 A/Parish E Sent to 13 GA. Horse Deveroft on Camp 10 pm. Necessary action taken. Weather fine.	T/3
"	5	18	" Baggage " 8.30 pm. MO o/p'd tps. maj. for Cavellem 2 pm. Weather fine.	T/3

Army Form C. 2118.

WAR DIARY
or
INTELLIGENCE SUMMARY.
(Erase heading not required.)

Instructions regarding War Diaries and Intelligence Summaries are contained in F. S. Regs., Part II. and the Staff Manual respectively. Title pages will be prepared in manuscript.

Place	Date	Hour	Summary of Events and Information	Remarks and references to Appendices
ESQUERDES	Sept 6	18	Supplies by Supply Sec. at fm 8.30am weather fine.	TC
"	7	18	" Baggage " T9SR0140S Sq1My Wilston T. joined m36 fr drus vis 742S1786 " Truck A broke down & no L. lry 9 spare drivers received examine by M.O. 6 for fitness for Infantry. weather fine.	TC
"	8	18	" Supply Sec " 41st Div Race Meeting 2.15. au Ruinds Gemmitere to attend 23rd Mot. Supply staging trips to joined units also 23 & Res. weather fine.	TC
"	9	18	" Baggage Sec " T9Q2440 A1 Pardish E. wounded in hot shaving Stopbeer & Driver t/20 from the Sgt. OC 3 cog. medical forward area in connection with transport. T/44445 D. Goodall J T3/022127 Dr. Heath C.F. joined from base. weather fine	T/8

WAR DIARY
or
INTELLIGENCE SUMMARY.
(Erase heading not required.)

Army Form C. 2118.

Place	Date	Hour	Summary of Events and Information	Remarks and references to Appendices
ESQUERDES	July 10th	18	Supplies to troops see ref. file 830 am. 1 NCO & 5 Ornes Returned from 1st Cornwall Units 12 noon. Hostile Aircraft over Camp 5.45 pm. Several premises taken. weather fine	T/2
"	11	18	" " " 830 am. 214885 Sgt ROSEN A. ctd as Interp. returned. T228 Labour Coy. rejd. Pte JAMES T. weather fine	T/2
"	12	18	" " " 1HP horsed to 3 coy. T/2 died MAIN E. attached 63 by j.r. duties. weather fine	T/3
"	13	18	" " of file 830 am. 1NCO & 1st 6 interpreters to unit's stunts 6.S'OMAR 85 am. 1HP 85. to 52 MA Va. 1NCO reported to Slay. 1HP 123"JR. to Balium. Baggage wag. of food ruits 5 am. weather fine	T/3
STAPLES	14	31	Supplies load moved HQ arrived HQ arrived in advance of 3 coy moved to camp 173 STAPLE area 7.15 am. 719 GOH DY NEILL T returned to duties of Pioneer Bn planed	T/3
X LATX	15	31	" by supplies see ref. file 10th inst Y. L+X return now of reinforcements 10.30 am.	T/3

WAR DIARY
or
INTELLIGENCE SUMMARY.
(Erase heading not required.)

Army Form C. 2118.

Place	Date	Hour	Summary of Events and Information	Remarks and references to Appendices
R4A7.6	16	18	Supplies Canvas to units by Supply Officer. Arrived 9.30am to camp Area 37. Huron Camp. Supplies received 12pm & 4pm. Weather fine.	T/O
Huron Camp	17	10	Supply to Supply Sec. delivered to units 7.30am. thence to Rouleans OUDERDOM to Camps. Bdy. rations to troops at Hill 1.30pm. T/69S N° LIMB L. Awarded 28 days F.P N° 1 to OC 410 Div. Train. Weather fine.	T/O
"	18	16	units 8.15am. then to Rouleans + then to troops re-fill. 1.30pm. Coy. rations Cars departs to T.H.Q. daily. 2 pm. took Tpe wagon to report CRE 41st Div. dump for Advanced RE Greenhill. Weather fine.	T/O
"	19	10	units. thence to Roulhank & Camps rations to troops re-fill 1.30pm. T/ Lieut. B. LeM. ANDREW proceeded to RE Surrey. Depot on 1 mth. formation. S4.555699 PTE GREENHILL A. to BASE DEPOT. S.355.835 PTE CARPENTER M.A. London L.3 Wg. from BASE DEPOT. 4 4.5 Swaps for Advanced CRE work.	T/O

WAR DIARY
or
INTELLIGENCE SUMMARY
(Erase heading not required.)

Army Form C. 2118.

Place	Date	Hour	Summary of Events and Information	Remarks and references to Appendices
LION CAMP 9D	15		Supplies to Supply Sec. Delivered rations to units & thence to Railhead, ret. here 1.30 p.m. Bus carried from Sharon Camp to Lion Camp. 9 a.m. Baggage wagon re-joined us. TS 7727 WHLR-BY. PUMFREY. W. proceeded to England on leave. T/18883 S.S.M. PERRY. A.R. returned to Coy for duty from T.H.Q. Italian aeroplane over camp 10 p.m. Usual precaution taken, weather wet.	TO
"	18		Deliveries ration to units & thence to Railhead ret. here 1.30 p.m. 3 prs Hrs Transp for R.E. advanced Transport. Hostile aircraft over Camp 9.20 p.m. Usual precaution taken. Weather fine.	TO
"	22	15	Delivered ration to units & thence to Railhead ret. here 1.30 p.m. 3 prs Hrs Transp for advanced R.E. Transport. Baggage wagon re-joined units. Storm, weather fine	TO

Army Form C. 2118.

WAR DIARY
or
INTELLIGENCE SUMMARY.
(Erase heading not required.)

Instructions regarding War Diaries and Intelligence Summaries are contained in F. S. Regs., Part II. and the Staff Manual respectively. Title pages will be prepared in manuscript.

Place	Date	Hour	Summary of Events and Information	Remarks and references to Appendices
LION CAMP.	23	18	Supplies carried to hulls by Supply Coy. Turned with Coy from Lion Camp 10.25am arrived at P.24.a.6.3 at 5pm. Rations delivered to units 6pm. weather fine.	T/O
	24	19	Supplies by Supply Coy. 8.15 to Railhead for Rations at Pulls 1.25pm. weather fine.	T/O
	25	18	" " at 10.30am. Baggage party & pack mules gun incorporated at 10.30am. Baggage party & pack mules gun incorporated. Turned with Coy from Camp P.24.a.63. Coy arrived at HARTFORT 6pm.	T/O
			a bay Staff Capt. to Bullets. Coy arrived at HARTFORT 6pm.	
	26	18	" Arrived a hulls by Supply Coy. Turned with Coy at 8am from HARTFORT to Hulls J.7.D.5.8 at 2.30am. Supplies re-fw. Coy arrived to Hulls J.7.D.5.8 at 2.30am. Supplies delivered to units same night. weather fine.	T/O
			11.30pm. and delivered to units same night. weather fine.	
	27	18	" By supply Coy. Re-fw. 7am. Turned with Coy 9.15am from Hulls J.7.D.58 to Hulls D.3.c.6.5 am. 2pm. Supplies delivered to units 3.15pm. Baggay way re-fwd Coy. Hostile aircraft overhead. 9.30pm. no casualties. Taken. weather fine.	T/O

WAR DIARY
or
INTELLIGENCE SUMMARY
(Erase heading not required.)

Army Form C. 2118.

Place	Date	Hour	Summary of Events and Information	Remarks and references to Appendices
DBCGS	28th	18	Supplies by supply dr retd. Pm. Following OR's prisoners on leave on XV Corps now allotment to England. T/213473 Dr GRAY. J. T/357626 Dr TAYLOR G.C. T/404326 Dr SHERRIF. C. S/403038 Pte BARBER G. H.M. Supplies received rather slower to units 9pm-onwards from	TO
	29th	8	1 Offr + 2 NCOs + 11 OR's wagon reported to Supply Offr on Railhead. For supplies in trucks 7.15am. Traffic cavaryh on line 9-10pm received supplies by supply lor. at nr 9pm precaution taken.	TO
	30	9am	Detail as 29th.	TO

Lt. McNeill
Lt. & QM., 4/10 Div. Train.

Army Form C. 2118.

WAR DIARY
or
INTELLIGENCE SUMMARY.
(Erase heading not required.)

Instructions regarding War Diaries and Intelligence Summaries are contained in F. S. Regs., Part II. and the Staff Manual respectively. Title pages will be prepared in manuscript.

Place	Date	Hour	Summary of Events and Information	Remarks and references to Appendices
Sheet 19 D3C.6.5.	Oct 1/21	18.	1 W.O. 2 NCOs 11 Pts & 11 G.S. Wagons reported to Supply Officer Railhead for Supplies in Bulk 7.15 Am. Supplies by Supply Sec: Refill 2pm, Supply Wagon of the 123 M.G. Coy rejoined Coy. "Weather Fine"	T13
	2	19.	1 W.O. 2 NCOs 11 G.S. Wagons reported to Supply Officer Railhead for Supplies in Bulk 7.30 Am. Supplies by Supply Sec: Refill 1pm. Following O.Rs proceeded on leave T4/065203 A/Cpl LONGHURST.E.G.H. T4/054475 Dr GENDERS.C.G. T4/SR/01405 C.S.M. WIGSTON.T. TS/1303 Far.Dr. NUNN. A.C. "WEATHER FINE"	T13
	3	18.	1 Officer 2 NCOs 11 G.S. Wagons reported to Supply Officer Railhead for Supplies in Bulk 7.15 Am. Supplies by Baggage Sec: Refill 1pm. 1 NCO 4 Pts & G.S. Wagons reported 2 R.S. Army Drops Coy Rk 9 A.M. for duty with 232 Rk. 2 P.S. 2 G.S. Wagons reported at R.S.O. Office LEFFRANCK HOUCKE at 4.30. 1 P.R. 1 G.S. Wagon reported at GHYVELDE to convey Ration to GHYVELDE Ration Dump. 1 P.R. 1 G.S. Wagon reported at GHYVELDE Ration Dump, at 8 A.M. to convey Rations to 36 C.C.S. Sanatorium ZUYDCOOTE. 2 Journeys. WEATHER DULL.	T13

Army Form C. 2118.

WAR DIARY
or
INTELLIGENCE SUMMARY.

(Erase heading not required.)

Instructions regarding War Diaries and Intelligence Summaries are contained in F. S. Regs., Part II. and the Staff Manual respectively. Title pages will be prepared in manuscript.

Place	Date	Hour	Summary of Events and Information	Remarks and references to Appendices
D3C65	4th	18.	1 W.O. 1 Cpl. 18 Prs. 12 G.S. Wagon 1 Limb G.S. reported to S.O. Officer Railhead for Supplies in Bulk. Paraded 7.15 a.m. Supplies by Supply Sec. Refill 1 p.m. 1 N.C.O. 7 Prs 1 G.S. Wagon reported at NEFFRINCKHOUCKE Railhead to convey Ration to GHYVELDE Ration Dump. Paraded 7.30. 1 N.C.O. N° 85. evacuated 13.9.17.T. Struck off Strength from that date. G.O.C. made inspection of Camp with O.C. Train. Weather Showery.	110
WKC57	5th	18.	Coy. moved from D3C65 with Supplies arrived W18C57 at 12.30 pm. Issued to Units. Supplies drawn from OOSTKERKE Railhead by N° 2 Coy. to Dump. Refill 2.30 pm by Supply Sec. Issued to Units. 1 N.C.O. N° 99. DIED. "C.O." took over Camp. Weather Showery.	113
"	6th	18.	Supplies by Supply Sec. Ration drawn from OOSTKERKE Railhead paraded 7.45 Am. Refill from Dump. 12 noon Issued to Units. F.P.O. 123 Bn attached to Bu Train. Coy re 4th Army Standing Orders N° 778. of 20/6/17. R+ 4th Army S.O. N° 208. Traffic Arrows marked HORSE T. Complied with. Weather Cold & Showery. 2nd 2 G.S. Wagon carried Baggage for Trench Mortars to forward area.	113

Army Form C. 2118.

WAR DIARY
or
INTELLIGENCE SUMMARY.
(Erase heading not required.)

Instructions regarding War Diaries and Intelligence Summaries are contained in F. S. Regs., Part II. and the Staff Manual respectively. Title pages will be prepared in manuscript.

Place	Date	Hour	Summary of Events and Information	Remarks and references to Appendices
W18C51	7th	18	Supplies No Refill, the extra days rations being Consumed for the 8th inst Transport Duties: 1 NCO. 6 Prs 6 G.S. Wagon conveying baggage for the 19th Middlesex to OOST DUENKERKE BAINS. 1 Pr 1 G.S. Wagon working under orders for Divl Gas Officer and 1 Pr 1 G.S. Wagon for Divl Salvage Officer. 1 Pr 1 G.S. Wagon reported at ST. IDESBALD. RLY HEAD. to Convey Rum for Bde, to 123 B.H.Qr. WINTER TIME came into force at 1. AM WEATHER WET & COLD.	TG
"	8th	18	Supplies by Supply See. Refill 9 Am from Dump Transport Duties 2 Prs working Sand Scoops for CF XV Corp. 1 Pr drew Water Cart from BRAY DUNES to DTQ. 1 R. 1 fml. H2 DADOS. 1 Pr 1 G.S. reported at ST IOFSBALD RNHD. for Rum for the 123 116HQr. CO. inspected Camp. WEATHER WET & COLD.	TG
"	9	18.	Supplies by Supply See. Refill 8 Am from Dump Transport Duties 2 Prs working Sand Scoops for CF XV Corp. 2 Prs 2 G.S. Waggon wanted 233 Coy RE. 1 Pr 1 G.S. Wagn TMQ 2 Pr 2 G.S. reported OC Divl Baths WEATHER WINDY & COLD.	TG

WAR DIARY
or
INTELLIGENCE SUMMARY.

Army Form C. 2118.

Place	Date	Hour	Summary of Events and Information	Remarks and references to Appendices
W/18 C.57	10th	18.	Supplies by Supply Sect. Refill 8 am from Dump. Transport Duties 2 Ors Working Sand Scoops for C.E. XV Corps 2 Ors 2 G.S. reported to 233 Coy R.E. 1 N.C.O 6 prs G.S. Corps Detail reported 228 Coy R.E. Weather (Fine & Cold)	TVS
"	11th	18	Supplies by Supply Sect. Refill 8 am from Dump. Transport Duties 2 Ors 2 G.S. reported 233 Coy R.E. 1 N.C.O. 8 Ors 8 G.S. reported 228 Coy R.E. Following O.R.s proceeded on Leave T/9946 2/Sap. Sadd. Nicholls W.H. T/044149 Corpl Kempton T.4/088705 Dr Andrews J. T/8125 Dr with West G.S. T/3692 Dr Collins & Transfd & Tresley T/30362 Dr Stirgrafe from Cy to T/83 Coy Weather (Windy & Cold)	TVS
"	12th	18	Supplies by Supply Sect. Refill 8 am from Dump. Transport Duties. 2 Ors 2 G.S reported 233 Coy R.E. 1 N.C.O 8 Ors 8 G.S. Corps Detail. Weather (Cold & Rain)	TVS
"	13th	18.	Supplies by Supply Sect. Refill 8 am from Dump. Transport Duties 2 Ors 2 G.S. reported 233 Coy R.E. 1 N.C.O 8 Or 8 G.S. Corps Detail Weather (Wet & Cold)	TVS

Army Form C. 2118.

WAR DIARY
or
INTELLIGENCE SUMMARY.
(Erase heading not required.)

Instructions regarding War Diaries and Intelligence Summaries are contained in F. S. Regs., Part II. and the Staff Manual respectively. Title pages will be prepared in manuscript.

Place	Date	Hour	Summary of Events and Information	Remarks and references to Appendices
W 18 C 5 7.	14th	18	Supplies by Supply Sect. Refill 8am from Dump. Transport Duties 1 R. 1 G.S. R.E. Workshops 1 R. 1 G.S. Blacksmiths Shop from Camp to D.A.D.O.S. 2 R. 2 G.S. 233 Coy R.E. Weather (Fine)	NB
"	15th	18.	Supplies by Supply Sect. Refill 7:30am from Dump. Transport Duties 2 R. 2 G.S. 233 Coy R.E. Baggage Sect. moved Sole unit T/1659 Dr. Lomb L T/063203 L-cpl Longhurst E.94. T/4/057475 Dr Senders E.g. 4 T3203 Q Mss Munn. A.E. Hollamy Weather (Fine) Released from Detention the undermentioned Returned from Leave T.2.R. / 011405 B.S.M. Wigston. T. OR proceeded on Leave T/939 Pt Hss Coates T/55394 L-cpl Smith.T/565285 Dr Jones. A.E.	NB
"	16th	18.	Supplies by Supply Sect. Refill 7:30 from Dump. Transport Duties 2 R. 2 G.S. 233 Coy R.E. Weather (Fine & Cold)	NB
"	17th	18	Supplies by Supply Sect. Refill 7:30 from Dump. Transport Duties 2 R. 2 G.S. 233 Coy R.E. 1 N.C.O 6 Rn 6 G.S. Corps Detail. Weather (Fine)	NB
"	18th	18	Supplies by Supply Sect. Refill 7:30am from Dump. Transport Duties 2 Rn 2 G.S. 233 Coy R.E. 1 N.C.O 6 Rn 6 G.S. Corps Detail S/070492 Pt Bradbury returned off Leave. Weather (Fine)	NB

Army Form C. 2118.

WAR DIARY
or
INTELLIGENCE SUMMARY.
(Erase heading not required.)

Instructions regarding War Diaries and Intelligence Summaries are contained in F. S. Regs., Part II. and the Staff Manual respectively. Title pages will be prepared in manuscript.

Place	Date	Hour	Summary of Events and Information	Remarks and references to Appendices
W.18.C.5.7.	19th	18.	Supplies by Supply Sect Refill 7.30 am from Dump 2 Res 2 G.S. 233 Coy R.E. 24. 34.D. 1 6 Riders Clipped at Dust Clipping Stable. Transport Duties 2 Res Weather (Fine)	T/S
"	20th	18	Supplies by Supply Sect Refill 7.30 am from Dump 2 G.S. 233 Coy R.E. 1 R. 1 G.S. Supplies for A.P.M. 3 Res 3.8.5. Y Corps R.E. Dump. 2 Res Marker Posted to Normal S/O. N2 63 Returned from 52= Mot. Vet. the undermentioned O Ranks proceeded on leave to England T961 Dr Sadd Dickinson T057023 Dr Edwards T057 153th Dr Hope W9 736546 Dr Horsely W. Transport Duties 2 Res Weather (Fine)	T/O
"	21st	18	Supplies by Supply Sect Refill 7.30 am from Dump. 2 Res 2 G.S. 233 Coy R.E. 2 pr XV Corps Working Band Scoops 1 R. 1 G.S. Manchester R.E. Dump. Transport Duties Church of England Service 2pm. Weather (Fine)	T/O
"	22nd	19	Supplies by Supply Sect Refill 7.30 am from Dump R.E. Dump 1 R. 1 G.S. Railhead 2 G.S. 233 Coy R.E. 1 R. 1 G.S. Manchester Transport Duties 2 Res Weather (Fine)	T/O

Army Form C. 2118.

WAR DIARY
or
INTELLIGENCE SUMMARY.
(Erase heading not required.)

Instructions regarding War Diaries and Intelligence Summaries are contained in F. S. Regs., Part II. and the Staff Manual respectively. Title pages will be prepared in manuscript.

Place	Date	Hour	Summary of Events and Information	Remarks and references to Appendices
W.18.C.5.7.	23rd	18	Supplies by Baggage Sect. Refill 7.30.am. from Dump. Transport Duties 2 G.S. 233 Coy R.E. H.Q. 1 Rider Clipped at Divl Clipping Stable (weather wet) 2 G.S. 2 O.Rank proceeded for Remounts & returned same day	TVB
	24.	18.	Supplies by Supply Sec. Refill 7.30 A.m. Transport Duties 2 trs. 2 G.S. 233 Coy R.E. 1 Gr. 1 G.S. APM Supplies 2 G.S. Area Commandant LA PANNE. 2 Gr. 2 G.S. Coal to Dul Baths. The following O.Rs. proceed on LEAVE T/3. 024064 Cpl. Johnson W.J. T/4. 065236 D/Hopley J.T. T/5. 36273 D/Morsley N. T/4. 057428 D/Yulf G. " returned off LEAVE S/SGT. KEATE. S/SGT-SHOR. NICHOLLS. W.H. WEATHER. FINE.	TVB
"	25.	18.	Supplies by Supply Sec. Refill 7.30 A.M. Transport Duties. 3 Gr. 3 G.S. Reported No.1 Coy Dump to Convey Rations to 156 Sea Pk. 2. 2. reported to Brig Observation Officer at R30 Central at 6.pm. The following O.Rs. returned off LEAVE T/044169 Cpl Kimpton F. T/058/05 D/Andrews G.F. T/5. 8125. D/Whlr. West. G.F. WEATHER Fine & Windy	TVB

WAR DIARY
or
INTELLIGENCE SUMMARY.
(Erase heading not required.)

Army Form C. 2118.

Place	Date	Hour	Summary of Events and Information	Remarks and references to Appendices
W18.C57	26th	18	Supplies by Supply Sec. Refill 7.30 A.m. Transport duties 1 Gr. GS Wagon reported to R.S.O. St. Desibalde Reilway @ 7.30 a.m. 2 " " " " at Manchester Dump " " " " to OC 87 Labour Coy. 1st Mules & feeder stores delivered rations for the Bombing School WEATHER FINE	TV3
"	27th	18	Supplies by Supply Sec. Refill 7.30 a.m. Transport Duties:- 1 NCO 4 Prs 4 GS Wagon reported at Rail Siding Dump H.Pn. 2 " " 1 GS Wagon reported at M.D.O. B.C. 5 at 8.30 a.m. 1 " " " " to R.S.O. St Desibalde at Manchester Dump. Weather Fine	TV3
"	28th	18	Supplies by Supply Sec. Refill 7.30 a.m. Transport Duties:- 2 Prs 2 GS. reported to OC Aircraft Pac W21 Dro Shut 11.9 A.m. 2 " 2 " " CRE 8 A.m. 2 " 2 " " Fd FC St. Desibalde 8 A.m. Baggage Sec. Joined their respective Units at 5 P.M. Church parade O/E at 2 P.M. Weather Fine T.35594 Act Cpl Smith JF returned off leave.	TV3

Army Form C. 2118.

WAR DIARY
or
INTELLIGENCE SUMMARY.
(Erase heading not required.)

Instructions regarding War Diaries and Intelligence Summaries are contained in F. S. Regs., Part II. and the Staff Manual respectively. Title pages will be prepared in manuscript.

Place	Date	Hour	Summary of Events and Information	Remarks and references to Appendices
WK C8.7	29	18.	Supplies by Supply Sec. Repu 7.30 am. The following O.R's returned from LEAVE T.S. 9369 2nd Cpl Coates R.L. T/4. 065285 Dr Jones A/b. Weather fine	T/B
	30.	18	Supplies by Supply Sec. Repu 7.30 am. Lieut Andrew B/b Schluck off Strength of the Coy. Weather fine	T/O
	31	Noon	Supplies by Supply Sec. Repu 7.30 am.	T/O

T Blewing
Capt
O.C. No 3 Coy 4th Div. Train

// Army Form C. 2118.

WAR DIARY
INTELLIGENCE SUMMARY.
(Erase heading not required.)

Instructions regarding War Diaries and Intelligence Summaries are contained in F. S. Regs., Part II. and the Staff Manual respectively. Title pages will be prepared in manuscript.

Place	Date	Hour	Summary of Events and Information	Remarks and references to Appendices
CAMPO SAMPIERO	MARCH 1st	18	General Routine. Horse Exercise prior to Entraining. WEATHER. Fine.	T/O
"	2nd	"	Coy Moved from billet at (CAMPO SAMPIERO) at 10 am to Entrain at (CAMPOSAMPIERO) Station. Train Departed at 1.39 p.m. WEATHER. Fine	T/O
"	3rd	"	—do— WEATHER. Fine	T/O
"	4th	"	Train Collapsed at 4h 5 am between the Stations of Muldon & St Michel. Several trucks wrecked incl. No Casualties to Coy. 1 Dr. 41 9/Cav Loader attached to 1th 123rd Inf. Bde. Had Os Wounded. Train Divided into 2 parts from wreckage 1st Proceeded to St Michel Station No 2 Arrived at St Michel Station at 4.30. Returned to Muldon at 12.30 pm No.1 Arrived at 4 pm No 2 to Muldon at 4 pm No 2 at 4.30. WEATHER. Fine & Cold.	T/O

Army Form C. 2118.

WAR DIARY
or
INTELLIGENCE SUMMARY.
(Erase heading not required.)

Instructions regarding War Diaries and Intelligence Summaries are contained in F. S. Regs., Part II and the Staff Manual respectively. Title pages will be prepared in manuscript.

Place	Date	Hour	Summary of Events and Information	Remarks and references to Appendices
ST. MICHEL	5th	18	Horses Entrained from Wreckage	T/3
	6th	"	Train Departed from St Michel at 10.40 am WEATHER Fine	T/3
	7th	"	Train Rejoined the other portion at (St JEAN) at 1 am & Departed at 12.00 am WEATHER Fine	T/3
	8th	"	Train Detrained at DOULLENS at 1.30 pm & arrived at (IVERGNY) at 7.15 pm WEATHER Fine	T/3
IVERGNY	9th	"	Supplies by Supply Sect. Refill 9.30 am Delivered to Stations was done WEATHER Fine	T/3
	10th	"	Supplies by Supply Sect. Refill 9.30 am Delivered to Units & Returned to camp Baggage Wagons Rejoined Coy. from Units (WEATHER Fine)	T/6
"	11			

WAR DIARY
or
INTELLIGENCE SUMMARY.
(Erase heading not required.)

Army Form C. 2118.

Instructions regarding War Diaries and Intelligence Summaries are contained in F.S. Regs., Part II. and the Staff Manual respectively. Title pages will be prepared in manuscript.

Place	Date	Hour	Summary of Events and Information	Remarks and references to Appendices
(IVERGNY)	11th	18	Supplies by Supply Sect. Refill 9.30am & Delivered to Units (WEATHER Fine)	T/3
"	12th	"	Supplies by Supply Sect. Refill 9.30am & Delivered to Units. The under-mentioned o.ranks proceeded on Leave to the United Kingdom. 78935 Pte Thomas 84172 Dr Thomas 286 Dr Sawdon J 70416 Pte Daw W. B.Sergt Taylor W.J. 36248. WEATHER Fine	T/3
"	13th	"	Supplies by Supply Sect. Refill 9.30am & Delivered to Units. 311296 Pte Wood a Admitted to 139th Fld Amb. (WEATHER Fine)	T/3
"	14th	"	Supplies by Supply Sect. Refill 9.30am & Delivered to Units. 29781 Pte Bryant Proceeded on Leave to the United Kingdom. WEATHER Dull & Cold	T/3
"	15th	"	Supplies by Baggage Sect. Refill 9am & Delivered to Units. The undermentioned o.ranks Proceeded on Leave to the United Kingdom 15183 T.S.Sm. Bryant R/2483/ Dr Cassidy B. ~ I/75528 Dr Minnis W. (WEATHER Fine)	T/3

Army Form C. 2118.

WAR DIARY
or
INTELLIGENCE SUMMARY.
(Erase heading not required.)

Instructions regarding War Diaries and Intelligence Summaries are contained in F. S. Regs., Part II. and the Staff Manual respectively. Title pages will be prepared in manuscript.

Place	Date	Hour	Summary of Events and Information	Remarks and references to Appendices
IVERGNY.	16th	18.	Supplies by Supply Sect. Refill 9 am & Delivered to Units the undermentioned Ranks Returned off leave from the United Kingdom T/64709 Pte Moles T. T/46958 Cpl. Peat T/40 259994 Cpl Gray T T/6647 Cpl Gray E. T/259 Dr Kent L. T/36393 Dr Mears W. T/36348 Dr Stanage W. T/36138 Dr Woodcock W. WEATHER fine	T/O
"	17th	"	Supplies by Baggage Sect. Refill 9 am & Delivered to Units WEATHER fine	T/O
"	18th	"	Supplies by Supply Sect: Refill 9 am & Delivered to Units 2nd Refill 3pm & Returned to Camp. WEATHER fine	T/O
"	19th	"	Supplies by Baggage Sect. Delivered Rations to Units at 9 am. Refill 3pm & Returned to Camp. Wagons of the 233rd Hd Coy R.F.A. 123rd MGC Detached to Units (WEATHER. WET & Cold)	T/O

Army Form C. 2118.

WAR DIARY
or
INTELLIGENCE SUMMARY.
(Erase heading not required.)

Instructions regarding War Diaries and Intelligence Summaries are contained in F. S. Regs., Part II. and the Staff Manual respectively. Title pages will be prepared in manuscript.

Place	Date	Hour	Summary of Events and Information	Remarks and references to Appendices
MARIEUX	20th	18.	Supplies by Supply Sect. Delivered to Units at 8am. Refill 11.30am. Baggage Wagons Proceeded to Units at 8am. Loaded & Returned to Camp. Coy. Moved from (IVERGNY) at 1pm with Supply & Baggage Sect. Loaded. And arrived at (MARIEUX) at 6pm. N.º T/36323 Dr. Reynolds.T. Returned off Leave from the United Kingdom. (WEATHER RAINY)	T/S
BOUZINCOURT	21st	18.	Coy. Moved from (MARIEUX) at 8.30am With Supply & Baggage Sect & Arrived at BOUZINCOURT at 12.10pm. Supply & Baggage Sect. Delivered Rations & Baggage to Units. Supply Sect. Refilled at 5.30pm & Returned to Camp. WEATHER Fine	T/S
ACHIET LE PETIT	22nd	18	Coy Moved from (BOUZINCOURT) at 8am with Supply Sect. at 8am. Baggage Sect Joined Coy on Line of March. Coy arrived at (ACHIET-LE-PETIT) at 3.15pm. Supply & Baggage Sect Delivered Rations & Baggage to Units at 5pm. & Supply Sect Returned to Camp. (WEATHER Fine)	T/O
"	23rd	18	Supplies by Supply Sect. Proceeded to Refilling Point at 12 noon. Refill 1pm & Delivered to Units. WEATHER Fine	T/O

Army Form C. 2118.

WAR DIARY
or
INTELLIGENCE SUMMARY.
(Erase heading not required.)

Instructions regarding War Diaries and Intelligence Summaries are contained in F. S. Regs., Part II. and the Staff Manual respectively. Title pages will be prepared in manuscript.

Place	Date	Hour	Summary of Events and Information	Remarks and references to Appendices
ACHIET LE PETIT	24th	18	Supplies by Supply Sect. Forwarded to Railhead at 8 am. 1st Refill 9 am Rations Conveyed to Units by Bde. Transport. 2nd Refill 2 pm by Supply Sect. 1 Returns of 16 Camp. Coy. Moved from (ACHIET LE PETIT) at 6.15 pm and Sub Station Opened at (BUC QUOY) at 8 pm. WEATHER Fine T/04387 Sub Warehouse & S/3817S Retn. of Goods Coy from Base Depot.	⊗
ST. AMAND	25th	19th	Coy Moved from (BUC QUOY.) at 3 am and Arrived at (BIENVILLERS) at 10 am and Supply Sect. Delivered Rations to Units. Coy moved from (BIENVILLERS) at 4 pm & arrived at (ST AMAND.) at 6 pm. WEATHER Fine + Cold	⊗
Mr BAILLEULMONT	26th	19st	Supplies by Supply Sect. Refill 9 am. Returned to Camp. Coy Moved from (ST AMAND.) at 10 am & Arrived at Camp Nr BAILLEULMONT at 6 pm. Supply Sect. Delivered Rations to Units (WEATHER Fine + Cold)	⊗
"	27th		Supplies by Supply Sect. Refill 1 pm & Delivered Rations to Units (WEATHER Fine + Cold)	⊗

Army Form C. 2118.

WAR DIARY
or
INTELLIGENCE SUMMARY.
(Erase heading not required.)

Instructions regarding War Diaries and Intelligence Summaries are contained in F.S. Regs., Part II. and the Staff Manual respectively. Title pages will be prepared in manuscript.

Place	Date	Hour	Summary of Events and Information	Remarks and references to Appendices
SAULTY	28th	18	Coy Moved from Camp (NR. BAVILLEMONT.) at 10 a.m. & Arrived at SAULTY. at 12.30 p. Supply Sect Refill 12 noon & Delivered to Units. (WEATHER Dull & Cold)	TB
AUTHIE	29th	18	Supplies by Supply Sect. Refill Noon Coy Moved from (SAULTY) with Supply Sect Delivered to Units at 12.30 p. & Arrived at (AUTHIE) at 4 p.m Supply Sect Delivered to Units (WEATHER Dull & Cold)	TB
"	30th	18	Supplies by Supply Sect Refill 9 a.m. & Delivered Rations to Units WEATHER Wet & Cold	TB
"	31st	14	Supplies by Supply Sect Refill 9.30 a.m. & Delivered Rations to Units Transport Duties 2 A.S.C. 2 G.S. C.R.E. (WEATHER Fine.)	TB

J B ——— Capt
O.C. No 3 Coy. 111st Divl. Train R.C.—

WAR DIARY
or
INTELLIGENCE SUMMARY.

Army Form C. 2118.

Place	Date	Hour	Summary of Events and Information	Remarks and references to Appendices
	April			
THIEVRES	1st	18th	Supplies by Supply Sect. Refill 8.30am. Coy Moved from (AUTHIE) at 4 pm & arrived at (THIEVRES) at 5.15 pm. Supply Sect Delivered Rations to Units & Refilled 6pm & Returned to Camp. (WEATHER Dull)	AA
"	2nd	"	Supplies by Supply Sect. Delivered Rations to Units at 9am & Refilled 2pm & Delivered to Units. Supply Sect Detached to Units. (WEATHER Fine)	AA
(PETIT-NOUVIN)	3rd	"	Coy Moved from (THIEVRES) at 9am & arrived at (PETIT-NOUVIN) at 6pm. (WEATHER Dull)	AA
EECKE	4th	"	Coy Entrained at (PETIT-NOUVIN) at 2.30am. Train Departed at 6am. Coy Detrained at (PESEKHOCK) at 11.15am, & proceeded to (EECKE) arriving at 6.30pm. Supplies by Supply Sect. Refilled 6.30pm. Delivered Rations to Units & Reported Coy the undermentioned Officers & NCOs returned off leave from the United Kingdom 2/Lieut H.B. Aston. 735883 TSSM Bryant. & 6933 Tom.S. Sergt Taylor W.S. (WEATHER Rainy)	AA
"	5th	"	Supplies by Supply Sect. Refill 8.30am & Delivered Rations to Units the undermentioned O.Ranks Returned off leave from the United Kingdom. M2536 T/Cpl. Chidgey H. 24/86. Dr. Bowden J. 793526. Pte. Driver W.J. 993416. Pte. Drew W.J. Pte. Bryant. (WEATHER Fine)	AA

Army Form C. 2118.

WAR DIARY
or
INTELLIGENCE SUMMARY.
(Erase heading not required.)

Instructions regarding War Diaries and Intelligence Summaries are contained in F.S. Regs., Part II. and the Staff Manual respectively. Title pages will be prepared in manuscript.

Place	Date	Hour	Summary of Events and Information	Remarks and references to Appendices
EBCKE	6th	10.	Supplies by Supply Sect Refill 8.30 am. Delivered to Units Extra Wagons Rejoined Coy from Units. Dr Thomas EM Struck off Strength of Coy 1 Dr Cassidy B. Admitted to Hosp. (WEATHER Fine.)	NIL
"	7th	18	Supplies by Supply Sect Refill 9.30 am. Deliveries Rations to Units Dr Amos C Admitted to 130 Fy HA and Lieut Harris Rejoined Coy 4 Drs 8 ATO ADS Detached from Coy Surplus Transport. (WEATHER Dull.)	NIL
SHEET 28. 3.h. AA 3.0	8th	18	Supplies by Supply Sect Refill 8.30 am Returned to Camp. Coy Moved from (ECKE) at 10.30 am & arrived at Camp 6.h AA 30 at 3.15 pm Supply Sect Delivered Rations to Units 43.10 Dr Fry N & 1933/Pt Blake W.9 Struck off Strength of Coy (WEATHER Fine.)	NIL
"	9th	18	Supplies by Supply Sect Refill 10 am. Delivered Rations to Units 2045/6 Sinjt Sturrup Returned off Leave from the United Kingdom. Corpl Young C Admitted to Hos. 139th Fld Amb. (WEATHER Fine.)	NIL

Army Form C. 2118.

WAR DIARY
or
INTELLIGENCE SUMMARY.
(Erase heading not required.)

Instructions regarding War Diaries and Intelligence Summaries are contained in F. S. Regs., Part II. and the Staff Manual respectively. Title pages will be prepared in manuscript.

Place	Date	Hour	Summary of Events and Information	Remarks and references to Appendices
SHEET 2% G.H, A.3.0.	10th	18.	Supplies by Supply Sect. Proceeded to Railhead at 9am & Conveyed Rations to Refilling Point. Refill 2pm & Returned Rations to Units. (WEATHER Dull)	R.H
"	11st	18	Supplies by Supply Sect. Proceeded to Refilling Point at 2pm Refill 2.30pm & Returned Rations to Units. WEATHER fine	R.H.
"	12th	18.	Supplies by Supply Sect Proceeded to Refilling Point at 2pm Refilled at 2.30pm & Returned Rations to Units Baggage Wagons Reported by from Units Capt Ty Jenning R.E Corpl Smith Q.E. 1 Dr Noble Detached to the 2nd Army. (WEATHER fine)	R.H.
"	13st	18	Supplies by Supply Sect Proceeded to Refilling Point at 1.45pm Refilled 2pm & Returned to Units. Supply & Baggage Wagons of the following Units attached to Coy vi* DNA & Supply 2 Baggage Wagons of 6th H.L.I Regt Oct 26- 1 Water 32" Mob Vet Sect. 1 Limber of 51st H.F.A C.R.E WEATHER fine	(R)

Army Form C. 2118.

WAR DIARY
or
INTELLIGENCE SUMMARY.
(Erase heading not required.)

Instructions regarding War Diaries and Intelligence Summaries are contained in F. S. Regs., Part II. and the Staff Manual respectively. Title pages will be prepared in manuscript.

Place	Date	Hour	Summary of Events and Information	Remarks and references to Appendices
SUEZ TS. OH. ANZO.	14/4	18	Supplies by Baggage test proceeded to Refilling Point 4 to 15 pm. Refill 4.30 to 6 Reserve Rations to Unit. 7/h. Unmentioned O.R. as be reported to this Company from eye as general Cupt. Heavy from M.H. Coy. Pte. Brimning from M.H. Coy. Pte. Ashcroft from M.H. Coy. 1/3 Btn. N.Z.P. T93365 Dv. Bannon E. Proceeded to 139th F.A. to undergo a course of instructions.	(WEATHER Dull & rainy)
"	15/4	18	Supplies by Supply test proceeded to Refilling Point at 2.45 pm. Refill 3 pm & Delivered Reserve Rations to Unit. 1 N.Co. 2 B.s 2 G.S. Wagons from Blair Baggage Wagons Detailed to Unit. T2/7037 Dv. Ames Returned to Duty from the 46th D.R.S.	(WEATHER Dull)
"	16/4	18	Supplies by Supply test. Proceeded to Refilling Point at 12.45 pm. Refill 1 pm & Delivered Rations to Units.	(WEATHER Dull)
"	17/4	18	Supplies by Supply test Proceeded to (RESERVOIR) Railhead at 7.30 am will had to return to Camp owing to heavy Shell fire at Railhead Proceeded to Refilling Point at 2.45 pm. Refill 3 pm & Delivered Rations to Units Ration Convoy to Refilling Point (4) M.T. trans. Nos. 119-54.39.40.25 Sgt. Refer W. Admitted to the 139th F.A. with Scalp wound received at Railhead	(WEATHER Dull)

Army Form C. 2118.

WAR DIARY
or
INTELLIGENCE SUMMARY.
(Erase heading not required.)

Instructions regarding War Diaries and Intelligence
Summaries are contained in F. S. Regs., Part II.
and the Staff Manual respectively. Title pages
will be prepared in manuscript.

Place	Date	Hour	Summary of Events and Information	Remarks and references to Appendices
SHEET 2.S				
GH. ADZ.B.	18th	18	Supplies by Supply Sect. Proceeded to (PROVEN) Railhead at 8.30am & Conveyed Rations to Refilling Point. Refill 2pm & Delivered Rations to Units. 11 a.m. 18	(WEATHER Dull)
"	19th	18	Supplies by Supply Sect. Proceeded to Refilling Point at 1.45 pm. Refill 2pm & Delivered Rations to Units.	(WEATHER Snowy.)
"	20th	18	Supplies by Supply Sect. Proceeded to Refilling Point at 12.45pm Refill 1pm & Delivered Rations to Units. 2043970. B. Sergt. KEEFE W. having been evacuated to the C.C.S. is struck off the strength from the M.T. coast T.29.30.65 & Retoned from the 139th Fld Amble. having completed a course of state Cadu. & 4 No ammte.	(WEATHER Fine.)
"	21st	18	Supplies by Baggage Sect. Proceeded to Refilling Point at 1pm Refill 1.30pm & Delivered Rations to Units. M.COS feelives & Demonstration on (HOTCHKISS. GUN.)	(WEATHER fine.)
"	22nd	18	Supplies by Supply Sect. Proceeded to Refilling Point at 12.45pm Refill 1pm & Delivered Rations to Units. 2 H.D. Horses Nos 24 & 123 evacuated from the 52nd M.V.S. N.C.O.S feature & Demonstration on (HOTCHKISS. GUN.) Transport Duties 1NCO 3No 3 G.S. Wagons & ORS for Salvage.	(WEATHER fine.)
"	23rd	18	Supplies by Baggage Sect Proceeded to Refilling Point at 12.45 pm Refill 1pm & Delivered Rations to Units. Transport Duties 1NCO 3No 3 G.S. Wagons for Salvage.	WEATHER fine
"	24th	18	Supplies by Supply Sect. Proceeded to Refilling Point at 12.45pm Refill 1pm & Delivered Rations to Units. 2 H.D. Horses Nos 24 & 123 having been evacuated from the 52nd M.V.S. are struck off ch. Strength from the 21st inst.	WEATHER fine

WAR DIARY
INTELLIGENCE SUMMARY

Army Form C. 2118.

Place	Date	Hour	Summary of Events and Information	Remarks and references to Appendices
SHEET 28. G.H. AA3.0	25th	18	Supplies by Baggage Sect. Proceeded to Refilling Point at 12.45 pm Refill 1pm & Delivered Rations to Units. Bathing Parade 9am 50% of Company at light the unemployed oRanks & Rose did to Coins pr Ramounts Cpl Bidgey N (S?) Hunt 10 & Amo. C. (WEATHER fine)	R4
A.16. A.8.4.	26th	21	Supplies by Supply Sect. Proceeded to Refilling Point 12.45pm Refill 1pm & Delivered Rations to Units. Baggage Wagons Departed to Units by Road from G.H. AA3.0 at 7.30 pm. Arrived at A.16.A.8.4 at 9pm. WEATHER fine	R4
F.28. b.4.c.	27th	18	Supplies by Supply Sect. Proceeded to Refilling Point at 12.45pm Refill 1pm & Delivered Rations to Units (3rd [illegible]) Moved from A.16.A.8.4 at 1.30pm & arrived at F.28 b.4.c. at 3pm (Col Young B.R. Troops) Struck off Strength from 19th inst. WEATHER fine	R.4
	28th		Supplies by Supply Sect. Proceeded to (PROVEN) Refilling Point at 9.am. Convoy & Rations in bulk to Refilling Point. Refill 1pm & Delivered to Units. The undermentioned ORs having joined from Base Depot and taken on our Coy Strength 17 Gun Dr Fisher W.Y T.73951 Dr. McCaul. J.D. B.340. Horses having joined from Remount Depot are taken on our Coy Strength 119 Stroh Ok Stole & Other out (from 401 Coy Remounts) & Ranks returns from Coins & Adams to be Struck Our. WEATHER fine	R3

Army Form C. 2118.

WAR DIARY
or
INTELLIGENCE SUMMARY.
(Erase heading not required.)

Instructions regarding War Diaries and Intelligence Summaries are contained in F. S. Regs., Part II. and the Staff Manual respectively. Title pages will be prepared in manuscript.

Place	Date	Hour	Summary of Events and Information	Remarks and references to Appendices
SHEET 27. F.29. B.40	29th	18	Supplies by Supply Sect. Proceeded to (PROVEN) Railhead at 8 am but had to return to Camp owing to Heavy Shell fire. Dr. 147205 Dr. Whitford 1 attached from No.1 Coy wounded. Supply Sect. Proceeded to Refilling Point at 10 pm. Refill 10.0 pm & Delivered Rations to Units (WEATHER. fine.)	
"	30th	16	Supplies by Supply Sect. Proceeded to Refilling Point at 4 pm. Refill came & Delivered rations to Units. 32nd Regd. 2 Bdes Returned loaded to Camp. (WEATHER. fine.)	

Warin Lieut for
O.C. No 3 Coy
41st Divisional Train

In the field
30/4/1918.

Army Form C. 2118.

WAR DIARY
or
INTELLIGENCE SUMMARY.

(Erase heading not required.)

Instructions regarding War Diaries and Intelligence Summaries are contained in F. S. Regs., Part II. and the Staff Manual respectively. Title pages will be prepared in manuscript.

Place	Date	Hour	Summary of Events and Information	Remarks and references to Appendices
SHEET. 27 F.21.C.11.	MAY 1st	18th	Supplies by Supply Sect. Delivered Rations to Units at 8.30 am and Coy Moved from SHEET 27 F.28.b.40. at 3 pm and arrived at Camp SHEET 27 F.21.C.11. at 3.30 pm. Supply Sect. Refilled at 6 pm & Returned Loaded to Camp. No 33294 Pte. FOOTE. F. Attached from N° 2 Company Admitted to one 139th Field Ambula N° 421831 Pte CASSIDY. B. having been admitted to Hosp. on 24th while on leave in U.K. is struck off the strength from that date. (WEATHER FINE.)	1BA
"	2nd	18th	Supplies by Supply Sect. Delivered Rations to Units at 9 am. Supply Sect. Refilled at 3.30 pm & Returned Loaded to Camp. NCO's Lecture & Demonstration on (HOTCHKISS.) Gunnery. (WEATHER FINE)	2BA
"	3rd	18th	Supplies by Supply Sect. Delivered Rations to Units at 9 am. Supply Sect. Refilled 2.30 pm & Returned Loaded to Camp. Transport Duties. 1 N.C.O. 2 Pte 2 G.S. Wagons T.H.Q. Detail. (WEATHER FINE)	2BA
"	4th	18th	Supplies by Supply Sect. Delivered Rations to Units at 9 am Supply Sect Refilled at 2 pm Returned Loaded to Camp. N° 354211 Pte WILLIAMS. W.9. joined Company from the 238 Employment Company Baggage Wagons Rejoined Company from Units NCOs Lecture & Demonstration in (HOTCHKISS) Gunnery. (WEATHER FINE)	2BA
"	5th	18th	Supplies by Baggage Sect. Delivered Rations to Units at 9 am. Baggage Sect. Refilled at 2 pm & Returned Loaded to Camp. N° 654709 Corpl. FISHER. T. Proceeded to the II Corps Schools to undergo a course in (HOTCHKISS) Gunnery. Lieut. J.B Aston Transport Officer at Pulheads (WEATHER WET)	2BA

Army Form C. 2118.

WAR DIARY
or
INTELLIGENCE SUMMARY.
(Erase heading not required.)

Instructions regarding War Diaries and Intelligence Summaries are contained in F. S. Regs., Part II. and the Staff Manual respectively. Title pages will be prepared in manuscript.

Place	Date	Hour	Summary of Events and Information	Remarks and references to Appendices
SHEET 27 F21.C.11.	6th	18	Supplies Delivered to Units by Baggage Sect at 9am Supply Sect Proceeded to (ROUSBRUGGE) Railhead & Conveyed Rations in bulk to Refilling Point. Refill 2pm & Returned Loaded to Camp. The following are appointed ranks as stated T35394 a/Lce SMITH J.E. to 2/Cpl. n T088656 Dr. KENT A.T. to 2/Lce Corpl Loaded Replaced N° 133952 Pte NEW B/Y N° T2 357249 Pte QUARRY replaces N°201489 Pte BLAKE J. N°201363 Pte CASSIDY J. Reported to the 238th Employment Coy. Transport Duties 1.R.1.B.S. 7Kg Detail. N°20806 Pte CASSIDY J. returned unable to proceed to the 238th Employment Coy through injury to knee. (WEATHER FINE)	93A
"	7th	18	Supplies Delivered to Units by Baggage Sect at 8.30am Supply Sect Proceeded to ROUSBRUGGE Railhead & Conveyed Rations in bulk to Refilling Point. Refill 2pm & Returned Loaded to Camp. (WEATHER FINE)	93A
"	8th	18	Supplies Delivered to Units by Baggage Sect at 8.30am Supply Sect Proceeded to (ROUSBRUGGE) Railhead & Conveyed Rations in bulk to Refilling Point. Refill 2pm & Returned Loaded to Camp. (WEATHER FINE)	93A
"	9th	18	Supplies Delivered to Units by Baggage Sect at 8.30am Supply Sect Proceeded to ROUSBRUGGE Railhead & Conveyed Rations in bulk to Refilling Point. Refill 2pm & Returned Loaded to Camp. (WEATHER FINE)	93A
"	10th	18	Supplies Delivered to Units by Baggage Sect at 8.30am Supply Sect Proceeded to (ROUSBRUGGE) Railhead at 8am & Conveyed Rations in bulk to Refilling Point Refill 2pm & Returned Loaded to Camp. Capt J.Y. Fleming N° T 257/81 D.A.C.&s was returned from 2nd Army. (WEATHER FINE)	93A

Army Form C. 2118.

WAR DIARY
or
INTELLIGENCE SUMMARY.
(Erase heading not required.)

Instructions regarding War Diaries and Intelligence Summaries are contained in F. S. Regs., Part II. and the Staff Manual respectively. Title pages will be prepared in manuscript.

Place	Date	Hour	Summary of Events and Information	Remarks and references to Appendices
SHEET 27. F 21. C.11.	11th	18	Supplies Delivered to Units by Baggage Sect at 8.30am Supply Sect Proceeded to ROUSBRUGGE Railhead at 9am & Conveyed Rations in bulk to Refilling Point. Refill 1.30pm Returned Loaded to Camp. N.o.T. 35594 A/Corpl SMITH.J.F. Returned from 2nd Army. Lieut. J.B. Aston Transport Officer at Railhead. (WEATHER. FINE)	JBA
"	12.	18	Supplies Delivered to Units by Baggage Sect at 8.30am Supply Sect Proceeded to (ROUSBRUGGE) Railhead at 9am & Conveyed Rations to Refilling Point. Refill 1.30pm Returned Loaded to Camp. N.o.T.35651 Dr APPLEBEE. H. having joined the formation from Hospital also day is taken on the Strength of Coy 1 W.D. Horse attached from N27 Company having been destroyed on the 11th inst to Strength. WEATHER FINE.	JBA
"	13th	18	Supplies Delivered to Units by Baggage Sect at 9am Supply Sect Proceeded to (ROUSBRUGGE) Railhead at 8am & Conveyed Rations in bulk to Refilling Point. Refill 1.30pm & Returned Loaded to Camp. ILieut. R. Harris Transport Officer at Railhead. WEATHER. (WET. 9pm)	JBA
"	14th	18	Supplies Delivered to Units by Baggage Sect at 9am Supply Sect Proceeded to (ROUSBRUGGE) Railhead at 9am & Conveyed Rations in bulk to Refilling Point Refill 1.30pm LaCorpl Kent.A.T.T.35631 Dr Harris.A Proceed to Calais for Remounts. WEATHER. FINE)	JBA

Army Form C. 2118.

WAR DIARY
or
INTELLIGENCE SUMMARY.
(Erase heading not required.)

Instructions regarding War Diaries and Intelligence Summaries are contained in F. S. Regs., Part II. and the Staff Manual respectively. Title pages will be prepared in manuscript.

Place	Date	Hour	Summary of Events and Information	Remarks and references to Appendices
SHEET 24 F.21.C.1.1.	15th	18	Supplies Delivered to Units by Baggage Sect & an & Conveyed Rations in bulk to Refilling Point. Refill 1.30pm Supply Sect Proceeded to (ROUSBRUGGE) Railhead at 8am & Returned loaded to Camp. No T.037109 Corpl. FISHER T. Returned from II Corps School, having completed a course in (HOTCHKISS) Gunnery Lt/Lieut. J.M.B. ASTON Transport Officer at Railhead. He undermentioned having been returned to the 238th Ent Coy on Strength 20/680 Cpl. HEANEY J. N.T.28N/6 Pte DAW. W. (WEATHER FINE)	9BA
"	16th	18	Supplies Delivered to Units by Baggage Sect at 8am & Conveyed Rations in bulk to Refilling Point. Refill 1.30pm & Returned loaded to Camp. No.S.4/6046 Cpl ROSSER J.O. Attended on Special Leave T/Lieut. R. Harris to I.Captain. B. O.G. waited Camp short time. Supply Sect Proceeded to (ROUSBRUGGE) Railhead (WEATHER FINE)	9BA
"	17th	18	Supplies Delivered to Units by Baggage Sect. at 8am Supply Sect Proceeded to (ROUSBRUGGE) Railhead at 8am & Conveyed Rations in bulk to Refilling Point Refill 1.30pm & Returned loaded to Camp. Capt. T.V. Fleming Proceeded to the U.Kingdom on Leave T/Capt R. Harris T.088856. L/a Cpl KENT. A.T. L.T/326371 Dr FERRIS A.J. Returned from CALIS with Remounts. (WEATHER FINE)	9BA
"	18th	18	Supplies Delivered to Units by Baggage Sect at 8am & Conveyed Rations in bulk at Refilling Point. Supply Sect Proceeded to (ROOSBRUGGE) Railhead Refill 1.30pm & Returned loaded to Camp. No T.326731 Dr FERRIS A.J. L/Rider Returned to No.1 Coy. WEATHER. FINE.	RH.

Army Form C. 2118.

WAR DIARY
or
INTELLIGENCE SUMMARY.
(Erase heading not required.)

Instructions regarding War Diaries and Intelligence Summaries are contained in F.S. Regs., Part II. and the Staff Manual respectively. Title pages will be prepared in manuscript.

Place	Date	Hour	Summary of Events and Information	Remarks and references to Appendices
SHEET. 2.4. F.21.C.1.1.	19th	18.	Supplies Delivered to Units by Baggage Section at rear. Supply Sect. Proceeded to (ROUSBRUGGE) Railhead & Conveyed Rations in bulk to Refilling Park. Refill 1.30p.m. Returned loaded to Camp 2 that YB.actn transport Officers at Railhead. T.N.1099 Q. AMOS Proceeded to 139th FA to undergo a course of Instruction in SELECTION. (WEATHER FINE)	P.A.
—	20th	18	Supplies Delivered to Units by Baggage Sect. at rear. Supply Sect. Proceeded to ROUSBRUGGE) Railhead & Conveyed Rations in bulk to Refilling Park Refill 2.0p.m. Returned loaded to Camp. (WEATHER FINE)	P.A.
—	21st	18	Supplies Delivered to Units by Baggage Sect. at rear. Supply Sect. Proceeded to (ROUSBRUGGE) Railhead & Conveyed Rations in bulk to Refilling Park. Refill 1.30p.m. Returned loaded to Camp. T.N.2395 Q. McCul Proceeded to 125th Fty BHQ to return N.031436 Dr. DALE & admitted to Hosp. Inspection by T.C. Coy of Equipment. (WEATHER FINE)	A.N
—	22nd	18	Supplies Delivered to Units by Baggage Sect. at rear. Supply Sect. Proceeded to (ROUSBRUGGE) Railhead at 14.30 and Conveyed Rations in bulk to Refilling Park Refill 1.30p. Returned loaded to Camp. O.C. train Visited Camp. (WEATHER FINE)	A.I.
—	23rd	18	Supplies Delivered to Units by Baggage Sect. at rear. Supply Sect Proceeded to (ROUSBRUGGE) Railhead and Conveyed Rations in bulk to Refilling Park. Refill 1.30p. Returned loaded to Camp. (WEATHER FINE)	ABA

WAR DIARY
or
INTELLIGENCE SUMMARY.

Army Form C. 2118.

(Erase heading not required.)

Place	Date	Hour	Summary of Events and Information	Remarks and references to Appendices
SHEET 27 F21.C.11.	24th	18	Supplies Delivered to Units by Baggage Section at 8am Supply Section Proceeded to (ROUSBRUGGE) Railhead at 7.45am & Conveyed Rations in bulk to Refilling Point. Refill 1.30pm & Returned & Loaded to Camp. No.T29701 D. Mac Cord. P. Returned to Coy as NoT90574.36 D. Dale N. having been returned to duty from Hosp. (WEATHER RAINY)	9BA
	25th	18	Supplies Delivered to Units by Baggage Section at 8am Supply Section Proceeded to (ROUSBRUGGE) Railhead at 7.45am & Conveyed Rations in bulk to Refilling Point. Refill 1.30pm & Returned Loaded to Camp. (WEATHER FINE)	9BA
	26th	18	Supplies Delivered to Units by Baggage Section at 8am Supply Section Proceeded to (ROUSBRUGGE) Railhead at 7.45am & Conveyed Rations in bulk to Refilling Point. Refill 1.30pm & Returned Loaded to Camp. Church of England Service in Camp at 6pm. (WEATHER FINE)	9BA
	27th	18	Supplies Delivered to Units by Baggage Section at 8am Supply Section Proceeded to (ROUSBRUGGE) Railhead at 7.45am & Conveyed Rations in bulk to Refilling Point. Refill 1.30pm & Returned Loaded to Camp No.T070959 Dr. AM08. C. Returned from II Corps School of Sanitation having completed 6 weeks course. Lt. following N.Co. having joined this formation from Base Depot a S.C. &c. taken on the Strength of Coy S.T.0439.90. S. Sergt M.E. F.E.W. Court of Inquiry on the Loss of two Bicycles Nos. B.22045 & No.T9228. (WEATHER FINE)	9BA
	28th	18	Supplies Delivered to Units by Baggage Section at 9am Supply Section Proceeded to (ROUSBRUGGE) Railhead at 7.45am & Conveyed Rations in bulk to Refilling Point. Refill 1.30pm & Returned Loaded to Camp Transport Details 1.R.1 G.S. Green Forage. (Punishment) NoT9604 Dr. KELLY. J.J. awarded 14 Days F.P. No.2 Forfeits 1 G.C. Badge. (WEATHER FINE.)	9A

Army Form C. 2118.

WAR DIARY
or
INTELLIGENCE SUMMARY.
(Erase heading not required.)

Instructions regarding War Diaries and Intelligence Summaries are contained in F.S. Regs., Part II. and the Staff Manual respectively. Title pages will be prepared in manuscript.

Place	Date	Hour	Summary of Events and Information	Remarks and references to Appendices
SHEET 27 F.21.C.1.1.	29th	18	Supplies Delivered to Units by Baggage Sect at 8am. Supply Sect. Proceeded to (ROUSBRUGGE) Railhead at Y.HOP & Convoyed Rations in bulk to Refilling Point. Refill 1.30pm. Returned Loaded to Camp. The Bosl. Br. LAKIN W. Admitted to the 139th F.A. transport Details 1 NCO. 1R. 1SS. Green Forage. (WEATHER FINE)	9BA
	30th	18	Supplies Delivered to Units by Baggage Sect at 8am. Supply Sect Proceeded to ROUSBRUGGE Railhead at Y.HOP & Convoyed Rations in bulk to Refilling Point. Refill 1.30pm. Returned Loaded to Camp. Reversion No S/H/064816 A/Cpl Jarvis R.B. reverts to rank of A/L Cpl from 3/8, owing to No S/M/D/2289 Corpl Ashcroft J. having returned for Duty 3/8. Appointment No S/H/4896 A/L Cpl Jarvis R.B. appointed A/Cpl from 10/8 vice No S/H/60466 Cpl Roser J.C. evacuated to CCS 9/8. Reversion No S/H/064816 A/Corpl Jarvis R.B. reverts to rank of A/L Cpl from 28/8 acting to No S/H/60465 Cpl Roser J.C. having rejoined for duty 28/8. Re Appointment. No S/H/064816 A/L Cpl Jarvis R.B. appointed A/Corpl from 29/8 vice 110570 Cpl Young G.R. evacuated to CCS 19/8. Capt E.M.Wood joined Company from N°1 Coy transport. Outfit 1 NCO 1/R 1SS. Green Forage. (WEATHER FINE)	9BA
	31st		Supplies Delivered to Units by Baggage Sect. at 8am. Supply Sect. Proceeded to ROUSBRUGGE Railhead at Y.H.500 & Convoyed Rations in bulk to Refilling Point. Refill 1.30pm. Returned Loaded to Camp. 2/Lieut. G.B. Aston Transport Officer at Railhead & Capt R. Harris proceeded to the 58th Division transport. Detail 1 NCO. 1R. 1SS. Green Forage. (WEATHER FINE)	9NW.

In the field
31. 5. 18

E.M.Wood Capt.
O.C. N°3 Coy 41 Divisional Train.

Army Form C. 2118.

WAR DIARY
or
INTELLIGENCE SUMMARY
(Erase heading not required.)

Instructions regarding War Diaries and Intelligence Summaries are contained in F.S. Regs., Part II. and the Staff Manual respectively. Title Pages will be prepared in manuscript.

Place	Date	Hour	Summary of Events and Information	Remarks and references to Appendices
SHEET 27. F21 C.1.1	JUNE. 1st.	18.	Supplies Delivered to Units by Baggage Sect at 9am. Supply Sect Proceeded to Railhead at 4.45am & Conveyed Rations in bulk to Refilling Point. Refill 1.30pm & Returned loaded to Camp. Baggage Wagons Detached to Units No 040959 Dr Ames & Having completed a course on Sanitary Duties at II Corps School of Sanitation, is Classified (Good.) Inspection by O.C. of the 1st Box Respirators. Transport Details 1 NCO 1 A/NCO & Been Large. (WEATHER FINE.)	W.S.
	2nd	18	Supplies Delivered to Units by Supply Sect at 7.30am & Supply Sect Refilled 2.30pm & Delivered Rations to Units No T/260486 Cpl ROSSER JD Returned off leave from the U.K. Kingdom. WEATHER FINE	T.S.
SHEET 27. B.20. B.1. 8.	3d	18	Coy Moved from Camp F21 C.1. at 9am & arrived at Camp B.20. B.1. 8. at 4.15pm. Supply Sect Refilled at 5pm & Returned loaded to Camp No T/46601 D. Moore EF Proceeded to M.U.K. on leave WEATHER FINE	T.S.
SHEET 27. G.33. D.0.3.	4t	18	Coy Moved from Camp B.20 B1.8. at 9.15am with Supply Sect Loaded & arrived at Camp SHEET 27. G.33. D.O.3. at 11.30am Supply Sect Delivered Rations to Units Refilled at 2.30pm & Returned loaded to Camp (WEATHER FINE)	T.S.
"	5t	18	Supply Sect Delivered Rations to Units at 8.30am Refilled 1.30pm & Returned loaded to Camp. No 76791 Dr KELLY JJ admitted to the 139th F.A. ~ No T/4 7317 Dr DEACY M. attached from No1 Coy admitted to the 139th F.A. WEATHER FINE	T.S.
"	6t	18	Supply Sect Delivered Rations to Units at 9am Refilled 1.30pm & Returned loaded to Camp. No T/ 051741 Dr ORKLE W.H. St/O516 P.D. COLE H.M. T/023846 Dr HARDMAN ~ T/8125 with WEST OF admitted to the 139d. F.A. Baggage Wagons Rejoined Coy from Units	T.S.

WAR DIARY
or
INTELLIGENCE SUMMARY

Army Form C. 2118.

(Erase heading not required.)

Place	Date	Hour	Summary of Events and Information	Remarks and references to Appendices
SHEET 27 G.33.D.0.5.	7th	18	Supplies Delivered to Units by Supply Sec at 9am Refill 1.30pm Returned Loaded to Camp. N°3 A.S.C. Coy Nunn M. Admitted to the 139th F.A. Supply of Baggage Wagons of the 4th D.H.Q. & 18th Div. Sig. Coy. & C.R.E. Transferred to N° 2 Coy Train. Supply of Baggage Wagons of the 19th MIDDLESEX, 4th M.G. BATT. & D.A.C. attached from N°1 Coy. WEATHER FINE.	NS
"	8th	16	Supplies Delivered to Units by Supply Sec at 6.30 am. Baggage Sec Proceeded to (WATTEN) Railhead at 8.30 am & Convoy Rations in bulk to Refilling Point. 2015 & Pte Jones Admitted to the 139th F.A. (WEATHER FINE.)	NS
"	9th	18	Supply Sec Proceeded to (WATTEN) Railhead at 8.30 am & Conveyed Rations in bulk to Refilling Point. Refill 2pm. Rations Conveyed to Units by N°2 Coy Transport. Supply of Baggage Wagons of the 19th MIDDLESEX, 4th M.G.B. & D.A.C. Returned to Units N° 1502698 Pte 18mb. G.W. Proceeded to II Corps School to undergo a Course in HOTCHKISS GUNNERY (WEATHER FINE)	NS
ST MARTIN-AU-LAERT.	10th	18	Coy Moved from Sheet 27. G.33. D.0.5. at 12 noon & Arrived at ST MARTIN at 2.30pm. Capt Y.P. Fleming returned off Leave from the U.K. & Capt J.P. Fleming Awarded the (M.C.) Supply Sec Refilled at 3pm & Delivered Rations to Units. (WEATHER DULL)	NS
"	11th	18	Supplies by Supply Sec. Refill 1.30pm & Delivered to Units Baggage Wagons of the 123rd B.H.Q. 11th R.W. Surreys & 23rd Middx reported Coy. (WEATHER FINE.)	NS

Army Form C. 2118.

WAR DIARY
or
INTELLIGENCE SUMMARY
(Erase heading not required.)

Instructions regarding War Diaries and Intelligence Summaries are contained in F. S. Regs., Part II. and the Staff Manual respectively. Title Pages will be prepared in manuscript.

Place	Date	Hour	Summary of Events and Information	Remarks and references to Appendices
ST MARTIN-AU-LAERT	12th	18	Supplies by Supply Sect. Refill 1.30pm & Delivered to Units No T8 8126-with WhoS G.S. T92584 Q Amm M. returned to duty from the 139th Fld Amb. (WEATHER FINE)	NS
"	13th	18	Supplies by Supply Sect. Refill 1.45pm & Delivered to Units No T24981 Dr Able. W.H. S/T80016 Pte Bode AM. No T64354 Dr Hardman. E. having been evacuated to ... stationary hosp. are struck off the G. Strength 201690 Pte Jones J. 236 Employment Coy having been xxx to No 8 I.O.S. is struck off W. Strength. Baggage Wagons sent to "P.W.M.N.G." signed by No 27547101 Pte Middleton at proceed to H.G. Kingdom on leave. (WEATHER FINE)	NS
"	14th	18	Supplies by Supply Sect. Refill 1.45pm & Delivered to Units (WEATHER FINE)	NS
"	15th	18	Supplies by Supply Sect. Refill 1.45pm & Delivered Rations to Units (WEATHER FINE)	NS
"	16th	18	Supplies by Supply Sect. Refill 1.45pm & Delivered Rations to Units (WEATHER FINE)	NS
"	17th	18	Supplies by Supply Sect. Refill 1.45pm & Delivered Rations to Units No T8 637008 Dr Naylor W.S. proceed (WEATHER FINE)	NS
"	18th	18	Supplies by Supply Sect. Refill 1.4 5pm & Delivered Rations to units No T8 023905 Cpl Pant. F.W. returned from N Corps School having completed a course in (HOTCHKISS) Gunnery H co Classified (good) & Kent period coy (WEATHER FINE)	NS

WAR DIARY
or
INTELLIGENCE SUMMARY

(Erase heading not required.)

Army Form C. 2118.

Place	Date	Hour	Summary of Events and Information	Remarks and references to Appendices
ST. MARTIN-AU-LAERT.	19th	18	Supplies by Supply Sect. Refill 4.15 pm & Delivered Rations to Units (WEATHER FINE)	NS.
"	20th	18	Supplies by Supply Sect. Refill 1.30pm & Delivered Rations to Units. Both Show of 12.3rd Inty Bde of Horses & Vehicles. Boy took prizes as follows 1st for Wate Cart - & 1st & 2nd for Single H.D. Horses. (WEATHER FINE)	NS.
"	21st	18	Supplies by Supply Sect. Refill 1.35 pm & Delivered Rations to Units. N° T/M.M. 16520 Dr Millerwh & Provided to the U.Kingdom on Leave. (WEATHER FINE)	NS.
"	22nd	18	Supplies by Supply Sect. Refill 1.30pm & Delivered Rations to Units. N° T/18650 Dr Moore C.W.H & Returned of Leave from the U.Kingdom. Inspection by OC Coy of Rifles & Box Respirators (WEATHER FINE)	NS.
"	23rd	18	Supplies by Supply Sect. Refill 1.30 pm & Delivered Rations to Units (WEATHER FINE)	NS.
"	24th	18	Supplies by Supply Sect. Refill 11.30am & Delivered Rations to Units Baggage Wagons Detached to Units (WEATHER FINE)	NS
"	25th	18	Coy Moved from ST. MARTIN-AU-LAERT. at 10am & Arrived at (KINDERBELK.) at 1.15pm Supplies by Supply Sect. Refill 3.30pm & Delivered Rations to Units. Supply Wagon of the 233rd Ind Coy R.E. Rejoined Company (WEATHER FINE)	NS
KINDERBELK.	26th	18.	Coy Moved from KINDERBELK. at 9.30am & Arrived at Camp Map. Ref. Sheet 27. N23. tr S.O at 12 noon. Supplies by Supply Sect. Refill 4.30pm. & Delivered Rations to Units. (WEATHER FINE)	NS
Sheet.27. N23.B.S.O	27th	18	Supplies by Supply Sect. Refill 3pm & Delivered Rations to Units (WEATHER FINE)	NS

Army Form C. 2118.

WAR DIARY
or
INTELLIGENCE SUMMARY

(Erase heading not required.)

Instructions regarding War Diaries and Intelligence Summaries are contained in F. S. Regs., Part II. and the Staff Manual respectively. Title Pages will be prepared in manuscript.

Place	Date	Hour	Summary of Events and Information	Remarks and references to Appendices
SHEET.24 H.23.D.5.0.	28th	15	Supplies by Supply Sect. Refill 2.30 pm & Delivered Rations to Units. No. T/4/065289 Dr. Hooper A.N. Proceeded on leave to the United Kingdom. (WEATHER FINE)	TO
"	29th	18	Supplies by Supply Sect. Refill 2 pm & Delivered Rations to Units. Supply Wagons of the 11th R.W. Surreys Detached to Units. (WEATHER FINE)	TO
SHEET.24 K.21.D.7.4.	30th	14	Coy. Moved from Camp Map Ref. Sheet 24 N.23.b.5.0 at 6.15 am & Arrived at Camp Map Ref. Sheet 24 K.21.D.7.4. at 11.45 am Supply Sect. Drew Rations in Bulk from (STEENWOORDE) Railhead Refill 3 pm & Delivered to Units. (WEATHER FINE)	TO

Murray Capt
O.C. No.3 Coy 41st Divisional Train

2449 Wt. W14957/M90 750,000 1/16 J.B.C. & A. Forms/C.2118/12.

Army Form C. 2118.

WAR DIARY
or
INTELLIGENCE SUMMARY

(Erase heading not required.)

Instructions regarding War Diaries and Intelligence Summaries are contained in F.S. Regs., Part II. and the Staff Manual respectively. Title Pages will be prepared in manuscript.

Place	Date	Hour	Summary of Events and Information	Remarks and references to Appendices
SHEET 24 K21 D.7.4.	JULY 1st	18	Second Refill @ 2.30pm. 30" Supplies by Supply Sect. Delivered Rations to Units at 6.30am. Drew Rations in bulk from (STEENVOORDE) Railhead at 11am & Convoyed same to Camp. Refill 2pm. Supply wagons remained loaded. WEATHER. FINE.	T/S
"	2nd	18	Supplies by Supply Sect. Delivered Rations to Units at 8am. Drew Rations in bulk from (STEENVOORDE) Railhead at 11am & Convoyed same to Refilling Point. Refill 2.30pm. Returned loaded to Camp. Baggage Wagons Reported Company Smith Capt. J.T. Fleming M.C. Transport Officer at Railhead. N.C°892nd Co. Middx Reg. Returned officer & men from the United Kingdom. WEATHER. FINE.	T/S
"	3rd	18	Supplies by Baggage Sect. Delivered Rations to Units at 8am. Drew Rations in bulk from (STEENVOORDE) Railhead at 11am & Convoyed same to Refilling Point. Refill 2.30pm & Returned loaded to Camp. The undermentioned having joined from the O.S.C. Base Depot on the 1st inst are taken on the Strength of Company. N°384804 Dr CONWAY W.T. N°625776 Dr CREWE C.W. N°384809 Dr CHURCHWARD T.H. N°386951 Dr HARDISTY L.W. N°308163 Pte STINTEN A.J. N°635035 Sgm BENDALL M. 79R 5em BENGAL attang.Pam to 139? yld amb. WEATHER FINE)	T/S
"	4th	18	Supplies by Supply Sect. Delivered Rations to Units at 8am. Drew Rations in bulk from (STEENVOORDE) Railhead at 11am & Convoyed same to Refilling Point. Refill 2pm & Returned loaded to Camp. WEATHER. FINE.	T/S
"	5th	18	Supplies by Baggage Sect. Delivered Rations to Units at 8am. Drew Rations in bulk from (STEENVOORDE) Railhead at 11am & Convoyed same to Refilling Point. Refill 1.30pm & Returned loaded to Camp. Capt. J.T. Fleming M.C. Transport Officer at Railhead. WEATHER. FINE.	T/S

Army Form C. 2118.

WAR DIARY
or
INTELLIGENCE SUMMARY
(Erase heading not required.)

Instructions regarding War Diaries and Intelligence Summaries are contained in F. S. Regs, Part II. and the Staff Manual respectively. Title Pages will be prepared in manuscript.

Place	Date	Hour	Summary of Events and Information	Remarks and references to Appendices
SHEET 24 K21.D 7.4.	6th	18	Supplies by Supply Sect. Delivered Rations to Units at 8am. Drew Rations in bulk from (STEENVOORDE) Railhead at 11am. & Conveyed same to Refilling Point. Refill 1.30pm. & Returned Loaded to Camp. Transport Duties 2.P.S. 2.G.S. Coal Convoy 2.A.S. 2.G.S. Green Forage 1/S. G.O.C. inspected Camp with O.C. Train. No. T0346 Dr. SHARP B. transferred to 123rd Inf B.H.Q. (WEATHER. FINE)	T/S
"	7th	18	Supplies by Baggage Sect. Delivered Rations in bulk from (STEENVOORDE) Railhead at 11am & Conveyed same to Refilling Point. Refill 2pm & Returned Loaded to Camp. Transport Duties 1.N.C.O. 6.P.S. 6.G.S. T.N.B. Details. Church of England Service in Camp at 6pm. No T334705 Dr. NAYLOR W.S. Returned off leave from the U. Kingdom. (WEATHER. FINE)	T/S
"	8th	18	Supplies by Supply Sect. Delivered Rations to Units at 8am. Drew Rations in bulk from (STEENVOORDE) Railhead at 11am. & Conveyed same to Refilling Point. Refill 1, 3pm. & Returned Loaded to Camp. Transport Duties 1.4.G.S. T.H.Q. Detail. Capt. J.V. Fleming M.C. Transport Officer at Railhead. (WEATHER. FINE)	T/S
"	9th	18	Supplies by Baggage Sect. Delivered Rations to Units at 8am. Drew Rations in bulk from (STEENVOORDE) Railhead at 11am & Conveyed same to Refilling Point. Refill 2pm. & Returned. Transport Duties H.A.P.6. 1.4.G.S. T.H.Q. Detail. (WEATHER. SNOWERY.)	T/S
"	10th	18	Supplies by Supply Sect. Delivered Rations to Units at 7.45am. Drew Rations in bulk from (STEENVOORDE) Railhead at 11am & Conveyed same to Refilling Point. Refill 2pm. & Returned Loaded. Transport Duties 1.N.C.O. 3.P.S. 3.G.S. 3 Lorries. T.H.Q. Detail. 1.N.C.O. 10 pro 11.G.S. 6 Lorries R.F.A. No T063705 Dr. MULLOCH(M.M.)Returned off leave from the 150th Army Brigade attached from the United Kingdom. (WEATHER. SNOWERY.)	T/S

Army Form C. 2118.

WAR DIARY
or
INTELLIGENCE SUMMARY

(Erase heading not required.)

Instructions regarding War Diaries and Intelligence Summaries are contained in F. S. Regs., Part II. and the Staff Manual respectively. Title Pages will be prepared in manuscript.

Place	Date	Hour	Summary of Events and Information	Remarks and references to Appendices
SHEET 27. K21 D.7.4	11th	18	Supplies by Baggage Sect. Delivered Rations to Units at 4.30am. Drew Rations in bulk from (STEENVOORDE) Railhead at 11am & Convoyed same to Refilling Point. Refill 2pm. & Returned Loaded to Camp. Transport Duties 1 Officer 1 N.C.O. 3 Pr. 3.G.S. T.H.Q. Blind, Capt. Y.Y. Fleming M.C. Fleming M.C. Medical Inspection at 6pm for Classifying Category of Company. 1st Taylor with Cpl. Mundy Proceeded on leave to the United Kingdom. (WEATHER SHOWERY.)	T/B
"	12th	18	Supplies by Supply Sect. Delivered Rations to Units at 4.30am. Drew Rations in bulk from (STEENVOORDE) Railhead at 11am & Convoyed same to Refilling Point. Mounted Inspection by O.C. Train at 2.30am. Refill 3.30 pm & Returned Loaded to Camp. (WEATHER SHOWERY.)	T/B
"	13th	18	Supplies by Baggage Sect. Delivered Rations to Units at 4.30am. Drew Rations in bulk from (STEENVOORDE) R.H. at 11am & Convoyed same to Refilling Point. Refill 1.30pm & Returned Loaded to Camp. Box Respirator Inspection at 3.30pm. WEATHER FINE.	T/B
"	14th	18	Supplies by Supply Sect. Delivered Rations to Units at 4.30am. Drew Rations in bulk from (STEENVOORDE) Railhead at 11am & Convoyed same to Refilling Point. Refill 1.30pm. Returned Loaded to Camp. Capt. J.Y. Fleming M.C. Transport Officer at Railhead. (WEATHER SHOWERY.)	T/B
"	15th	18	Supplies by Baggage Sect. Delivered Rations to Units at 4.30am. Drew Rations in bulk from (STEENVOORDE) Railhead at 11am & Convoyed same to Refilling Point. Refill 1.30pm & Returned Loaded to Camp. (WEATHER SHOWERY)	T/B
"	16th	18	Supplies by Supply Sect. Delivered Rations to Units at 4.30am. Drew Rations in bulk from (STEENVOORDE) Railhead at 11am & Convoyed same to Refilling Point. Refill 1.30pm & Returned Loaded to Camp. (WEATHER SHOWERY)	T/B
"	17th	18	Supplies by Baggage Sect. Delivered Rations to Units at 4.30am. Drew Rations in bulk from (STEENVOORDE) Railhead at 11am. Convoyed same to Refilling Point. Refill 1.30pm & Returned Loaded to Camp. Transport Details 1 N.C.O. 3 Pr. 3 G.S. T.H.Q. Detail Pt. Taylor on leave. J Accused on leave to the U. Kingdom. Capt. J.Y. Fleming M.C. Transport Officer at Railhead. Baggage Sect Detached to Units. (WEATHER FINE.)	T/B

Army Form C. 2118.

WAR DIARY
or
INTELLIGENCE SUMMARY

(Erase heading not required.)

Instructions regarding War Diaries and Intelligence Summaries are contained in F. S. Regs., Part II. and the Staff Manual respectively. Title Pages will be prepared in manuscript.

Place	Date	Hour	Summary of Events and Information	Remarks and references to Appendices
SHEET 24 K21.D.7.4	18th	16	Supplies by Supply Sect. Delivered Rations to Units at 7.30am. Drew Rations from (STEENVOORDE) Railhead at 11am. Convoyed same to Refilling Point. Refill 1.30pm. Returned Loaded to Camp Supply Wagons of the 150 Bde A.F.A. Transport to Refl. Cav. Supply Wagons of the 19th MIDDLESEX ~ S.A.A. Sect DAC. firing Company. Lewis Guns returned to Camp from N.4 by Hostile Aircraft our Camp at 11.10 & 11.15am. All bombs dropped in vicinity of Camp. WEATHER FINE	TO
"	19th	16	Supplies by Supply Sect. Delivered Rations to Units at 7.30am. Drew Rations from (STEENVOORDE) Railhead at 11am No. JTy. 065299 Lt. Hooper. All Returned of Convoyed same to Refilling Point. Refill 1.30pm. Returned Loaded to Camp ~ off Leave from the United Kingdom. WEATHER FINE	TO
"	20th	16	Supplies by Supply Sect. Delivered Rations to Units at 7.30am Drew Rations from STEENVOORDE) Railhead at 11am of Convoyed Same to Refilling Point. Refill 1.30pm. Returned Loaded to Camp Sept. J. Pythering M.C. Transport officer at Railhead. WEATHER FINE	TO
"	21st	16	Supplies by Supply Sect. Delivered Rations to Units at 4.30am Drew Rations in bulk from (STEENVOORDE) Railhead at 11am & Convoyed Same to Refilling Point Refill 1.30pm. Camp Church of England Service in Camp at 6pm No Tow 288 Lt Bagshaw 109 Brocedes on Leave to the United Kingdom. (WEATHER FINE)	TO
"	22	18	Supplies by Supply Sect. Delivered Rations to Units at 7.30am Drew Rations in bulk from (STEENVOORDE) Railhead at 11am & Convoyed Same to Refilling Point. Refill 1.30pm & Returned Loaded to Camp. The 118th Divisional Concert Party (the Duds) gave a performance in Camp at 6pm No T026908 Cpl Pink J.M. Proceeded to CALAIS with Remount Party 2 Brass Remounts (WEATHER FINE)	TO
"	23rd	18	Supplies by Supply Sect Delivered Rations to Units at 4.30am Drew Rations in bulk from (STEENVOORDE) Railhead at 11am & Convoyed Same to Refilling Point. Refill 12.30pm Returned Loaded to Camp. Capt J.P. Fleming Transport Officer at Railhead. (WEATHER. WET.)	TO

Army Form C. 2118.

Instructions regarding War Diaries and Intelligence Summaries are contained in F.S. Regs., Part II. and the Staff Manual respectively. Title Pages will be prepared in manuscript.

WAR DIARY
or
INTELLIGENCE SUMMARY
(Erase heading not required.)

Place	Date	Hour	Summary of Events and Information	Remarks and references to Appendices
SHEET 24 K.21.O.7.4.	24th	18	Supplies by Supply Sect. Delivered Rations to Units at 4.30am. Drew Rations in bulk from (STEENVOORDE) Railhead at 11am & Conveyed same to Refilling Point. Refill 12.30pm & Returned loaded to Camp. Transport Duties 1.R.1.25. T.H.Q. Detail. (WEATHER FINE)	T/S
"	25th	18	Supplies by Supply Sect. Delivered Rations to Units at 4.30am. Drew Rations in bulk from (STEENVOORDE) Railhead at 11am & Conveyed same to Refilling Point. Refill 12.30pm & Returned Loaded to Camp. The undermentioned man having joined this formation from the A.S.C. Base Depot are to be on the Companys Strength No 390690 B.Cooke No 8 No 723500 B.Beckwin S. No 732850 A B.Oakley A.H. + No 732860 B.Plunder V.H.B. No 621988 Cpl Back H.V. Returned from Calais with Remounts. (WEATHER FINE)	T/S
"	26th	18	Supplies by Supply Sect. Delivered Rations to Units at 4.30am. Drew Rations in bulk from (STEENVOORDE) Railhead at 11am & Conveyed same to Refilling Point. Refill 12.30pm & Returned Loaded to Camp. B.M. Doe B. M.D.H joined Coy from the 106 Regt 29th American Division. Capt J.P. Fleming M.C. Transport Officer at Railhead Inspection of Mules & Brass Dispatches at 3.30pm No 78mp57 B units Admitted to cell 139th Hos Amb. (WEATHER SHOWERY)	T/S
"	27	18	Supplies by Supply Sect. Delivered Rations to Units at 4.30am. Drew Rations in bulk from (STEENVOORDE) Railhead at 11am & Conveyed Same to Refilling Point. Refill 2.30pm & Returned Loaded to Camp & Baggage Wagons of the 106 Regt 29th American Division rejoined Regt. (WEATHER SHOWERY)	T/S
"	28th	18	Supplies by Supply Sect. Delivered Rations in bulk from (STEENVOORDE) Railhead at 11am & Conveyed Same to Refilling Point. Refill 1/12.30pm & Returned Loaded to Camp. No T/2649448 Cpl Plumb A.J. Returned off leave from the United Kingdom. Cap pkm B. Urquhart. Admitted to the 135th Fld Amb. Church of England. Service in Camp at 6.30pm. (WEATHER SHOWERY)	T/S
"	29th	18	Supplies by Supply Sect. Delivered Rations to Units at 4.30am. Drew Rations in bulk from (STEENVOORDE) Railhead at 11am & Conveyed Same to Refilling Point. Refill 2pm & Returned Loaded to Camp Transport Duties 1.R.1.25. T.H.Q. Detail. (WEATHER FINE)	T/S

WAR DIARY
INTELLIGENCE SUMMARY

Army Form C. 2118.

Place	Date	Hour	Summary of Events and Information	Remarks and references to Appendices
SHEET 27. K21. D.7.4	30th	18	Supplies by Supply Sect. Delivered Rations to Units at 4.30 a.m. Drew Rations in bulk from (STEENVOORDE) Railhead at 11am & Conveyed same to Refilling Point. Refill 2 pm & Returned to Camp. Capt. J.H. Fleming M.C. Transport Officer at Railhead. (WEATHER FINE)	
"	31st	15	Supplies by Supply Sect. Delivered Rations to Units at 4.30am. Drew Rations in bulk from (STEENVOORDE) Railhead at 11am & Conveyed same to Refilling Point. Refill 2pm & Returned to Camp. 2Lieut Emly attached to Company M/T S/5954 Dr Evans R.W. Proceeded on leave to the United Kingdom. (WEATHER FINE)	

[signature] Capt.
O.C. No 3 Coy 41st Divisional Train

Army Form C. 2118.

WAR DIARY
or
INTELLIGENCE SUMMARY
(Erase heading not required.)

Instructions regarding War Diaries and Intelligence Summaries are contained in F. S. Regs., Part II. and the Staff Manual respectively. Title Pages will be prepared in manuscript.

Place	Date	Hour	Summary of Events and Information	Remarks and references to Appendices
SHEET. 24. K21.D.4.4.	AUGST. 1st	18	Supplies by Supply Sect. Delivered Rations to Units at 7.30am Drew Rations in bulk from (STEENVOORDE) Railhead at 11am & Conveyed same to Refilling Point. Refill 2pm & Returned Loaded to Camp Baggage Wagon of the 10th R.W. Kent & 11th R.W. Surrey N 123 1" Infy BHQ regained Company from Unit. Supply Wagon of the 2.33" Fld Coy R.E. Detached to Unit. (WEATHER FINE)	T/O
"	2nd	18	Supplies by Supply Sect. Delivered Rations to Units at 7.30am, Drew Rations in bulk from (STEENVOORDE) Railhead at 11am & Conveyed Same to Refilling Point. Refill 2 pm & Returned Loaded to Camp. Transport Details 1 NCO 3 pns 3 f.s. — L.O Detail. (WEATHER VERY WET.)	T/O
"	3rd	18	Supplies by Supply Sect. Delivered Rations to Units at 7.30am Drew Rations in bulk from (STEENVOORDE) Railhead at 11am & Conveyed same to Refilling Point. Refill 2 pm & Returned Loaded to Camp. Transport Details 2 Pns 2 ss. T.H. L.s Detail. Baggage Wagons of the 10th MIDDLX Regt joined Coy from Unit. 2 Do 2 Ns 2 GS 2 London attached to Coy from 2nd Batt. 101st Bgd of American Division (WEATHER SHOWERY.)	T/O
"	4th	18	Supplies by Supply Sect. Delivered Rations to Units at 7.30am Drew Rations in bulk from STEENVOORDE Railhead at 11am & Conveyed same to Refilling point. Refill 2 pm & Returned Loaded to Camp. Capt. J.P. Fleming M.C. of the 5th/6th Dr. Landon J. represented the Company on Genl Plumers C.B. G.C.M.G. A.D.C. Church Parade & March Past. on the Anniversary of the 4th year of the War. 293365 Pr. Brannen E. Proceeded on leave to the United Kingdom. (WEATHER FINE)	T/O
"	5th	18	Supplies by Supply Sect. Delivered Rations to Units at 7.30am Drew Rations in bulk from STEENVOORDE Railhead at 11am & Conveyed Same to Refilling Point. Refill 2 pm & Returned loaded to Camp. N 301062 Pt Stenton A. having been returned to a S.C. Base Depot. Surplus to Establishment is Struck off the Strengl of Company (WEATHER SHOWERY)	T/O

WAR DIARY
or
INTELLIGENCE SUMMARY

Army Form C. 2118.

Place	Date	Hour	Summary of Events and Information	Remarks and references to Appendices
SHEET 24. K.21.D.9.4.	6th	18	Supplies by Supply Sect. Delivered Rations to Units at 7.30 am. Drew Rations in bulk from (STEENVOORDE) Railhead at 11 am. Conveyed same to Refilling Point. Refill 2 pm. Returned loaded to Camp. NTT 02/100. Train J. Returned off Leave from the United Kingdom. Pianos fu. N° 4207 26 Pte Stone Pte from N° 1109 10 103 Coy. (WEATHER SNOWERY).	M
"	7th	18	Supplies by Supply Sect. Delivered Rations to Units at 7.30 am. Drew Rations in bulk from (STEENVOORDE) Railhead at 11 am. Conveyed same to Refilling Point. Refill 2 pm. Returned loaded to Camp. Cpl.Sjt. Fleming M.C. transport officer at Railhead. Baggage for 2 Wagons of M.T. "M" Surreys detached to Unit. Sup N° 119 Struck off Strength of Company. Lieut. W. Enily formed N° 2 Company Capt. M.B. Pollard Unquhead returned from ch. 138 F.A. is taken off it 3rd list. (WEATHER FINE.)	M
"	8th	18	Supplies by Supply Sect. Delivered Rations to Units at 7.30 am. Drew Rations in bulk from STEENVOORDE Railhead at 11 am. & Conveyed same to Refilling Point. Refill 2 pm. Returned loaded to Camp. Lieut. R.S. Peacock Proceeded on 7 days leave to the United Kingdom. 2 Pios. 2 Pios. 2 B.S. Baggage Detached to Unit. 10 R.W. Kents. Inspection of Rifles Box Respirators Water Bottles at 3.30 pm. Supply R. Wagon Reported by from the 233'd H.A Coy R.E. (WEATHER FINE)	M
"	9th	18	Supplies by Supply Sect. Delivered Rations to Units at 7.30 am. Drew Rations in bulk from (STEENVOORDE) Railhead at 11 am & Conveyed same to Refilling Point. Refill 2 pm. Returned loaded to Camp. N° 20156A Pte. Hill, J.H. 238' Employment Coy attached to Company Proceeded on leave to the United Kingdom. N° 7984 238 Pte. Bagshaw W.H. Returned off Leave from the 10 R.W. Kents Regt. The United Kingdom. Baggage One Box Wagons Reported by from the 10 R W Kents Regt. (WEATHER FINE)	M
"	10th	18	Supplies by Supply Sect. Delivered Rations to Units at 7.30 am. Drew Rations in bulk (STEENVOORDE) Railhead at 11 am & Conveyed same to Refilling Point. Refill 2 pm. Returned Loaded to Camp. N° Sjt. 643910 S Sergt. Keyt. W. Proceeded on leave to the United Kingdom. Supply R. Wagons of Ch. 108 Regt 2nd American Division Reported from London. (WEATHER FINE)	M

WAR DIARY or INTELLIGENCE SUMMARY

Army Form C. 2118.

(Erase heading not required.)

Place	Date	Hour	Summary of Events and Information	Remarks and references to Appendices
SHEET 27. K21 D 7.4	11th	18	The undermentioned Category "B" Drivers having joined this formation from the A.S.C. Base Depot are taken on the Strength of Company:— No. T/455133 Q. Perry.S. No. T/366456 Q. Pullinger B.H. T/370110 Q. Preston.J.E. T/67025 Q. Pratt.L.W. T/69076 Q. Pink.H.W. Proceeded to the XIX. Corps School to undergo a Course of (A.S) No. T/04290 Q. Roser.A. Accepted on leave to the United Kingdom Supplies by Supply Col. Delivered Rations to Units at 7.30 a.m. Drew rations in bulk from (STEENVOORDE) Railhead at 11 a.m. Convoyed same to Refilling Point. Refill 2 p.m. Returned to Camp by 3 p.m. The following Q M.S. T/26 Q Rolfe.R. 10757 Q Roff.B. Returned to United Kingdom to Preparations to take Up M.T. Transport offices of Railhead transit. of England (WEATHER FINE)	T/O
"	12th	18	Supplies by Supply Sect. Delivered Rations to Units at 7.30 a.m. Drew Rations in bulk from (STEENVOORDE) Railhead at 11 a.m. Convoyed same to Refilling Point. Refill 2 p.m. Returned to Camp. No. T/37925 with Work.T.E. No. T/992326 A. Munn. M. Proceeded on leave to the United Kingdom. No. T/59133 Q Sarge.H. Coy.B having joined this formation from the A.S.C. Base Depot is taken on the Strength the following Category "A" Drivers having Returned to the A.S.C. Base Depot are struck off the Strength of Coy. T/36346 Q. Moraly.W T/69 Q. Knot. L 563111 Q Mead T5147 Q Minchull. T5 62330 M only M. T/356192 9/2 Cpl. Melville E 238 Employment Coy posted to Company. (WEATHER FINE)	T/O
"	13th	18	Supplies by Baggage Sect. Delivered Rations to Units at 7.30 a.m. Drew Rations in bulk from (STEENVOORDE) Railhead at 11 a.m. Convoyed same to Refilling Point. Refill 2 p.m. Returned to Camp. Rifle &130 exe Respiratoral Inspection at 3.30 p.m. (WEATHER FINE)	T/O
"	14th	18	Supplies by Supply Sect. Delivered Rations to Units at 7.30 a.m. Drew Rations in bulk from STEENVOORDE Railhead at 11 a.m. Convoyed same to Refilling Point. Refill 2 p.m. Returned. No.9369 Aux Corpl Coats.R.L Recuited to HArmy Rest Camp. located to Camp. (WEATHER. FINE.)	T/O

Army Form C. 2118.

WAR DIARY
or
INTELLIGENCE SUMMARY
(Erase heading not required.)

Instructions regarding War Diaries and Intelligence Summaries are contained in F. S. Regs., Part II. and the Staff Manual respectively. Title Pages will be prepared in manuscript.

Place	Date	Hour	Summary of Events and Information	Remarks and references to Appendices
SHEET 27. K.21.D.14.	15th	18	Supplies by Supply Sect. Delivered Rations to Units at 7.30 am. Drew Rations in bulk from (STEENVOORDE) Railhead at 11 am & Conveyed same to Refilling Point. Refill 2 pm & Returned to Camp. M.T.82160 A. Morotin No.13. Transferred to N.E. 1 Coy. Capt. J.R. Fleming M.C. Transport Officer Proceeded on Leave to the United Kingdom at Railhead. Capt. M.B. Pollact Wynhart Proceeded (WEATHER. FINE)	nil
"	16th	18	Supplies by Baggage Sect. Delivered Rations to Units at 7.30 am. Drew Rations in bulk from (STEENVOORDE) Railhead at 11 am & Conveyed same to Refilling Point. Refill 2 pm & Returned to Camp. Transport Details: Ms. G.S.S. Green Forage Nº7890 9 23 B. amos C. Returned to Duty from M.H. at Dunmow Reception Camp. (WEATHER. FINE)	nil
"	17th	18	Supplies by Supply Sect. Delivered Rations to Units at 7.30 am. Drew Rations in bulk from (STEENVOORDE) Railhead at 11 am. Conveyed same to Refilling Point. Refill 2 pm & Returned to Camp. Transport Details: 2 Rs 2 G.S. 1 Limber Green Forage. (WEATHER. FINE)	nil
"	18th	18	Supplies by Baggage Sect. Delivered Rations to Units at 7.30 am. Drew Rations in bulk from (STEENVOORDE) Railhead at 11 am & Conveyed same to Refilling Point. Refill 2 pm and Returned to Camp Nº T/63958 Corpl. Boal Geo. Returned from XIX Corps School having completed a course of Gas Instruction. Transport Details 2 Rs 2 G.S. 1 Lorry. Green Forage. Church of England Service in Church Army Hut at 6 pm. (WEATHER. FINE)	nil
"	19th	18	Supplies by Supply Sect. Delivered Rations to Units at 7.30 am. Drew Rations in bulk from (STEENVOORDE) Railhead at 11 am. Conveyed same to Refilling Point. Refill 2 pm & Returned to Camp. Transport Details: 2 Rs 2 G.S. 1 Lorry. Green Forage Nº T/63138/ D. Evans Rev. Returned off Leave from the United Kingdom. Capt. J.R. Fleming M.C. Transport Officer at Railhead Supply Reptd. (WEATHER. FINE)	nil

WAR DIARY
or
INTELLIGENCE SUMMARY

(Erase heading not required.)

Army Form C. 2118.

Instructions regarding War Diaries and Intelligence Summaries are contained in F.S. Regs., Part II. and the Staff Manual respectively. Title Pages will be prepared in manuscript.

Place	Date	Hour	Summary of Events and Information	Remarks and references to Appendices
SHEET 24. K.21.D.7.A.	20th	18	Supplies by Baggage Sect. Delivered Rations to Units at Y 20am. Drew Rations in bulk from (STEENVOORDE) Railhead at 11am & Conveyed same to Refilling Point. Refill 2pm & Returned Loaded to Camp. Transport Duties 7&T/29566 Dr Broomer & Returned off leave from the United Kingdom 7&T/6301 Dr Lorimer F attached from 101 Coy admitted No 136 Fd Amb. (WEATHER FINE)	nil
"	21st	18	Supplies by Supply Sect. Delivered Rations to Units at Y 3am & Drew Rations in bulk from (STEENVOORDE) Railhead at 11am & Conveyed same to Refilling Point. Refill 2pm & Returned Loaded to Camp. Transport Duties NCO & 2 R. & F. for Potates 2 Ars 2 SS Green Forage. (WEATHER FINE)	nil
"	22nd	18	Supplies by Baggage Sect. Delivered Rations to Units at Y 30am & Drew Rations in bulk from (STEENVOORDE) Railhead at 11am & Conveyed same to Refilling Point. Refill 2pm & Returned Loaded to Camp. Transport Duties 3 Ars 3 SS Green Forage 7&T/23313 Pte Hacking S proceeded to the United Kingdom on leave. Capt J.T. Hemming MC Transport officer at Railhead. Asst Bee Respirator Inspection at 3.30pm. WEATHER FINE	nil
"	23rd	18	Supplies by Supply Sect. Delivered Rations to Units at Y 20am & Drew Rations in bulk from (STEENVOORDE) Railhead at 11am & Conveyed same to Refilling Point. Refill 2pm & Returned Loaded to Camp. Transport Duties NCO 2 Ars 2 SS Brown Forage. 1/2/20351 Pte Jessett J 2 SS Employment S Proceeded on Leave to the United Kingdom. Issue of Probationary. The following NCO having Completed a Course of Instruction at XIX Corps Gas School is Classified as isolated 315900 Cpl. Past HW. Round. WEATHER FINE.	nil

WAR DIARY
or
INTELLIGENCE SUMMARY

(Erase heading not required.)

Army Form C. 2118.

Place	Date	Hour	Summary of Events and Information	Remarks and references to Appendices
SHEET 24. K.21.D.4.4	24th	18.	Supplies by Baggage Sect. Delivered Rations to Units at 7.30am & Drew Rations in bulk from (STEENVOORDE) Railhead at 11 and Conveyed same to Refilling Point. Refill Point Returned Load to Camp. 2/Lieut R.J. Bacot Returned off Leave from the United Kingdom.	110
"	25th	18	Supplies by Supply Sect. Delivered Rations to Units at 7.30am & Drew Rations in bulk from (STEENVOORDE) Railhead at 11.00am & Conveyed same to Refilling Point. Refill 2pm & Returned Loaded to Camp. Transport Duties 2P to 2.55. 1 Horse Broken Forage Church of England Service on Church Army Hut. WEATHER FINE	110
"	26th	18	Supplies by Baggage Sect. Delivered Rations in bulk from (STEENVOORDE) Railhead at 11 am & Conveyed same to Refilling Point. Refill 2pm & Returned Loaded to Camp Transport Duties 2P to 2.55. 1 Horse Grew Forage No. 20,361 Pte Neil J.M. attached to 238 Employment Coy Returned off Leave from the United Kingdom. No. 353, 535 Pte Carpenter M.A. Attached from T.H.Q. Transferred to 7th 2 Coy Train No. 23,948 Sgt Brown C. Proceeded on Leave to the United Kingdom. Capt J.P. Fleming M.C. Transport Officer at Railhead. (WEATHER FINE) WEATHER SNOWERY.	110
"	27th	18.	Supplies by Supply Sect. Delivered Rations to Units at 7.30am & Drew Rations in bulk from (STEENVOORDE) Railhead at 11 and Conveyed same to Refilling Point. Refill 2pm & Returned Loaded to Camp Transport Duties 2Ho 2.55 Horse Drew Forage. WEATHER SNOWERY	110

Army Form C. 2118.

WAR DIARY
~~INTELLIGENCE SUMMARY~~
(Erase heading not required.)

Instructions regarding War Diaries and Intelligence Summaries are contained in F. S. Regs., Part II. and the Staff Manual respectively. Title Pages will be prepared in manuscript.

Place	Date	Hour	Summary of Events and Information	Remarks and references to Appendices
SHEET 27 K21.D.7.4	28th	18	Supplies by Supply Sect. Delivered Rations to Unit at 7.30am & Drew Rations in bulk from STEENVOORDE Railhead at 11am & Conveyed same to fulfilling Point. Refill 2nd & Returned to Unit. Refilled 10 Baggage Wagons detailed by Coy HqrS. 1 W Returned off loan from the United Kingdom. 19 Supply Wagons of the 19th Middlesex 4233 Sta Coy attached to N°2 Coy from Supply Wagons after the 110th M.G.C. Pack Horse Company (WEATHER Showery)	NIL
	29th	19	Supplies by Supply Sect. Drew Rations in bulk from STEENVOORDE Railhead at 5-12.15 & moved from SHEET 27 K21.D.7.4 at 1-12 noon. Supply Sect 3 rng Coy in Lorries arrived at RENESCURE at 6.30pm. U.T.O 65221 & Lord Lt R.A. Lewin J.B. Son proceeded the United Kingdom on 11.66292 & Rodd A N59202 & N.num on return off leave from the United Kingdom. WEATHER FINE	NIL
RENESCURE,	30th	18	Coy moved from RENESCURE at 7.30am & arrived at ST MARTIN AU LAERT at 10.30am. N°516.9 ton Gpl lorries to R.L. returned from II Army Rest Camp. Supply Sect Drew Rations & Refill 10m & Returned & conveyed Supply Wagons & to Pt. attached to N° 118 N° 2 Coy (WEATHER FINE)	NIL
ST.MARTIN AU LAERT	31st	13	Supplies by Supply Sect. Delivered Rations to Units at 6.30am & Drew Rations in bulk from LUMBRES Railhead at 10am and conveyed same to Refilling Point Refill 2pm & Returned loaded to Camp Baggage Wagons Regimental Company Same (WEATHER FINE)	NIL

T. Mumm Capt.

O.C. N° 3 Coy 41st Divisional Train.

2449 Wt. W14957/M90 750,000 1/16 J.B.C. & A. Forms/C.2118/12.

WAR DIARY or INTELLIGENCE SUMMARY

Army Form C. 2118.

(Erase heading not required.)

Instructions regarding War Diaries and Intelligence Summaries are contained in F.S. Regs, Part II. and the Staff Manual respectively. Title Pages will be prepared in manuscript.

Place	Date	Hour	Summary of Events and Information	Remarks and references to Appendices
ZERMEZEELE	SEPT. 1st	19	Supply Sect. Delivered Rations to units at 7am. Baggage Wagons Delivered O.R. kits to units Returned afterwards to unit from which obtained. Aug/Smr Coy Company arrived from ST NAZAIRE at 11 a.m. Left again at ZERMEZEELE at 6.30pm. Supply of 4 and K refilled at 2pm at Pierre Jarnier to Camp B/205436 M. Buick land T. Returned to N.E. 2 Coy Supp. M.T. Pillard Migratory Horses (Brevard to Calais) (WEATHER FINE)	(10)
SHEET 2A K.18. C.9.7.	2nd	18	Proceed with Supply Sect Loaded from (ZERMEZEELE) at 9am arrived at Camp Shap Ref Shed at K.18. C.9.7. at 4 pm Supply Sect Delivered Rations to units. (WEATHER FINE)	(10)
SHEET 2A K.14 & 7.1	3rd	18	Supplies by Supply Sect M.H.C. 9am & delivered Rations to units Coy am Loaded from Camp K.18. C.9.7. at 9 & am & arrived at Camp K.14 & 7.1 at 2.30 pm Sect refilled 2.30pm & Returned loaded to Camp.	(10)
"	4th	18	Supplies by Supply Sect Delivered Rations to Units at 9 am & Refill 3pm & Returned loaded to Camp Pt Teybis S/Sgt Shuttleworth H. Proceeded on Leave & left unit at 11.30pm Baggage Wagons Reported Company from work. (WEATHER FINE)	(10)
"	5th		Supplies Delivered to Units by Supply Sect as 9am Bagge Sect Returned WINNEZEELE Arrived at 9am & Began Rations in Truck at 10.15 am & Coyyed same to Parts in Refill 2pm. Returned loaded to Camp Rations 15 M. Villegal unit & delivered Rations from Calais with Rations (WEATHER FINE)	(10)

Army Form C. 2118.

WAR DIARY
or
INTELLIGENCE SUMMARY

(Erase heading not required.)

Instructions regarding War Diaries and Intelligence Summaries are contained in F. S. Regs., Part II. and the Staff Manual respectively. Title Pages will be prepared in manuscript.

Place	Date	Hour	Summary of Events and Information	Remarks and references to Appendices
SHEET 24 K17.b.4.1	6th	18	Supplies by Supply Sect. Delivered Rations to Units at 9am. Baggage Sect Proceeded to (WINNEZEELE) for Mess at 9am. Drew Rations in bulk at 10.45am & Emerged same to Refilling Point. Refill Pt. Supply Sect at 3pm. Returned loaded to Camp. D. Mason J. Detached from 1 Coy Ridewelle on leave to Gt. Britain 6pm. (WEATHER FINE)	TW
SHEET 2Y L23.a.5.2	7	18	Supplies Delivered to Units by Supply Sect at 9am. Baggage Sect Brought 1st (WIPPENHOEK) Railhead. Drew Rations in bulk & Emerged same to Refilling Pt. Refill Pt 2p. Entrained for Camp from Camp B K17.b.4.1. at 9.30am. Arrived at 10.45am. Camp L23 a.5.2 at 11.25am. 10th Mnuter Cast Detached to 2 M.B. (WEATHER SHOWERY)	TW
"	8	18	Supplies Delivered to Units by Supply Sect at 9.45am. Baggage Sect Proceeded to WIPPENHOEK Railhead. Drew Rations in bulk at 8 am and Emerged same to Refilling Pt. Refill Pt 2.30pm. Returned loaded to Camp. M53335 Pte Hacking Gr. 20155 Pte Cassidy J. Returned off Leave from the United Kingdom. (WEATHER SHOWERY)	TW
"	9	18	Supplies Delivered to Units by Supply Sect at 9.15am. Baggage Sect Proceeded to WIPPENHOEK Railhead at 7.30 am. Drew Rations in bulk off & and Emerged same to Refilling Point. Refill 10.30am. Returned loaded to Camp. M245315 Pte Gallagher W. Proceeded on leave to the United Kingdom. WEATHER SHOWERY	TW

WAR DIARY
or
INTELLIGENCE SUMMARY

(Erase heading not required.)

Army Form C. 2118.

Place	Date	Hour	Summary of Events and Information	Remarks and references to Appendices
SHEET 27 L23 a 5.2	10th	16	Supplies Delivered to Units by Supply Sect at 4.45am & Drew Rations both & Conveyed same to Refilling Point. Sgt. Arrived at WIPPENHOEK Rail 18.30am & Returned Loaded to Camp No. 376/57/B. Callaghan W Proceeded on leave to England United Kingdom Natural Transport Duties NCO 2R + 2 P.S. RE Waiting 17. C.O. 3R + 3S RE Due 2 Horses. (WEATHER SNOWERY)	TD
	11th	18	Supplies Delivered to Units by Supply Sect at 4.30am Baggage Sect Received @ WIPPLIN HOEK Railhead at 11.00am Drew Rations in bulk at 10.45am. J.G. Hughson to Thorlay Camp No.383/289 R. Hooper O.H. Admitted to the Refilling Pt. 40 239948 Sgt. Burner C. Returned off leave from the United Kingdom Transport Duties NCO 2R + 2 PS RE Transport Duties NCO 2 + 2 PS RE 1B 1SS Gun Forge. WEATHER SHOWERY.	TD
	12th	18	Supplies Delivered to Units by Supply Sect at 4.30pm Baggage Sect Proceeded @ WIPPENHOEK Railhead at 10 am & Drew Rations in Bulk R at 10.15am & Conveyed same to Refilling P.t. 40 363289 R. Hooper all Returned to Duty from No 38601 Pte Cakley ad Admitted to UK 139 FA 40 G 66 56 Pte Cpl. Rent 27 Proceeded on leave to the United Kingdom Transport Duties NCO 2R + 2PS RE 1/3 1 SS Gun Forge WEATHER SHOWERY.	TD
"	13th	18	Supplies Delivered to Units by Supply Sect at 4.30am Supply Sect Proceeded to WIPPENHOEK Railhead at 10am. Drew Rations in bulk at 10.15am & Conveyed same to Refilling Point Pte 1131 J.C. Cray Sig Cpl Jarvis S.E. Reported Sick TS 27890 Sgt Cpl Jarvis S.E. Returned to duty from T2 2 Disc Employment Coy 27326/4 Master J 236 G 44578 Mather F.A. Gun Forge WEATHER. FINE.	TD
"	14th	18	Supplies Delivered to Units by Supply Sect at 4.30am Supply Sect Received to WIPPENHOEK Railhead at 10am & Drew Rations in Bulk at 10.15am & Conveyed same to Refilling Point Pte 11.30am T. Lindsy B. Baker V No 75.201 R. Goodliffe O. Returned off leave from Returned to old Camp 2" Lindsy P Dept, No 70.8231 R. Goodliffe O. Returned off leave from the United Kingdom Transport Duties 2A 2 SS Agriculture. WEATHER. SHOWERY	TD

WAR DIARY
or
INTELLIGENCE SUMMARY

(Erase heading not required.)

Army Form C. 2118.

Instructions regarding War Diaries and Intelligence Summaries are contained in F.S. Regs., Part II. and the Staff Manual respectively. Title Pages will be prepared in manuscript.

Place	Date	Hour	Summary of Events and Information	Remarks and references to Appendices
SHEET 27 L.23.a.5.2.	13th	18	Supplies Delivered to Units by Supply Sect at 4.30am. Supply Sect Proceeded to WIPPENHOEK Railhead at 10am. Drew Rations in bulk at 10.15am. Convoyed same to Refilling Point. Refill 11.30am applications loaded to Camp. No T2 SBy C.Sgn Dispatched Proceeded on Leave to the United Kingdom. Transport Duties 2R 2TS Horses Carting 1 A.1.S.C. Supplies to the W.Y. Bn Reception Camp. WEATHER FINE	TR
"	16th	18	Supplies Delivered to Units by Supply Sect at 4.30am. Drew Rations in bulk at 10.15am. Convoyed same to Refilling Point. Refill 11.30am. Returned to Camp. Pte 149426 Pte Henry Ryn admitted to the 139th Field Ambulance. N? 55967 Pte H. Attatchd Coy N? 273 238... Empty Coy Proceeded on Leave to the United Kingdom. Transport Duties 2R 2.9.S. Horses Carting 1 A.1.S.C. Supplies to the W.Y. Bn Reception Camp 1 A.1.S.C. Supplies to 123" Bde School. WEATHER FINE	TR
L.33 CENTRAL	17th	18	Supplies Delivered to Units by Supply Sect at 4.30am. Supply Sect Proceeded to WIPPENHOEK Railhead at 10am. Drew Rations in bulk at 10.15am. Convoyed same to Refilling Point. Company moved from Camp Map Ref Sheet 27 L.23.a.5.2. at 9.30am Arriving at L.33 Central at 10.30am. Supply Sect Refills 11.30am. Returned to Camp. Transport Duties 2R 2.9.S. Horses Carting 1 A.1.S.C. Supplies to W.Y. Bn Reception Camp. 1 A.1.S.C. Supplies to 123" Bde School. (WEATHER FINE)	TR
"	18th	18	Supplies Delivered to Units by Supply Sect at 6.30am. Drew Rations in bulk by Refilling Point. Refill 11.30am. Returned. Loaded to Camp. Transport Duties 2R 2.5.S. Horses Carting 1 A.1.S.C. to 123 "Bde School. 1 A.1.S.C. Supplies to W.Y. Bn. Bn Reception Camp 2Pts 255 Horses Carting 1A 1BS Bde School. 1A. 1BS Supplies to Unit. N? 375041 Q. Cpl by a.d. Kenny Hts attached to Unit. N? 375041 Q. Cpl by a.d. Kenny Ryn evacuated Baggage 12 w Wagons of the 10 R.W. Kent. Attached to the Strength of Company. N? 3 L.213 w.w.2 w struck off the strength of Company. (WEATHER FINE)	TR
"	19th	18	Supplies Delivered to Units by Supply Sect at 6.30am. Drew Rations in built from WIPPENHOEK Railhead at 10am. Convoyed same to Refilling Point. Refill 11.30am. Returned. Loaded to Camp. Baggage Wagons Detached to Units Transport Duties 2pts 2 I.S. Horses Carting 1 A.1.S.C. Supplies to the 41" Divl Reception Camp. 1 A.1.S.C. Supplies to the 123 "Bde School. 1A 1BS Supplies to the 41" Divl Reception Camp. 1A 1BS Supplies to the 3" Aust. Cas? on the 13 inst. N? 375041 Q. Cpl by a.d. Henry Ryn evacuated to the 3" Aust. Cas? on the 13 inst. to which a Ret? of the Strength of Company. WEATHER FINE	TR

Army Form C. 2118.

WAR DIARY
or
INTELLIGENCE SUMMARY
(Erase heading not required.)

Instructions regarding War Diaries and Intelligence Summaries are contained in F. S. Regs., Part II. and the Staff Manual respectively. Title Pages will be prepared in manuscript.

Place	Date	Hour	Summary of Events and Information	Remarks and references to Appendices
L33 Control	20th	18	Supplies Delivered to Units by Supply Sect. at 7.30am. & Drew Rations from WIPPEN HOEK Railhead at 10am. & Conveyed same to M.T. Reserve Depot at STEENVOORDE. Transport XAII TT. 2A 2/5. Harvest Carting 2A 2/5. Reserve Rations for 124 "Inf" Bde 1A/R. Supply to 123 Bde School MT/S/7603.1016 S/Sgt Shuttleworth W. Returned 1A/S. Supplies to 41st Divnl Reception Camp from leave to the United Kingdom.	TO (WEATHER FINE)
"	21st	18	Supply Sect. Proceeded to WIPPEN HOEK Railhead at 9.30am & Drew Rations in bulk at 10am & Conveyed same to Refilling Point. Refill 11.30am & Delivered Rations to Units. Men proceeding to United Kingdom on Leave to the United Kingdom. Transport Carting 2A, 2/5 Harvest Carting 1A, 2/5 Supplies to the 123rd Inf/Bde School 2A 1/S. Supplies to the 2nd Divnl Reception Camp MT/7603333. A. Minor Railway moved from the A.S.C. 1300 10spot to be on the Strength of Company.	(WEATHER FINE)
"	22nd	18	Supply Sect. Proceeded to WIPPEN HOEK Railhead at 9.30am & Drew Rations in bulk at 10am. Conveyed same to Refilling Point. Refill 11.30am & Delivered Rations to Units. Transport Carting 2A 2/5 Harvest Carting 1A 1/S. Supplies 1A/S.S. Supplies to 123 Inf Bde School 1A/S.S. Supplies to 41st Divnl Reception Camp.	TO WEATHER FINE
"	23rd	18	Supply Sect. Proceeded to WIPPEN HOEK Railhead at 10am & Drew Rations in bulk at 10.45am. & Conveyed same to Refilling Point. Refill 12 noon & Delivered Rations to Units. Harvest Carting 2A/2/5 Harvest Carting 1A/ 3/S. Supplies to the 123 Bde School 1A/S.S. Supplies to 41st Divnl Reception Camp.	TO (WEATHER FINE)
"	24th	18	Supply Sect. Proceeded to WIPPEN HOEK Railhead at 10.10am & Drew Rations in bulk at 10.45 am & Conveyed same to Refilling Point. Refill 12 noon & Delivered Rations to Units. Transport Carting 1A 1/S. Supplies to the 41st Divnl Reception Camp.	TO (WEATHER FINE)

WAR DIARY
or
INTELLIGENCE SUMMARY

(Erase heading not required.)

Army Form C. 2118.

Place	Date	Hour	Summary of Events and Information	Remarks and references to Appendices
L33 Central	25th	18	Supply Sect Proceeded to WIPPENHOEK Railhead at 10am & Drew Rations in bulk at 10:10am & Conveyed same to Refilling Point. Refill 2pm & Delivered Rations to Units Transport. Willis 1R.1 9.S. Supplies to 123 Bde School A/cds. Supplies to 4th Divnl Reception Camp. M/0356 143 9/c Cpl Mitchell E 238. Employment Coy Provided on Leave to the United Kingdom Nº 2075333 Dr Parry S. having been evacuated to the 10th C.C.S. in sick. Sgt Sleight & Company Nº 1914236 A. Callaghan W. Returned from Leave to the United Kingdom. Nº 354126 Pte. Nemo. Returned unfit. WEATHER SHOWERY.	10
"	26th	18	Supply Sect Proceeded to WIPPEN HOEK Railhead at 10am & Drew Rations in bulk at 10.45am. Conveyed same to Refilling Point. Refill 1.30pm & Delivered Rations to Units Transport Details 1R.1 9.S Supplies to 123 Bde School. 1A. 1 9.S. Supplies to 41st Divnl Recpt Camp. WEATHER FINE	10
"	27th	18	Supply Sect Proceeded to WIPPEN HOEK Railhead at 10.10am & Drew Rations in bulk at 10.45am & Conveyed same to Refilling Point. Refill 1:30pm & Delivered Rations to Units Transport Details 1R.1 9.S Supplies to 123 Bde School. 1A. 1 9.S Supplies to 41st Divnl Reception Camp. 9 m. 2 9.S. Supplies for 1214 Bde. N/s 29858 Compl Banks F.D.T.1 8110 Sadd Cpl Lawson JC Returned from II Army Rest Camp. N/s 5264133 Dr Rome B Admitted to 139 th F.A. WEATHER FINE	10
BRANDHOEK	28th	22.	Supply Sect Proceeded to WIPPEN HOEK Railhead at 10am & Drew Rations in bulk at 10.45am & Conveyed same to Refilling Point. Refill 1.30pm & Delivered Rations to Units. Company moved from Camp L.33. Central at 4pm & Arrived at BRANDHOEK at 9.30pm. (WEATHER FINE)	10
"	29th	18	Supply Sect Proceeded to Refilling Point at 8.30am Refill 9am & Delivered Rations to Units. Nº 874 05709 Cpl Lister T. believed to have been Wounded (cannot be traced) with 1 Riding Horse Killed & Dr Beckwith 2448 Horses attached from 491 Company Wounded by Enemy Bombs dropped on the night of the 28/29th inst. (WEATHER RAINY)	10

Army Form C. 2118.

WAR DIARY
or
INTELLIGENCE SUMMARY

(Erase heading not required.)

Instructions regarding War Diaries and Intelligence Summaries are contained in F. S. Regs., Part II. and the Staff Manual respectively. Title Pages will be prepared in manuscript.

Place	Date	Hour	Summary of Events and Information	Remarks and references to Appendices
BRANDHOEK	30	18.	Supply Sect. Proceeded to Refilling Point at 8.30am Refill 9 am & Delivered Rations to Units WEATHER. (VERY RAINY)	

T Blunn Captain.
O.C. No 3 Company 41st Divisional Train

Army Form C. 2118.

WAR DIARY
or
INTELLIGENCE SUMMARY.
(Erase heading not required.)

Instructions regarding War Diaries and Intelligence Summaries are contained in F. S. Regs., Part II. and the Staff Manual respectively. Title pages will be prepared in manuscript.

Place	Date	Hour	Summary of Events and Information	Remarks and references to Appendices
H24.C34.	Oct 1st	19"	Supply Sect. Proceeded to Kipling Point at 9.30 a.m. Refill 9 a.m. & Delivered Rations to Units. Company moved from Bandhoek at 12 noon & arrived at H24. C34. at 6.30p.m. 71 S.B. 909 Cpl. Jaken having been issued to the Cpl. C3 as to strength off the Strength of Company. (WEATHER FINE.)	113
"	2nd	18"	Supply Sect. Proceeded to Kipling Point with Head Qrs. at 7.30a.m. Refill 8.30am & Delivered Rations to Units. 7187 Pte. P.S.M. Kilgarlin returned from leave to the United Kingdom. 12634 Pte. Brookr N. attached to Company from the 936th Employment Company Proceeded on leave to the British Kingdom. (WEATHER FINE)	119
"	3rd	18"	Supply Sect. Proceeded to Kipling Point. Issued Rations at 7.30am. Refill 8.30am & Delivered Rations to Units. 36626 Pte. Taylor E.G. Proceded on leave to the United Kingdom. (WEATHER SHOWERY)	110
"	4th	16	Supply Sect. Proceeded to Kipling Point at 8.30 a.m. Refill 9.30 a.m. & Delivered Rations to Units with Leave men. (WEATHER SHOWERY)	105
"	5"	18	Supply Sect. Proceeded to Kipling Point at 8.10am. Refill 8.30am. & Delivered Rations to Units with Rail Pairs. (WEATHER SHOWERY)	118
"	6th	18	Supply Sect. Proceeded to Kipling Point at 8.15am. Refill 8.30am & Delivered Rations to Units with men. Company came into Camp at midnight. (WEATHER FINE)	116
"	7th	18	Supply Sect. Proceeded to Kipling Point at 8.30am. Refill 9.30am & Delivered Rations to Units & Baggage returned from Units. (WEATHER SHOWERY)	113
"	8th	18	Supply Sect. Proceeded to Kipling Point at 8.30am. Refill 9.30am & Delivered Rations to Units. (WEATHER FINE)	113
"	9th	18	Supply Sect. Proceeded to Kipling Point at 8.15am. Refill 9.30am & Delivered Rations to Units. (WEATHER FINE)	113
"	10th	18	Supply Sect. Proceeded to Kipling Point at 8.15am. Refill 9.30am & Delivered Rations to Units. N.E.947 Barsa Company to Relieved from leave to the United Kingdom. (WEATHER FINE)	105
"	11th	18	Supply Sect. Proceeded to Kipling Point at 8.30am. Refill 8.30am & Delivered Rations to Units. Baggage to Wagons of the 19th Middlesex Regt Reqnd. Company from Units 123 to 11 B. N.R. Carpor Wagon. (WEATHER SHOWERY.)	117
"	12th	16	Supply Sect. Proceeded to Kipling Point at 8.30 a.m. Refill 8.30am & Delivered Rations by Bay to 11th & 19th Sect. S.B. Nicholl C.441 Proceeded on leave to the United Kingdom. 2nd Lieut Col. Mitchell E. 238 Employment Company attached to Company to Company Returned off leave from the United Kingdom	119
"	13	18	Supply by Supply Sect. Refill 8.30am & Delivered Rations to Units. 17 Weather 7-23 P. Employment Attached to Company Returned off leave to the United Kingdom. (WEATHER SHOWERY)	117

WAR DIARY
or
INTELLIGENCE SUMMARY.

Army Form C. 2118.

(Erase heading not required.)

Place	Date	Hour	Summary of Events and Information	Remarks and references to Appendices
I.Q. Central	Sept 14	18	Supply Sect. Proceeded to YPRES. Railhead at 7.30 am & Drew Rations in bulk Refill R11&12 Delivered Rations to Units. Company Moved from Camp Map Ref. H2H C 34 at 2.30 pm & arrived at Camp Map Ref. I.9.C Central at 3.30 pm. (WEATHER FINE)	MX
"	15	18	Supply Sect. Proceeded to YPRES. Railhead at 7.15 am. Drew Rations in bulk & Conveyed same to Refilling Point. Refill R13 & R14 & Delivered Rations to Units. M.T. Lorry Cpl Kendall S.W. joined Coy from 3rd Grain Coy. WEATHER FINE	MX
K14 BB2	16	18	Supply Sect. Proceeded to YPRES. Railhead at 6.30 am & Drew Rations in bulk & Conveyed same to Refilling Point. Refill R15 & R16 & Delivered Rations to Units. Company Moved from Camp I.9.C Central at 9.45 am & arrived at K14 BB2 at 2 pm. WEATHER VERY WET.	MX
"	17	18	Supply by Supply Sect. Received to Refilling Point at 12.30 pm Refill R17 & R18 & Delivered Rations to Units. WEATHER DULL	MX
"	18	18	Supplies by Supply Sect. Proceeded to Refilling Point at K.14 B2 at Refill 7.30 am & Returned to Camp. WEATHER DULL	MX
SH 29	19	18	Supplies by Supply Sect. Delivered Rations to Units at 9 am. Refill 2 pm. VR Arrived Coy from M.T. Company to Independence for Remounts. WEATHER	MX
G.20.C	20	18	Supplies by Supply Sect. Delivered Rations to Units at 11 am. Company Moved from K.14.882 at 1.15 pm & arrived at G.20.C at 3.45 pm. Refill 5.30 pm & Returned to Camp. WEATHER SHOWERY	MX
G.29.6.62	21	20	Supplies by Supply Sect. Delivered Rations to Units at 8.30 am. Company moved from G.20.C at 1.15 pm & arrived at G.29.6.82 at 2.15 Supplies Refill 6 pm & Returned from WEATHER FINE	MX
"	22	19	Supplies by Supply Sect. Delivered Rations to Units at 8.30 am. Refill 6 pm & Returned Rations to Camp M.C.M.T.H for Hamlin & Returned with Remounts from Zeod Reens. WEATHER DULL	MX
"	23	18	Returned by Supply Sect. Delivered Rations Units at 8.30 am Refill to ben & Returned Loaded to Camp GE(MM)336 b& Dr Taylor GE(MM)336 b& Dr Jayler M.1263419 Pte Buckley LN1363419 Pte Jayler. Returned from Leave to the United Kingdom M.T. 762793 Pte Rosen is posted to RE Sect to alter the Strength. (WEATHER FINE)	MX

WAR DIARY
or
INTELLIGENCE SUMMARY

(Erase heading not required.)

Army Form C. 2118.

Instructions regarding War Diaries and Intelligence Summaries are contained in F. S. Regs., Part II. and the Staff Manual respectively. Title pages will be prepared in manuscript.

Place	Date	Hour	Summary of Events and Information	Remarks and references to Appendices
SHEET 29				
G.29.d.5.2.	24	18	Supplies by Supply Sect. Delivered Rations to Units at 8.30 am. Refill 3.30 pm & Returned Loaded to Camp. WEATHER FINE.	AB
"	25	18	Supplies by Supply Sect. Delivered Rations to Units at 8.30 am. NL Nº 090959 St Amos. C. Proceded on leave to the United Kingdom. WEATHER DULL	AB
"	26	18	Supplies by Supply Sect Proceeded to Refilling Point at 7 am & Refill 4.30 am & Delivered Rations to Units. WEATHER FINE	AB
"	27	18	Supplies by Supply Sect. Proceeded to Refilling Point at 6.2 am & Refill 6.3 am & Delivered Rations to Units. Supply Sect. Proceeded to LEDEGHEM at 12 noon & Drew Rations in bulk at 2 pm & Conveyed same to Refilling Point. Refill 3.30 pm & Returned loaded to Camp. Baggage Sec one Officer & Company from Run Rochester Units. WEATHER FINE.	AB
"	28	18	Supplies by Baggage Sect Delivered Rations to Units at 8 am. Capt J.S. Fleming M. Nº 92084 Corpl Landon Nº 2417 & Gemlin S. Attended the Worals of the Official landing crew of COURTRAI Baggage Sect. Proceeded to LE DRUM Railhead at 12 noon & Drew Rations in bulk at 2 pm Conveyed same to Refilling Point. WEATHER FINE	AB
H.32.D.10.2.	29	18	Supplies by Supply Sect Refill 9 am & Delivered Rations to Units at 9 am Baggage Sect Moved from BISSINGHEM Railhead at 6 pm & Drew Rations in bulk & Conveyed same to Refilling Point Company moved from Camp Nos. Refl.Nº SH29. G.29.d.5.2 at 1 pm & Arrived at G.29.X.70.99. My Rd Shut Nº H.32.d.10.2 at 2.30 pm Nº 103. 2nd Lt. S. Sgt Nicolls WH Returned from leave to the United Kingdom. WEATHER FINE	AB
"	30	18	Supplies by Supply Sect Refill 9 am & Delivered Rations from WL Proceeded to BISSINGHEN Railhead at 1.30 pm & Drew Rations in bulk at 2 pm & Conveyed same to Camp. Nº 314 102 Pumi B Having been evacuated to C.C.S. on 18 by 18 is struck off the Company strength. WEATHER FINE	AB
"	31	18	Supplies by Baggage Sect Refill 9 am & Delivered Rations to Units Proceeded to BISSINGHEM Railhead at 1.30 pm & Drew Rations in bulk at 2 pm & Conveyed same to Bissingherm Railhead. Captain M. C. Proceeded on leave to the United Kingdom. Capt G.N. Wood Attached to Company from 40. Company. WEATHER FINE	AB

Milward Captain

For O.C. Nº 3 Coy 41st Divisional Train

Army Form C. 2118.

WAR DIARY

INTELLIGENCE SUMMARY.

(Erase heading not required.)

Instructions regarding War Diaries and Intelligence Summaries are contained in F. S. Regs., Part II. and the Staff Manual respectively. Title pages will be prepared in manuscript.

Place	Date	Hour	Summary of Events and Information	Remarks and references to Appendices
SHEET 29 H32 a10.2	Nov. 1st	18	Supplies by Supply Sect. Refill 2pms & Delivered Rations to Units. Baggage last Rations 2nd. Sub. Section 4/2 SHT. D. Thornton Lt proceeded on leave to the United Kingdom. WEATHER FINE	Snow
SHEET 29 H34 C66	2nd	18	Supplies by Supply Sect. Refill 2am. & Delivered Rations to Units. Company moved from Billets Map 51 Sh 29H.32. a 10.2 at 10.30am d arrived at BILLETS Map Ref Sh 29 H34 C66. at 11.30am. Supply Sect. proceeded to BISSINGHEM Railhead at 12.30pm & Drew Rations (no. 1 & 2) Convoyed same to Refilling point. WEATHER DULL	Snow
"	3rd	18	Supplies by Supply Sect. Refill 2am d Delivered Rations to Units. Supply Sect. proceeded to BISSINGHEM Railhead at 12.30pm & Drew Rations & Convoyed same to Refilling Point. WEATHER DULL	Snow
"	4th	18	Supplies by Supply Sect. Refill 2am. d Delivered Rations to Units. Supply Sect. proceeded to BISSINGHEM Railhead at 12.30am d Drew Rations in bulk & Convoyed same to Refilling Point. No 33303 Lce Cpl Munro A.C. Proceeded on leave to the United Kingdom. WEATHER FINE	Snow
SHEET 29 I.32. C.38.	5th	18	Supplies by Supply Sect Refill 2am. & Delivered Rations to Units. Supply Sect. proceeded to BISSINGHEM Railhead at 12.30pm & Drew Rations in bulk & Convoyed same to Refilling Point. Company moved from Camp Map Ref Sh. 29 H34 C66. at 9.30am d arrived at Camp Map Ref. Sh 29 I.32 C.38 at 11.30am d Refill of 235 Rations & pay troop 2 attached to this company proceeded on leave to the United Kingdom. WEATHER VERY WET	Snow
"	6	18	Supplies by Supply Sect Refill 2am d Delivered Rations to Units. Service Rations & supplies & loaded to Camp. Rations Convoyed to Refilling point. Baggage by M.T. WEATHER VERY WET	Snow
SHEET 29 I.9a.4.4.	7	18	Supplies by Supply Sect. Delivered Rations to Units at 8am & proceeded to Refilling Point Railway Map Sh 29 I.9 Drew Rations in bulk d Convoyed same to Refilling point. Moved from Billets Map Ref Sh 29 I.32 C.38 at 8.11.30am d arrived at Billets Map Ref Sh 29 I.9a.4.4. at 2pm. No. 111933 Pte Savage H. Returned from leave. WEATHER SNOWY	Snow

WAR DIARY
INTELLIGENCE SUMMARY
(Erase heading not required.)

Army Form C. 2118.

Instructions regarding War Diaries and Intelligence Summaries are contained in F. S. Regs., Part II. and the Staff Manual respectively. Title pages will be prepared in manuscript.

Place	Date	Hour	Summary of Events and Information	Remarks and references to Appendices
SHEET 29. 19.0.9.9.	NOV. 8"	18.	Supplies by Supply Sect. Refit at 9am. Delivered Rations to Units. Second Refit 2pm Delivered. Loaded to Camp. Rations conveyed from Railhead to Railway Railhead M.T.S. 05.30.9.0. appx. we was detached to this Coy B.H.D. (WEATHER SHOWERY)	J. niv
"	9"	19	Supplies by Supply Sect. Delivered Rations to Units at 9am. Supply Sect. moved off to VINCLY Railhead at 10am. Whole Railway Railhead M.T. Company same to Coy B.H.D. 2nd Refit 6.15pm Delivered Rations to Camp. (WEATHER FINE)	J. niv
SHEET. 29.	10"	21.	Supplies by Supply Sect. Delivered Rations to Units. Company moved from Camp Map Ref Shut.29. J.23.9.9.0. at 9.30am & Arrived at Camp Map Ref. Shut.29. J.33.9.9.0. at 12.45. Supply Sect. Refit 8.30pm & Returned Rations to Camp. N0.05 05289 Pte. Hoosen QW Proceed on leave.	J. niv
SHEET.30. M.22.C	11	18.	Supplies by Supply Sect. Delivered Rations to Units at 6 am. Company moved from Camp Map Ref. Shut.29. J.33. 9.9.0 at 9.15am & Arrived at Camp Map Ref. Shut. 30 M22.C at 5.45pm (WEATHER FINE)	J. niv
"	12"	19	Supplies by Supply Sect. Refit 9am. & Delivered Rations Tumb at 2pm. (WEATHER SHOWERY)	J. niv
"	13"	18	Supplies by Supply Sect. Refit 11 pm & Delivered Rations to Units. N0.TS.5.355 M. Taylor. Transferred 0/3 to A.S.C./CP 4. (T.F.) 1354.3. Bsn York. Ch. Posted to Coy from 140th F.A. WEATHER FINE	J. niv
SHEET. 30. N.23.Q.9.9.	14"	18	Supplies by Supply Sect. Shut. 30. M.22. C. at 10 am. Arrived at Camp Map Ref. Shut. 30. N23. Q.9.9.0.0.4.45pm. Coy, Refit 9pm Delivered Rations to Camp. Capt. J. Fleming.(m.c.) Returned to detachment of this Unit. S.D. from London. Sapoto detail Nov 14 1916. Letter from London Sapoto detail Nov 14 1916 (A.S.C.)(T.F.) Nov 14 1916. (WEATHER FINE)	J. niv
"	15"	18	Supplies by Supply Sect. Delivered Rations to Units at 9am. Refit at 9pm Delivered Rations to Camp. (WEATHER FINE)	J. niv
"	16"	16	Supplies by Supply Sect. Delivered Rations to Units at 9am. Refit 4.30pm & Returned Loaded to Camp. No. TMR 03 Lce Cpl Leyhurst E.G.H. & T9959 Dr Annis C. Returned from Leave. WEATHER FINE)	J. niv
"	17"	19	Supplies by Supply Sect. Delivered Rations to Units at 9 am. Refit 2pm Returned Loaded to Camp. Supply Wagons of the 190th Bde R.F.A attached to Company. WEATHER FINE)	J. 28.

WAR DIARY

~~INTELLIGENCE~~ SUMMARY.
(Erase heading not required.)

Army Form C. 2118.

Instructions regarding War Diaries and Intelligence Summaries are contained in F. S. Regs., Part II. and the Staff Manual respectively. Title pages will be prepared in manuscript.

Place	Date	Hour	Summary of Events and Information	Remarks and references to Appendices
GAMMERAGES	18th	20	Supplies by Supply Sect. Delivered Rations to Units. Company Moved from Camp Map Ref Sheet 32	R.S.P
			N23 a 99, at 7am & Arrived at Camp at GAMMERAGES at 4.15 pm Supply Sect Refilled at MORBEKE Station & Returned Loaded to Camp. (WEATHER COLD)	R.S.P
"	19	22	Supplies by Supply Sect Delivered Rations to Units at 9 am Refilled at MORBEKE Station & Returned Loaded to Camp. No 33394 Cpl Smith J.C. proceeded on leave to the United Kingdom (WEATHER COLD)	R.S.P
LES DEUX ACREN	20	18	Supplies by Supply Sect. Delivered Rations to Units at 9 am Company Moved from GAMMERAGES at 9 am & Arrived at LES DEUX ACREN. 1.30 pm Supply Sect Refilled by B/V Returned Loaded to Camp. (WEATHER FINE)	R.S.P
"	21	18	Supplies by Supply Sect. Delivered Rations to Units at 9 am No 75369 Sen Cpl Conlin R.E. proceeded on leave to the United Kingdom. No 139939 A Amo C. admitted to the 139 FA (WEATHER FINE)	R.S.P
"	22	18	Supplies by Supply Sect Refill 9.30 am & Delivered Rations to Units No 44419 D. Thornton O.F.A. Jan B. Munn A.C. Returned from leave to the United Kingdom. (WEATHER FINE)	R.S.P
"	23	18	Supplies by Supply Sect Refill 9.30 am & Delivered Rations to Units. No 349981. Pte Bryan R.A Admitted to the 139th Field Ambulance. (WEATHER FINE)	R.S.P
"	24	18	Supplies by Supply Sect. Refill 9.30 am & Delivered Rations to Units. (WEATHER FINE)	R.S.P
"	25	18	Supplies by Supply Sect. Refill 9.10 am & Delivered Rations to Units (WEATHER DULL)	R.S.P

WAR DIARY
INTELLIGENCE SUMMARY.
(Erase heading not required.)

Army Form C. 2118.

Place	Date	Hour	Summary of Events and Information	Remarks and references to Appendices
LES DEUX ACREN	26	18	Supplies by Supply Sect. Refill 9.30 am Delivered Rations to Units. 719 T#70959 Pt Amos C. v 2991 Pt Bryant H evacuated to C.C.S admitted 41 Stat ft (WEATHER DULL)	Qs/-
"	27	18	Supplies by Supply Sect. Refill 9.10 am Delivered Rations to Units 41 T39539 Pt Gow L.P. T#803 Pt Munn O.E. v A9201665 Pt Jones W admitted 26/11 139 F.A. (WEATHER DULL)	Qs/-
"	28	18	Supplies by Supply Sect. Refill 9.30 am Received Rations to Units. (WEATHER DULL)	Qs/-
"	29	18	Supplies by Supply Sect. Refill 9.30 am Delivered Rations to Units 11 T/6125 Pt Smith Gilbert G.B. "City 26" Pt. Laundry J. Proceeded to the United Kingdom on Special Leave. 110 T#54083 Dvr Bernard C. A. Evacuated to the United Kingdom on Ordinary Leave. (WEATHER FINE)	Qs/-
"	30	18	Supplies by Supply Sect. Refill 9.30 am Delivered Rations to Units. (WEATHER DULL)	Qs/-

R.S. French W.M. Captain
a/. O.C. 423 Coy 41st Divisional Train

WAR DIARY or INTELLIGENCE SUMMARY

Army Form C. 2118.

(Erase heading not required.)

Place	Date	Hour	Summary of Events and Information	Remarks and references to Appendices
LES DEUX ACREN	DEC. 1st	18	Supplies by Supply Sect. Refill 9am & Delivered Rations to Units. Second Refill by 3.9am & Returned/Loaded to Camp. No T6532 G.D. Hooper A.H. Returned from Leave to the United Kingdom	9BA.
"	2nd	18	Supplies by Supply Sect. Delivered Rations to Units at 9am. Refill upon returned & Loaded B. Camp. WEATHER FINE	9BA.
"	3rd	18	Supplies by Supply Sect. Delivered Rations to Units at 9am. Capt C.M. Wood. Rose did on leave to the United Kingdom Lieut. B.A.Emly joined Company T16256 by Cpl. Flight on appointed of Corporal 1 N.H. Horse No 101. having been evacuated to base off the Coys strength. WEATHER FINE	9BA.
"	4th	18	Supplies by Supply Sect. Refill 9am & Delivered Rations to Units. No T6523J Dr Good with a Slip.No Mc.Coull Pitt Dr Jos No Fox Nunn a.c. having been evacuated to C.C.S. for various off the Coys strength. WEATHER SHOWERY	9BA.
"	5th	18	Supplies by Supply Sect. Refill 9am & Delivered Rations to Units. No T9444JB Gnr L. Kempster Joined Company from 141st HQ RFA. WEATHER DULL	9BA.
"	6th	18	Supplies by Supply Sect. Refill 9am & Delivered Rations to Units. No T96025 Dr Pratt W.E admitted to the 139 F.A. WEATHER FINE	9BA.
"	7th	18	Supplies by Supply Sect. Refill 9am & Delivered Rations to Units. Marching Order Inspection by O. Company. WEATHER FINE	9BA.

Army Form C. 2118.

WAR DIARY
or
INTELLIGENCE SUMMARY.
(Erase heading not required.)

Instructions regarding War Diaries and Intelligence Summaries are contained in F. S. Regs., Part II. and the Staff Manual respectively. Title pages will be prepared in manuscript.

Place	Date	Hour	Summary of Events and Information	Remarks and references to Appendices
LES DEUX ACREN	8th	18.	Supplies by Supply Sect. Refill 9am. & Delivered Rations to Units N° 272217 Cpl. Kendall S.A. transferred to N° 1 Coy & N° 36192 Lce Cpl Kirk from N° 1 Coy to N° 3 Coy. (Weather: Fine)	913A.
"	9th	18.	Supplies by Baggage Sect. Refill 9am. & Delivered Rations to Units. N° T/2 CQMS Smith Y.P.E. Received N° 056114 on leave to the United Kingdom. (Weather Fine.)	913A.
"	10th	18.	Supplies by Supply Sect. Refill 9am. & Delivered Rations to Units N° S/369 Van. Cpl. Crotz R.L. Returned from leave to the United Kingdom. N° S/5229 Dr. Goodliffe O. Returned from Hospital. (Weather Showery)	913A.
"	11th	18.	Supplies by Supply Sect. Refill 9am. & Delivered Rations to Units. Subsistence Wagons of the 199th R.F.A. joining N°1 Coy Train 19, 2nd L.S. Detached to the 233 Hd Coy R.E. 199 2nd L.S. Detached to the 139 Hd and Second Refill 5.30pm. & Returned Loaded to Camp R.D. Lipton (a Newly H. Attached from N°1 Coy Train Proceeded on Leave to the United Kingdom. The following having joined from the A.S.C. Base Depot are taken on the strength of Company N° 336419 Pard Pd S/5329 D Agent H. N° T/11822 Dr. Dawes W. Transferred to Ck 139 F.A. The following having joined Tull 392 D. Dawes W. Transferred to Ck 139 F.A. N° S/5293 D. Bowie O. N° S/5/231 Dr Goodliffe Q. (Weather Fine.)	98A.
St Pierre Capelle	12	19	Company moved from (Les Deux Acren) at 9.30 m & Arrived at (St Pierre Capelle) at 12.40pm Refill 6.15pm & Returned Loaded to Camp. by Supply Sec. Delivered Rations to Units. (Weather Showery)	98A.
Lembecq	13	18	Company moved from St Pierre Capelle at 9am Supplies by Supply Sec. Delivered Rations to Units en route & arrived at Lembecq at 2.20pm (Weather Showery)	95A.
Mont St Pont	14	18	Supplies by Supply Sect. Refill 11.45am. Company moved from Lembecq at 8.45am & Arrived at Mont St Pont at 12.45pm Supply Sec. Delivered Rations to Units at 1pm. (Weather Showery)	96A.

Army Form C. 2118.

WAR DIARY
or
INTELLIGENCE SUMMARY.
(Erase heading not required.)

Instructions regarding War Diaries and Intelligence Summaries are contained in F. S. Regs., Part II. and the Staff Manual respectively. Title pages will be prepared in manuscript.

Place	Date	Hour	Summary of Events and Information	Remarks and references to Appendices
MONT ST PONT	15"	18	Supplies by Supply Sect. Refill 9am & Delivered Rations to Units. (WEATHER FINE)	913A
HOUTAIN-LE-VAL	16"	18	Supplies by Supply Sect. Refill 7.45am Company moved from MONT-ST-PONT) at 8.30am & Arrived at HOUTAIN-LE-VAL at 11.50pm. Supply Sect Delivered Rations to Units at 1.45pm. (WEATHER SHOWERY)	913A
SOMBREFFE	17"	18	Supplies by Supply Sect. Refill 8am. Company moved from HOUTAIN-LE-VAL) at 8.30am & Arrived at SOMBREFFE at 1.10pm. Supply Sect Delivered Rations to Units at 1pm. (WEATHER SHOWERY)	913A
BOTHEY	18	18	Company moved from SOMBREFFE) at 8.45am & Arrived at BOTHEY at 9.20am. Supply Sect. Refilled 2pm & Delivered Rations to Units. (WEATHER SHOWERY)	913A
LEUZE	19	18	Supplies by Supply Sect. Refill 8am. Company moved from BOTHEY at Man & arrived at LEUZE at 4.45pm. Supply Sect. Delivered Rations to Units at 5pm. (WEATHER Showery)	913A
PITET	20.	18	Supplies by Supply Sect. Refill 9am & Delivered Rations to the Company marked for LEUZE at 8am & Arrived at PETET at 3.50pm. (WEATHER SHOWERY)	913A
"	21	18	Supplies by Supply Sect. Refill 9.30am. Delivered Rations to Units Baggage Platoon reported Company from Units 445B T.S.M York CH. A moved from Leuze to the 18th Kingdom. (WEATHER FINE)	913A
NEAR HUY on HUY-AMPSIN MAIN ROAD	22	18	Supplies by Supply Sect. Refill 10.15am & Delivered Rations to Units. Company moved from PITET) at 9.15am & arrived at Billet on HUY-AMPSIN Main Road at 12.10pm. Units 2B4 Drivers Saunders J. & Palmer from Special team to the United Kingdom. (WEATHER FINE)	913A

Army Form C. 2118.

WAR DIARY
or
INTELLIGENCE SUMMARY.
(Erase heading not required.)

Instructions regarding War Diaries and Intelligence Summaries are contained in F. S. Regs. Part II. and the Staff Manual respectively. Title pages will be prepared in manuscript.

Place	Date	Hour	Summary of Events and Information	Remarks and references to Appendices
NEAR HUY. ON HUY-AMPSIN MAIN ROAD.	23	18	Supplies by Supplies Sect. Proceeded to (HUY) Railhead at 9.30am & Drew Rations in bulk & Conveyed same to Refilling Point. WEATHER Showery	JBA
"	24	18	Supplies by Baggage Sect. Proceeded to HUY Railhead at 7.15am & Drew Rations in bulk & Conveyed same to Refilling Point. WEATHER FINE.	JBA
"	25	18	Christmas Day. Supplies by Supply Sect. Proceeded to (HUY) Railhead at 9.30am & Drew Rations in bulk & Conveyed same to Refilling Point. Nº 33910 Q. Man J. Proceeded to England to retrain as a Coal Miner. (WEATHER FINE)	JBA 1
"	26	18	Supplies by Baggage Sect. Proceeded to (HUY) Railhead at 7.30am & Drew Rations in bulk & Conveyed same to Refilling Point. Nº 330172 Pte Sutton E. & Cpl C.W.1 Nº 330172 Pte Sutton & Nº 7896 Dvr W. Dickinson Proceeded to the United Kingdom on (Coal Mining) Nº 7896 Dvr W. Dickinson Returned from leave to the United Kingdom.	JBA
"	27	18	Supplies by Supply Sect. Proceeded to HUY Railhead at 7.30am & Drew Rations in bulk & Conveyed same to Refilling Point. 1 Baggage Wagon delivered to each Batt. Nº 82/100 & train Nº 025776 & Croton C/O. Nº 388-92 Pte Sutton E. having proceeded to the United Kingdom as Coal Miners are struck off the Company strength. (WEATHER SHOWERY)	JBA
"	28	18	Supplies by Baggage Sect. Proceeded to (HUY) Railhead at 7.15am & Drew Rations in bulk & Conveyed same to Refilling Point. WEATHER SHOWERY	JBA
"	29	18	Supplies by Baggage Sect. Proceeded to HUY Railhead at 3.30pm & Drew Rations in bulk & Conveyed same to Refilling Point. (WEATHER Showery)	JBA

Army Form C. 2118.

WAR DIARY
or
INTELLIGENCE SUMMARY.
(Erase heading not required.)

Instructions regarding War Diaries and Intelligence Summaries are contained in F. S. Regs., Part II. and the Staff Manual respectively. Title pages will be prepared in manuscript.

Place	Date	Hour	Summary of Events and Information	Remarks and references to Appendices
NEAR (HUY) ON HUY-AMPSIN MAIN ROAD.	30"	18	Supplies by Baggage Sect: Proceeded to (HUY) Railhead at Y.30 and Drew Rations in bulk & Conveyed same to 1st Refilling Point: 71°Q.56704. 6 OR's Smith Y.W.C. Returned from Leave to the United Kingdom. 1 H.D. Horse No. 149 Evacuated to the 52nd M.V.S. 71°Q.78263. Pt. 102 Rr m/H. Q admitted to the 140th Field Ambulance. (WEATHER FINE)	JBA
"	31	18	Supplies by Supply Sect: Proceeded to (HUY) Railhead at Y.300 and Drew Rations in bulk & Conveyed same to Refilling Point: N°39Q490 60 O.Rs how S. Proceeded to the United Kingdom for Demobilisation on Release as a (Coal miner). (WEATHER DULL)	JBA

JW Colouston 2nd Lieut
O.C. N°3 Coy 41st Divisional Train R.A.S.C

No 3 Coy

Army Form C. 2118.

WAR DIARY

INTELLIGENCE SUMMARY.

(Erase heading not required.)

Place	Date	Hour	Summary of Events and Information	Remarks and references to Appendices
NEAR (HUY) HUY-AMPSIN MAIN ROAD	1919 Jan 1	18	Supplies by Baggage Sect: Proceeded to (HUY) Railhead at 4.45 a.m. v Drew Rations in bulk & conveyed same to Refilling Point. No. T/065205 Dr Mullock H.J Admitted to 14.0 Field Ambulance. A.D.S. No T/149. Having been evacuated to ch 52" M.V.3. on the 30 inst: is struck off the Company Strength. No T/39499 Q Orielation B (having proceeded to the United Kingdom for Demobilization on a 14 days miner) is struck off the Companys Strength.	9BA 9BA
"	2	18	(WEATHER FINE) Supplies by Supply Sect: Proceeded to (HUY) Railhead at 4.30am v Drew Rations in bulk & conveyed same to Refilling Point. No T/090454 Corpl. Johnson W.J Proceeded on Leave to the United Kingdom.	9BA
"	3	18	(WEATHER FINE) Routine as usual. No. T/065205 Pr. Mellersh H.J returned from 140H Fld Amb. No. T/36763 Pr. Gillam. T. Joined from Base Depot WEATHER FINE	9BA
"	4	18	Supplies drawn from Railhead at 7.45 am. Second drawing from Railhead at 2.30 PM. Supplies remaining in waggons overnight 12/12496 Dr Fallows R. } Joined 12/13893 " Evans W } from 14/108396 " Flight WH } No 2 LofC Area Reception Camp 13/030224 " Gerrard G.H } retransferred to 139. Field Ambulance. Weather fine	9BA

Army Form C. 2118.

WAR DIARY
or
INTELLIGENCE SUMMARY.
(Erase heading not required.)

Instructions regarding War Diaries and Intelligence Summaries are contained in F. S. Regs., Part II. and the Staff Manual respectively. Title pages will be prepared in manuscript.

Place	Date	Hour	Summary of Events and Information	Remarks and references to Appendices
Near HUY HUY-AMPSIN (MAIN ROAD)	5	18	Supplies delivered to dump. Rations drawn from Railhead 11.15 a.m. T4/166283 Pt. WEBSTER M.H. returned from 144th Fld Amb. Weather SHOWERY	JBA
	6	18	Supplies delivered to dump. No Supplies drawn from Railhead owing to non-arrival of Pack train. T4/065236 Pt. HOPLEY J.T. proceeded on leave to United Kingdom 5 km. Weather SHOWERY	JBA
	7	18	Supplies drawn from AMPSIN Railhead 8 a.m. & delivered to dump. Baggage Wagons of 11th Queens joined Unit. WEATHER FINE	JBA
	8	18	Supplies drawn from AMPSIN Railhead 12 noon & delivered to dump. Supply Wagons of 11th Queens joined Unit. S4/019402 Pte COJJARY H.C proceeded on leave. Baggage Wagons & 10th Kents joined Unit. WEATHER FINE	JBA
	9	18	Supplies drawn from AMPSIN R/head 8.30 a.m & delivered to dump. Second refill by Lorries 1 p.m. Third refill from HUY R/head by H.T. at 2 p.m. Baggage Wagons of 23rd Middlesex & 193rd Bde H. Qrs. Supply Wagons of 10th Kents joined Unit. WEATHER DULL	JBA
	10	18	Company entrained HUY Station 4 P.M. WEATHER FINE	JBA
	11	18	" detrained COLOGNE 11 a.m. Travelled by march route to MARIN arrived 6 P.m. WEATHER STORMY	JBA

Army Form C. 2118.

WAR DIARY
or
INTELLIGENCE SUMMARY.
(Erase heading not required.)

Instructions regarding War Diaries and Intelligence Summaries are contained in F. S. Regs., Part II. and the Staff Manual respectively. Title pages will be prepared in manuscript.

Place	Date	Hour	Summary of Events and Information	Remarks and references to Appendices
WAHN. GERMANY	12	18	Supplies drawn from No. 4 Coy at 9 am. Baggage & Supply Wagon returned from Units. T/145443 T/SSM YORK C.H. returned from leave. WEATHER FINE	JBA
"	13	18	Supplies Refill from dump at WAHN STATION at 9 am Rations for 11th QUEENS & 10th KENTs delivered by lorry. WEATHER STORMY	JBA
"	14	18	Supplies Refill 9 am No. T/n/057401 D/ MIDDLETON. W. & T/n/065236 D/ HOPLEY J.T. proceeded on leave to the U.K. WEATHER DULL	JBA
"	15	18	Supplies as usual. TS/7931 Far Dr HATTON. H joined from R.A.S.C. Base Depot Baggage & Supply Wagon of 4ol MG Batt Joined from No. 1 Coy WEATHER STORMY	JBA
"	16	18	Supplies as usual. No. T/3699R LCpl KIRK J proceeded on leave to U.K. WEATHER FINE	JBA
"	17	18	Routine as usual. WEATHER STORMY	JBA
"	18	18	Routine as usual. WEATHER STORMY	JBA
"	19	18	Routine as usual. WEATHER STORMY	JBA

Army Form C. 2118.

WAR DIARY
or
INTELLIGENCE SUMMARY.
(Erase heading not required.)

Instructions regarding War Diaries and Intelligence Summaries are contained in F. S. Regs., Part II, and the Staff Manual respectively. Title pages will be prepared in manuscript.

Place	Date	Hour	Summary of Events and Information	Remarks and references to Appendices
WAHN. GERMANY	20	18	Routine as usual N° T.4/35626 D. TAYLOR G.E. Admitted to the 139th Field Amb. WEATHER Stormy	JBA
"	21	18	Routine as usual WEATHER FINE	JBA
"	22	18	Routine as usual N° T.4/065205 D. MELLERSH H.J. Admitted to the 139th Field Amb. N° TS/8990 Sadd. Corpl LAWSON J.E. N T.4/065247 D. MORRIS F. Proceeded on leave to the U.K. WEATHER FROSTY.	JBA
"	23	18	Routine as usual N° T.3/021484 Cpl. JOHNSON W.J. Returned from Leave to U.K. WEATHER FINE, COLD	JBA
"	24	18	Routine as usual T.4/057384 Dr. EVANS R.W. proceeded to the U.K. for Demobilization as a Pivotal man. (WEATHER FINE, COLD.)	JBA
"	25	18	Routine as usual N° T./35626 D. TAYLOR G.E. Returned to duty from 139th Field Amb. N° T./120456 T/SERGT. STIRRUP J N T.4/60283 D. WEBSTER M. Proceeded on leave to the U.K. T/292326 D. DUNN. M Admitted 139 F.A. (WEATHER FINE, COLD)	JBA
"	26	18	Routine as usual N° S4./040422 Sgt. SATTERTHWAITE W. admitted to the 139th Field Ambulance (WEATHER Cold & Snowy)	JBA

WAR DIARY
or
INTELLIGENCE SUMMARY.

Army Form C. 2118.

Place	Date	Hour	Summary of Events and Information	Remarks and references to Appendices
WHAM. GERMANY	27	18	Routine as usual. T.4/065205 Dr MELLERSH. H.J. Returned to duty from the 139" Field Ambulance. (WEATHER SNOWY)	JBA
"	28"	18	Supplies drawn from HEUMAR Railhead at 8.30am by H.T. √ delivered to dump. Refill 10.45am √ Delivered to Units T.4/065236 Dr.1 HOPLEY. J.T. Returned from Leave to the U.K. (WEATHER SNOWY)	JBA
"	29"	18	Supplies drawn from HEUMAR Railhead at 8.45am by H.T. √ delivered to dump Refill 1pm √ Delivered to Units T.4/065205 Dr.MELLERSH. N.J. Admitted to no 139" Field Ambulance. S4/043902 Pte. COLLARD. H.C. Admitted to no 139" Field Ambulance. T.4/07/26/3 HENS Admitted to 139"A.B. (WEATHER DULL&COLD) Returned from Leave to the U.K.	JBA JBA
HEUMAR. (GERMANY)	30	18	Supplies drawn from (HEUMAR) Railhead at 8.45am by H.T. √ delivered to Dump. Refill 9.30am √ Delivered to Units. Second drawing from Railhead at 3.15pm Supplies Remaining in Wagons overnight. (WEATHER SNOWY)	JBA
	31		Supplies. REFILL 10am √ Delivered Rations to Units (WEATHER COLD)	JBA

Jno. Bolton 2nd Lieut
O.C. No 3 Coy 41st Divisional Train

Army Form C. 2118.

WAR DIARY
or
INTELLIGENCE SUMMARY.
(Erase heading not required.)

Place	Date	Hour	Summary of Events and Information	Remarks and references to Appendices
HEUMAR. GERMANY.	Feb. 1	18	Supplies delivered to Units at 8.30 am. Drew from Railhead HEUMAR at 10.45 am & delivered to dump. Refill 2 pm & Supplies Remaining in Wagons overnight. (WEATHER. COLD & SNOWY)	JBA
"	2nd	18	Supplies delivered to Units at 7.30 am. Drew from HEUMAR Rhead at 10.45 am & delivered to dump. Refill 2 pm Supplies Remaining in Wagons overnight. Baggage Wagons Rejoined Company from Units 2ND Horses Nos 128 & 138 having been evacuated to the 52" M.V.S. on the 30" inst. are struck off the strength (WEATHER COLD & SNOWY)	JBA
"	3rd	18	Supplies delivered to Units at 8.30 am & Drew from (HEUMAR) Railhead at 10.45 am & Delivered to Dump. Refill 2 pm Supplies Remaining in Wagons overnight. (WEATHER COLD & SNOWY)	JBA
"	4th	18	Supplies delivered to Units at 7.30 am & Drew from (HEUMAR) Railhead at 10.46 am & Delivered to Dump. Refill 12 noon Supplies Remaining in Wagons overnight. T4.1094105 Dr BRIGGS E. Proceeded on Leave to the U.K. T.S. 14424 W.H.R. Dr PUMFREY. W. admitted to the 138" FIELD AMBULANCE. WEATHER. COLD & SNOWY)	JBA

Army Form C. 2118.

WAR DIARY
or
INTELLIGENCE SUMMARY.
(Erase heading not required.)

Instructions regarding War Diaries and Intelligence Summaries are contained in F. S. Regs., Part II. and the Staff Manual respectively. Title pages will be prepared in manuscript.

Place	Date	Hour	Summary of Events and Information	Remarks and references to Appendices
HEUMAR. GERMANY	5th	18	Supplies delivered to Units at 7.30am Drew from Railhead at 10.45 am & Delivered to Dump Refill 12 noon Supplies remaining in Wagons overnight. T.S./6933 FARR S. Sgr. TAYLOR W. G. & T./36348 Dr. STONEAGE H. Proceeded on leave to the U.K. LIEUT. R.S. PEACOCK Proceeded on leave. LIEUT CAVANAGH Attached to Coy. (WEATHER SNOWY)	JBA
"	6th	18	Supplies as usual. Capt. T.V. FLEMING, M.C. Rejoined the Company from the United Kingdom. T./36333. Dr. MEARS. W. Proceeded on leave to the United Kingdom. WEATHER. FINE (COLD)	JBA
"	7th	16	Supplies as usual. T4/058023 Dr. EDWARDS C. Admitted to the 140" Field Amb. T4/1065205 Dr. MELLERS H. J. & T./292526 Dr. NUNN. M. having been evacuated to C.C.S. are struck off the Coys. strength. S4/090422 Sgt. SATTERTHWAITE. W. & T./407426 Pte HEMS. R. J. Rejoined Coy from Hosp. S4/064816 Cpl. JARVIS. R. B. Proceeded on leave to the U. K. (WEATHER. FINE+COLD)	JBA
"	8	18	Supplies as usual	WEATHER (FINE+COLD)
"	9	18	Supplies as usual T.S./4424 WHLR. Dr. PUMFREY W. WEATHER (FINE+COLD) having been evacuated to C.C.S. is struck off Coys Strength	JBA

Army Form C. 2118.

WAR DIARY
INTELLIGENCE SUMMARY.
(Erase heading not required.)

Instructions regarding War Diaries and Intelligence Summaries are contained in F. S. Regs., Part II. and the Staff Manual respectively. Title pages will be prepared in manuscript.

Place	Date	Hour	Summary of Events and Information	Remarks and references to Appendices
HEUMAR GERMANY	10th	18	Supplies as usual. Lieut. CAVANAGH Rejoined No. 4 Company, 1 H.D. Horse No. 144 having been destroyed on the 9th inst. is struck off the strength. 3 H.D. Horses having been received from the 139th Field Ambulance are taken on the Coys Strength. (WEATHER FINE & COLD)	TO
"	11th	18	Supplies as usual. WEATHER FINE & COLD.	TO
"	12th	18	Supplies as usual T.4./065247 Dr. MORRIS. F. Returned from Leave to the U.K. T.4./057023 Dr. EDWARDS. C. Returned to duty from the 140th Field Ambulance. WEATHER FINE & COLD	TO
"	13th	18	Supplies as usual. T./36992 L/Cpl KIRK J & T.4./057428 Dr. YULE G Returned from Leave to the U.K. T.3./026902 Dr. MACINTYRE. D. having joined this formation owing to Re-organization of the Field Ambulance is taken on the Coys Strength. (WEATHER FINE & COLD)	TO
"	14th	18	Supplies as usual. WEATHER FINE.	TO
"	15th	19	Supplies as usual T./20456 Sgt. STIRRUP J T.4./057401 Dr. MIDDLETON.W. & T.4./160283 Dr. WEBSTER. M.H. Returned from Leave to the U.K. (WEATHER. DULL)	TO

Army Form C. 2118.

WAR DIARY
or
INTELLIGENCE SUMMARY.

(Erase heading not required.)

Instructions regarding War Diaries and Intelligence Summaries are contained in F. S. Regs., Part II. and the Staff Manual respectively. Title pages will be prepared in manuscript.

Place	Date	Hour	Summary of Events and Information	Remarks and references to Appendices
HEUMAR. GERMANY.	16th	18	Supplies as usual. T.3/102698. Cpl. PANT. F.W. Proceeded on Leave to U.K. (WEATHER DULL)	T.B.
"	17th	18	Supplies as usual. Lecture by O.O. Train on Volunteering for Army of Occupation at 5pm (WEATHER SNOWERY)	T.B.
"	18th	18	Supplies as usual. T.S.18970 Sadd. Cpl. LAWSON. J.E. Returned from Leave to the U.K. T.1/36323 Dr. REYNOLDS. T. Proceeded on Leave to the U.K. (WEATHER SNOWERY)	T.B.
"	19	18	Supplies as usual. No. 133952 Pte NEWBY. J. Attached from 238 "Employ Coy. Proceeded on Leave to the U.K. (WEATHER DULL)	T.B.
"	20"	18	Supplies as usual. Chit. 1414. Dr. THORNTON. G Admitted to the 140" Fd Amb. Horse Inspection at 2pm by the 41st Divisional Horse Master (WEATHER FINE)	T.B.
"	21st	18	Supplies as usual. (WEATHER FINE)	T.B.
"	22"	18	Supplies as usual. (WEATHER Showery)	T.B.

Army Form C. 2118.

WAR DIARY
or
INTELLIGENCE SUMMARY.
(Erase heading not required.)

Instructions regarding War Diaries and Intelligence Summaries are contained in F. S. Regs., Part II. and the Staff Manual respectively. Title pages will be prepared in manuscript.

Place	Date	Hour	Summary of Events and Information	Remarks and references to Appendices
HEUMAR GERMANY	23rd	18	Supplies as usual. T4/108686 L/Cpl KENT. A.T. Admitted to 140th Field Amb. Lieut. R.S. PEACOCK Returned from Leave to the U.K. T.2./13473 Dr GRAY. J. & T./289981 Pte BRYANT. H. Proceeded on Leave to the U.K. (WEATHER FINE)	T/S
"	24th	18	Supplies as usual T4/185528 Dr MINNS. W.J. Proceeded on Leave to the U.K. (WEATHER FINE)	T/S
"	25th	18	Supplies as usual. T.S./6933 FARR S.Sgt. TAYLOR W.G. T./36345 Dr STONEAGE H. & T4/094105 Dr BRIGGS. E. Returned from Leave to the U.K. (WEATHER SHOWERY)	T/S
"	26	18	Supplies as usual T/36333 Dr MEARS. W. Returned from Leave to the U.K. T./384804 Dr CONWAY. W.T. Proceeded on Leave to the U.K. T/11651 AH ADAMS having joined from 46th Div'n TRN is taken on the Coy Strength. (WEATHER FINE)	T/S
"	27th	18	Supplies as usual T./384809 Dr CHURCHWARD T. & T4/186001 Dr MOORE. E.F. Proceeded on Leave to the U.K. WEATHER FINE	T/S

Army Form C. 2118.

WAR DIARY
or
INTELLIGENCE SUMMARY.
(Erase heading not required.)

Instructions regarding War Diaries and Intelligence Summaries are contained in F. S. Regs., Part II. and the Staff Manual respectively. Title pages will be prepared in manuscript.

Place	Date	Hour	Summary of Events and Information	Remarks and references to Appendices
HEUMAR GERMANY.	28th	18.	Supplies as usual. CHT:/417 D. THORNTON. G. Murray) (Weather Dull n Cold.) been evacuated to CCS is attached to Coys strength from 20th	WS

HEUMAR.
28. 2. 1919.

W Brown.
Captain.
O.C. No 3 Coy 41st Divisional Train

Army Form C. 2118.

WAR DIARY
INTELLIGENCE SUMMARY
(Erase heading not required.)

Instructions regarding War Diaries and Intelligence Summaries are contained in F. S. Regs., Part II. and the Staff Manual respectively. Title pages will be prepared in manuscript.

Place	Date	Hour	Summary of Events and Information	Remarks and references to Appendices
HEUMAR. GERMANY	MARCH 1st	18	Supplies delivered to Units at 4.30 am. Drew Supplies in bulk from (HEUMAR.) Railhead at 10.45am. Conveyed Same to Refilling Point. Company Paraded for Mounted Inspection at 2pm. Refill 3pm. Supplies Remaining in Wagons overnight. T/386451. Dr. HARDISTY. J.W. Proceeded on Leave to U.K. (WEATHER FINE)	A3
"	2nd	18	Summer Time came into use at 23.00 hours. Winter Time all clocks were put forward one hour. Supplies as usual. Refill 12 noon. (WEATHER FINE)	A3
"	3rd	18	Supplies as usual T/35647 Dr. BRAID. G.A. Proceeded on Leave to the U.K. (WEATHER. FINE & DULL)	A3
"	4th	18.	Supplies as usual. S.4./105991 Cpl. GRAY. L. T.S./9369 Farr Cpl. COATES R.L. Proceeded on Leave to the U.K. (WEATHER SNOWY)	A3
"	5th	18	Supplies as usual. T4./086856 9/Cpl. Kent A.T. Returned to duty from the 140th Field Ambulance (WEATHER SHOWERY)	A3

Army Form C. 2118.

WAR DIARY
or
INTELLIGENCE SUMMARY.
(Erase heading not required.)

Instructions regarding War Diaries and Intelligence Summaries are contained in F. S. Regs., Part II. and the Staff Manual respectively. Title pages will be prepared in manuscript.

Place	Date	Hour	Summary of Events and Information	Remarks and references to Appendices
HEUMAR GERMANY	6th	18	Supplies as usual. Refill 11 and T.4-/234948 Sgt BREWER C. Proceeded to the U.K. fr. Demobilization and is struck off the Coys strength. (WEATHER SHOWERY)	No
"	7	18	Supplies delivered to Units at Yard. Drew from HEUMAR Railhead of 9, 4.5 and Y convoyed same to Refilling Point. Refill 10.30 and delivered to Units. L.H.D. Horse 4" to having been destroyed on the 5th inst. is struck off the Coys strength. (WEATHER FINE)	No
"	8th	18	Supplies as usual (WEATHER Showery)	No
"	9	18	Supplies as usual. T3/026988 Corpl PART F.W. Returned from Leave to the U.K. (WEATHER SHOWERY)	No
"	10	18	Supplies as usual T/36323 Dr REYNOLDS. T. Returned from Leave to the U.K. T.4/065293 Dr ROSIER. A. Admitted to the 140th Field Ambulance (WEATHER FINER DULL)	No
"	11th	18	Supplies as usual. 133952 Dr NEWBY J Returned from Leave to U.K. (WEATHER FINE)	No
"	12th	18	Supplies as usual (WEATHER FINE)	No

WAR DIARY
or
INTELLIGENCE SUMMARY

Army Form C. 2118.

Place	Date	Hour	Summary of Events and Information	Remarks and references to Appendices
HEUMAR GERMANY	13	18	Supplies as usual. Ceremonial Parade at 2.30pm. C.O. Presented with (T.F.) Decoration by Major General [Sir] V.B. Lanford K.C.B. (WEATHER FINE)	AD
"	14	18	Supplies as usual. Lieut J.B. Aston proceeded to the UK for 10 mos hygiene (WEATHER FINE)	AD
"	15	18	Supplies as usual. T/289981 Pte BRYANT. H. Returned from Leave to the UK. (WEATHER FINE)	AD
"	16	18	Supplies as usual. T/4/185528 Dr. MINNS W.J. Returned from Leave to UK. (WEATHER FINE)	AD
"	17	18	Supplies as usual. T/384804 Dr. CONWAY C. Returned from Leave to the UK. (WEATHER FINE)	AD
"	18	18	Supplies as usual T2/134793 Dr. GRAY J. Returned from leave (WEATHER FINE)	AD
"	19	18	Supplies as usual. T.4./186501 Dr. MOORE E.F.N T./384809 Dr. CHURCHWARD T. Returned from Leave to the UK T.3/029008 Dr. NAYLOR W.S. Proceeded on Leave to the UK Lieut R.S. PEACOCK detached to N[?] Coy as S.O. (WEATHER FINE & COLD)	AD
"	20	18	Supplies as usual (WEATHER FINE)	

WAR DIARY
or
INTELLIGENCE SUMMARY.
(Erase heading not required.)

Army Form C. 2118.

Place	Date	Hour	Summary of Events and Information	Remarks and references to Appendices
HEUMAR GERMANY	21st	18	Supplies as usual T/386451 Dr HARDISTY J Returned from leave to the U.K. Baggage Wagons of the 23rd Middlesex Rgt detached to Unit. (WEATHER FINE)	NS
"	22	18	Supplies as usual Baggage wagons of the 23rd Middlesex Coy to Unit (WEATHER FINE)	NS
"	23	18	Supplies as usual (WEATHER FINE)	NS
"	24	18	Supplies as usual S4/059971 Cpl GRAY L ~ T/73647 Dr BRAID G.A. Returned from leave to the U.K. (WEATHER SHOWERY)	NS
"	25	18	Supplies as usual T/396193 Dr PRESTON J.E ~ 201506 Pte CASSIDY J Lieut RS Beakey and Coy. (WEATHER FINE) Proceeded on leave to the U.K	NS
"	26	18	Supplies as usual TS/19369 FARR Cpl COATES R L Returned from leave to the U.K. T4/065293 Dr ROSIER A Returned to duty from the 140 F.A. Baggage Wagons Detached to Unit (WEATHER FINE)	NS
"	27	18	Supplies as usual T4/065293 Dr ROSIER A Proceeded to Headquarters 123 Lt Bde for duty Supply Wagons of the 11th R.W. Surrey Regt remained with Unit after delivery WEATHER SHOWERY	NS

Army Form C. 2118.

WAR DIARY
or
INTELLIGENCE SUMMARY.
(Erase heading not required.)

Instructions regarding War Diaries and Intelligence Summaries are contained in F. S. Regs., Part II. and the Staff Manual respectively. Title pages will be prepared in manuscript.

Place	Date	Hour	Summary of Events and Information	Remarks and references to Appendices
HEUMAR GERMANY	28	18	Supplies as usual. N° T3/026902 Dr MACINTYRE D. N° T/386456 Dr PULLINGER G.H. Proceeded on leave to the U.K. Baggage Wagon of 1th Headquarters 123rd Infy Bde Reserved Company. WEATHER SNOWERY	NS
	29	19	Supplies drawn from Railhead at 9.45am Refill 10.30am & Delivered to Units by Rail. N° 12 S.R. Coy Wigston 1 Detached to London Rupp Conv of Reception Camp. Supply Wagons & 4 Medium Repair Coy. WEATHER SNOWING	NS
"	30	18	Supplies drawn from Railhead at 9.45am Refill 10.30am & Delivered to Units by Rail. Baggage Wagons of the Bde to Supply Wagons 14 "1" R.W Surveys Returned to Ford Lionels (WEATHER SNOWING.)	NS
"	31	18	Supplies drawn from Railhead at 9.45am Refill 10.30am & Delivered to Units by Rail. (WEATHER FINE/DULL.)	NS

M Denny Captain.
O.C. N° 3 Coy London Divisional Train.

3 Coy

WAR DIARY
or
INTELLIGENCE SUMMARY.
(Erase heading not required.)

Army Form C. 2118.

Place	Date	Hour	Summary of Events and Information	Remarks and references to Appendices
HEUMAR GERMANY	APRIL 1	18	Supplies drawn from Railhead at 9 a.m. Refill 10.30 am & Delivered to Units of Bde by Rail. No TS/74149 W/H/R Cpl PLUMB AS & T4/144288 Dr BAGSHAW W.F. Proceeded on Leave to the U.K. (WEATHER FINE)	Ref. App.
	2	18	Supplies as usual T4/233210 Dr ARGENT N & 201677 Pte McDONNEL RASC proceeded on Leave to the U.K. (WEATHER FINE)	Ref. App.
~	3	18	Supplies as usual T/CAPT W.R. ROBERSON M.C. RASC Joined Coy from the 19th Div.T.Train T/LIEUT G.C. COOKE Joined Coy from 20th Div.T.Train (WEATHER FINE)	Ref. App.
~	4	18	Supplies as usual. (WEATHER FINE)	(App.)
~	5	18	Supplies as usual. T4/293365 Dr BRAMMER proceeded on Leave to the U.K. Capt T/V FLEMING MC RASC having been transferred to the 19 Div.Train is struck off the strength from this unit. T4/066236 Dr HOPLEY JT. T4/057023 Dr EDWARDS C Admitted to the 140 Field Amb. (WEATHER FINE)	(App.) W.R.

Army Form C. 2118.

WAR DIARY
or
INTELLIGENCE SUMMARY.
(Erase heading not required.)

Instructions regarding War Diaries and Intelligence Summaries are contained in F. S. Regs., Part II. and the Staff Manual respectively. Title pages will be prepared in manuscript.

Place	Date	Hour	Summary of Events and Information	Remarks and references to Appendices
HEUMAR GERMANY	6th	18	Supplies as usual. 1112 158636 Pte TABERMAN. G. 236 Empty (y) Proceeded on Leave to the United Kingdom	W.R.
			(WEATHER FINE)	
—	7th	18	Supplies as usual. N T.3/027003 Dr NAYLOR. W.S. Returned from Leave to the United Kingdom	W.R.
			(WEATHER FINE)	
—	8th	18	Supplies as usual. S/355543 Pte HACKING. G. Proceeded on Leave to the United Kingdom T.4/065236 Dr HOPLEY. J.T. & T.4/057023 Dr EDWARDS. O. Returned to duty from the 140th Field Ambulance.	W.R.
			(WEATHER FINE)	
—	9th	18	Supplies as usual. T.4/057823 Dr GOODLIFFE. A. Proceeded on Leave to the United Kingdom	W.R.
			(WEATHER FINE)	
—	10th	18	Supplies as usual.	W.R.
—	11th	18	Supplies as usual. T.S/9613 WHKR.S.Sgt SHUTTLEWORTH. H. & T4/086656 Cpl KENT. A.T. Proceeded on Leave to the U.K.	W.R.
			(WEATHER DULL)	

Army Form C. 2118.

WAR DIARY
or
INTELLIGENCE SUMMARY.
(Erase heading not required.)

Instructions regarding War Diaries and Intelligence Summaries are contained in F. S. Regs., Part II. and the Staff Manual respectively. Title pages will be prepared in manuscript.

Place	Date	Hour	Summary of Events and Information	Remarks and references to Appendices
HEUMAR GERMANY	12	18	Supplies as usual. (WEATHER FINE)	WRR
	13	18	Supplies as usual. WEATHER FINE.	WRR
	14	18	Supplies as usual. T/390193 Dr PRESTON J.E. Returned from Leave to the United Kingdom. (WEATHER FINE)	WRR
-	15"	18	Supplies as usual. No T/358550 Pte FOSTER W. Attached to Company from I.H.Q. WEATHER DULL	WRR
-	16"	18	Supplies as usual. No 192621 Pte HART C. Attached to Company from No 238 Employment Coy. No T4/248315 Dr CALLAGHAN W. 126834 Pte FOWLER H. v 153611 Pte HUTLEY J.L. Proceeded on Leave to the United Kingdom. WEATHER DULL	WRR
-	17	18	Supplies as usual. T/386456 Dr PUHLINGER G.H. 1201506 Pte CASSIDY J. Returned from Leave to the United Kingdom. WEATHER FINE.	WRR

Army Form C. 2118.

WAR DIARY
or
INTELLIGENCE SUMMARY.

(Erase heading not required.)

Instructions regarding War Diaries and Intelligence Summaries are contained in F. S. Regs., Part II, and the Staff Manual respectively. Title pages will be prepared in manuscript.

Place	Date	Hour	Summary of Events and Information	Remarks and references to Appendices
HEUMAR GERMANY	18	18	Supplies as usual. The following having found from the Guard Divisional Train are taken on the Coys Strength T/4723 DWR RockyFT T/4893Y D. KEEVES. J. T/392617 D. CRAWFORD. A.H T/1432994 D. BOTTERILL. J. 4-5.2/018023 Sgt LEACH. T.W joined from the 20" Divisional Train these taken on the Coys strength 4/6 TS/4731 D. FARR. HATTON. H. Proceeded on leave to the U.K.	WKK
	19	18	Supplies as usual. WEATHER FINE	WKR
	20	18	Supplies as usual. WEATHER FINE	WKR
	21	18	Supplies as usual 4/6 TS 7649 WNLR Cpl PLUMB A.S.T T/44288 D. BAGSHAW. W.F. Returned from leave to the UK WEATHER FINE	WKR
	22	18	Supplies as usual. 4/6 74/1232210 D. ARGENT. H Returned from leave to the U.K. 4/6 T/384804. D. CONWAY W.T having been evacuated to 37" C.C.S. on the 19" inst. is struck off the Coys strength WEATHER FINE	WKR

Army Form C. 2118.

WAR DIARY
or
INTELLIGENCE SUMMARY.
(Erase heading not required.)

Instructions regarding War Diaries and Intelligence Summaries are contained in F. S. Regs., Part II. and the Staff Manual respectively. Title pages will be prepared in manuscript.

Place	Date	Hour	Summary of Events and Information	Remarks and references to Appendices
HEUMAR GERMANY	23rd	18	Supplies as usual. N° T.358550 Pte. FOSTER. W. Proceeded on leave to the U.K.	W.O.R.
"	24	18	Supplies as usual. N° T.364.682 Dr. NEWELL. A. having joined from the 26 Divisional train is taken on the Cadre strength. N° T.1392.617. Dr. CRAWFORD. A. Proceeded on leave to the U.K.	W.O.R.
			WEATHER FINE	
"	25th	18	Supplies as usual. The G.O.C. Division Inspected Company (WEATHER FINE)	W.O.R.
"	26th	18	Supplies as usual. N° T.3/026902 Dr. MACINTYRE. D. Returned from leave to the U.K. N° T4/248101 Dr. NEWEY. H. M. Coy. Admitted to the 140 Field Ambulance.	W.O.R.
			WEATHER FINE	
"	27	18	Supplies as usual. N° 201677 Pte. MACDONNELL C. 158635 Pte. TABERMAN. G. A. 4 10.R². 238 Employment Coy Returned from leave to the U.K. N° T4.32991 Dr. BOTTERILL. J. T.T4.20334 Dr. KEEVES. J. Proceeded on leave to the U.K.	W.O.R.
			WEATHER FINE & COLD.	

Army Form C. 2118.

WAR DIARY
or
INTELLIGENCE SUMMARY.
(Erase heading not required.)

Instructions regarding War Diaries and Intelligence Summaries are contained in F. S. Regs., Part II. and the Staff Manual respectively. Title pages will be prepared in manuscript.

Place	Date	Hour	Summary of Events and Information	Remarks and references to Appendices
HEUMAR. GERMANY	28	18	Supplies as usual. WEATHER FINE & COLD.	WRR
"	29	18	Supplies as usual. Baggage Wagons detached to Unit. R/Sgt T51 9613 WNLRS Sgt SHUTTLEWORTH JJ & Tpr 1086856 Corpl KENT A.E. Returned from leave to the United Kingdom. Lieut. O.H. Adams Returned from leave to the United Kingdom. WEATHER FINE & COLD.	WRR
"	30	18	Supplies as usual. Lieut. G.C. Cooke R.A.S.C. Admitted to the 140th Field Ambulance. WEATHER FINE.	WRR

WRR Weesem.
Captain
O.C. 423 Coy London Divisional Train.

Army Form C. 2118.

WAR DIARY
or
INTELLIGENCE SUMMARY.
(Erase heading not required.)

Instructions regarding War Diaries and Intelligence Summaries are contained in F. S. Regs., Part II. and the Staff Manual respectively. Title pages will be prepared in manuscript.

Place	Date	Hour	Summary of Events and Information	Remarks and references to Appendices
HEUMAR GERMANY.	MAY 1st	18	Supplies drawn from HEUMAR Railhead at 9:45ams & Conveyed to Refilling Point. Refill 10.30ams. Rations of the 2/4, 10, & 11 Queens Rgts & H.Q. 2nd London Inf Bde. Delivered to Units by Rail. Baggage Wagons of the Queens Regiment Coy from Unit. WEATHER FINE / DULL	WPR
"	2"	18	Supplies as usual. No. S/355573 Pte HACKING G. Returned from leave to the United Kingdom. Lieut A.H. ADAMS. R.A.S.C. having been transferred to the 14th Divisional Train is struck off the Company's Strength. WEATHER DULL.	WPR
"	3"	18	Supplies as usual. 10 ORks attached to Company from the 10 Queens Rgt for Transport Course. The following having proceeded to the United Kingdom for Demobilization are struck off the Coys strength. TS/16923 Sar. S/Sgt. TAYLOR W.G, TS/18961 Dr. Sadd DICKINSON J.G. TS/113443 Dr. GRAY J, J/174/063236 Dr. HOPLEY J.T. (WEATHER FINE.)	WPR

Army Form C. 2118.

WAR DIARY
or
INTELLIGENCE SUMMARY.
(Erase heading not required.)

Place	Date	Hour	Summary of Events and Information	Remarks and references to Appendices
HEUMAR GERMANY	MAY 4"	18	Supplies as usual. WEATHER FINE)	10PR
"	5"	18	Supplies as usual. 120 Ranks Attached to Company from 112 Reserve for Transport Course. WEATHER FINE)	10PR
"	6"	18	Supplies as usual. 7/33626 D. TAYLOR G.E. Proceeded on Leave to the United Kingdom. The following having joined from the 14 Army A(W) (H) Company are taken on the Coys strength T/4/236235 (Pt. JOHNSON.L. T/3/026438 D. HAINING T. T/4/262454 D. PEACE R. T/260043 D. POCOCK.NW. T/4/278103 D. ROWLANDS.A.C. WEATHER FINE)	10PR
"	7"	18	Supplies as usual. N° 153611 Pte HUTLEY J.L v N° 126834 Pt. FOWLER.H. Attached from N°238 Employment Coy Returned from leave to the United Kingdom. Medical Inspection 3pm All ranks attended. WEATHER FINE	10PR

Army Form C. 2118.

WAR DIARY
or
INTELLIGENCE SUMMARY.
(Erase heading not required.)

Place	Date	Hour	Summary of Events and Information	Remarks and references to Appendices
HEUMAR. GERMANY	MAY 8th	18	Supplies as usual. The following having been transferred to the 14'Army Aux. (H) Company on the 6' inst. are struck off the Company's Strength 7/35394 Cpl SMITH J.E. T4/065244 Dr MORRIS F. T3/026902 Dr MACINTYRE T4/059889 Dr ORR D. CHT. 1286 Dr SAWDON J. TS/1648 S^d.O S. Sgr NICHOLS W.N. Proceeded on leave to the U.K. M° T4/248315 Dr CALLAGHAN W. Returned from leave to the U.K. (WEATHER FINE)	WR
	9th	18	Supplies as usual. The following having been transferred to the 14' Army Aux H Company on the 6' inst. are struck off the Coys Strength 7/35644 Dr BRAID G.A. T4/144268 Dr BAGSHAW W.F. T4/059023 Dr EDWARDS C. T/7386456 Dr PULLINGER G.H. M° T4/066203 L/Cpl LONGHURST. E.G.H. Proceeded on leave to the United Kingdom. The following having Joined from the 14'Army Aux. (H)Coy this day is taken on to the Coys Strength T/346440 Dr JUNIPER W. (WEATHER FINE)	WR

Army Form C. 2118.

WAR DIARY
or
INTELLIGENCE SUMMARY.
(Erase heading not required.)

Instructions regarding War Diaries and Intelligence Summaries are contained in F. S. Regs., Part II. and the Staff Manual respectively. Title pages will be prepared in manuscript.

Place	Date	Hour	Summary of Events and Information	Remarks and references to Appendices
HEUMAR GERMANY	10"	18	Supplies as usual. The following having proceeded for Demobilzation on the 9" inst are struck off the Coys strength T4/056714 CQMS. SMITH V.H.C. T/80456 / Sgt STIRRUP J T3/024008 Dr NAYLOR W.S. T/370193 Dr PRESTON J.F. WEATHER FINE.	WBR
"	11"	18	Supplies as usual. (WEATHER FINE & THUNDERY.)	WBR
"	12"	18	Supplies as usual. No TS/4931 Dr. Van HATTON H. T M° T/392617 Q CRAWFORD. H. Returned from Leave to the United Kingdom Transport Detail 285 Wagons HEUMAR Aerodrome WEATHER FINE.	WBR
"	13"	18	Supplies drawn from HEUMAR Railhead 10°° hrs storaged by Rifle Killy Joint Refill 1000 hrs Rations Gprs 24", 10"/ 11" Lellows R91. C.2. London by Rail 9L° T/358550 Pte FOSTER W. L/cpl Bell A.D. delivered to Units by Rail 9L° T/358550 Pte FOSTER W. attached from T H.Q. Returned from Leave to the United Kingdom HEUMAR Aerodrome. Transport Detail 2 R 2 A.S. Wagons HEUMAR Aerodrome WEATHER FINE.	WBR

Army Form C. 2118.

WAR DIARY
or
INTELLIGENCE SUMMARY.
(Erase heading not required.)

Place	Date	Hour	Summary of Events and Information	Remarks and references to Appendices
HEUMAR COLOGNE GERMANY	14"	18	Supplies as usual. N° T/4/43299 Q. BOTTERILL J. & T./489337 Q. REEVES J. Returned from Leave to the United Kingdom. Transport detail 2/2 G.S. Wagons HEUMAR Aerodrome. WEATHER FINE)	WPR
"	15	18	Supplies as usual. N° T4/043290 Q. Mc HUGH. P. Attached from N°1 Coy. Returned from Leave to the United Kingdom. Transport detail 1 hvy 2 G.S. Wagons HEUMAR Aerodrome. (WEATHER FINE)	WPR
"	16"	18	Supplies as usual. The following Proceeded to England for Demobilization. TS/7649 Q/WKR PLUMB A.J. T4/040969 Q. AMOS C. T2/124969 Q. FALLOWS R. T4/06523/8. GOODLIFFE A. T/36963 Q. GILLAM T.E. T/36333 Q. MEARS W. T/36438 Q. STONEAGE N. T/405Y426 Q. YULE G. Transport detail 2 Pr. 2 G.S. HEUMAR Aerodrome. WEATHER FINE	WPR
"	17"	18	Supplies as usual. N° T4/436440 Q. JUNIPER W. N T4/276103 Q. ROWLANDS H.C. Proceeded on Leave to the United Kingdom. Transport detail 2 G.S. Wagons HEUMAR Aerodrome. WEATHER FINE)	WPR

Army Form C. 2118.

WAR DIARY
or
INTELLIGENCE SUMMARY.

(Erase heading not required.)

Instructions regarding War Diaries and Intelligence Summaries are contained in F. S. Regs., Part II. and the Staff Manual respectively. Title pages will be prepared in manuscript.

Place	Date	Hour	Summary of Events and Information	Remarks and references to Appendices
HEUMAR COLOGNE	18th	18	Supplies as usual. No/260985 Dr Neill having joined from the 14th Army Aux (H) Coy on the 14th inst: is taken on the Companys strength. (WEATHER FINE)	WRK
"	19th	18	Supplies as usual. No/74/238238 Cpl JOHNSON. L. Proceeded on leave to the United Kingdom. No.T/407736 Pte HEMS. R.J Proceeded to England HEUMAR Aerodrome for Repatriation to USA. Transport Detail 2h 2 G.S Wagons (WEATHER FINE)	WRK
"	20th	18	Supplies as usual. Transport Detail 2h 2 G.S Wagons HEUMAR Aerodrome (WEATHER FINE)	WRK
"	21st	18	Supplies as usual. Transport Detail 2h 2 G.S Wagons HEUMAR Aerodrome (WEATHER FINE)	WRK
"	22nd	18	Supplies as usual. Transport Detail 2h 2 G.S Wagons HEUMAR Aerodrome (WEATHER FINE)	WRK

Army Form C. 2118.

WAR DIARY
or
INTELLIGENCE SUMMARY.
(Erase heading not required.)

Instructions regarding War Diaries and Intelligence Summaries are contained in F. S. Regs., Part II. and the Staff Manual respectively. Title pages will be prepared in manuscript.

Place	Date	Hour	Summary of Events and Information	Remarks and references to Appendices
HEUMAR GERMANY	23"	18	Supplies as usual. Transport Details 2L DSS Wagons HEUMAR Cherrytown. Nº T3/026,708 D. Having J. Having been transferred to HQ 2 London Inf Bde is struck off the Coys Strength the following having proceeded to England for demobilization are struck of the Strength T4/044169 Cpl KIMPTON F. S4/064816 Cpl JARVIS R B. T4/042994 D. BOTTERILL J. Nº T7/020337 D. REEVES J. T4/160283 D. WEBSTER M H. T/157535 D. MANLEY P.A. WEATHER FINE	WKR
"	24.	18	Supplies as usual. Transport Details 2L DSS Wagons HEUMAR Cherrytown. Nº T2/019266 Sgt. PATTERSON J Transfer from 139" Field Amb. Nº T3/946 DSS NICHOLLS N T/383.36 D. TAYLOR G E Returned from leave to the United Kingdom. WEATHER FINE	WKR
"	25"	18	Supplies as usual. Nº T/340520 D. HANDLEY J having joined from the 14th Army Duce (H) Coy on the 24 inst is taken on the Company strength. Nº T/384804 D. CONWAY W T having joined from the 25" Gen'l Hosp on the 23" not to taken on the Coys strength. Nº S4/043902 Pte COLLARD N C Proceeded on leave to the United Kingdom (WEATHER FINE)	(9) R

WAR DIARY
or
INTELLIGENCE SUMMARY.

(Erase heading not required.)

Army Form C. 2118.

Place	Date	Hour	Summary of Events and Information	Remarks and references to Appendices
HEUMAR GERMANY	26	18	Supplies as usual. Transport Duties 2Pr. 2.E.S. HEUMAR Aerodrome. No T4/065203 L/Cpl. LONGHURST. E.G.H. Returned from leave to the United Kingdom. No T2/SR/104205 CSM WIGSTON. T. Proceeded on leave to the United Kingdom. WEATHER FINE	WAR
"	27.	18	Supplies as usual. Transport Detail 2Pr. 2.E.S. HEUMAR Aerodrome. 103999 Pte. STARLING. W.A. Joined Coy from No 238" Employment Coy. WEATHER FINE.	WAR
"	28	18	Supplies as usual. Transport Detail 2Pr. 2.E.S. HEUMAR Aerodrome. No 1512 571 Pte HARVEY. G.A./129374 Pte VINE. J.C.T. Joined Coy from No 238" Employment Company. Lieut R. Pitcock Proceeded to England for Demobilization. WEATHER FINE.	WAR
"	29"	18	Supplies as usual. Transport Details 2Pr. 2.E.S. Wagons HEUMAR Aerodrome. WEATHER FINE	WAR

Army Form C. 2118.

WAR DIARY
or
INTELLIGENCE SUMMARY.
(Erase heading not required.)

Instructions regarding War Diaries and Intelligence Summaries are contained in F. S. Regs. Part II. and the Staff Manual respectively. Title pages will be prepared in manuscript.

Place	Date	Hour	Summary of Events and Information	Remarks and references to Appendices
HEUMAR GERMANY	30	18	Supplies as usual. Transport details 2 fr. 2 B.S. Wagons HEUMAR Aerodrome. Baggage Party of the 10th Queens R.W. Surry Regt Rejoined Company from Unit the following proceed to England for demobly a/c AN 7/36323 D. Reynolds 7 73/626988 Cpl Pank Sut 7/392617 D. Crawford WEATHER FINE)	WRR
	31	18	Supplies as usual. Transport Details 2 fr. 2 B.S. Wagons HEUMAR Aerodrome. N.7/358404 Dr CONWAY W.T. having been transferred to H.Q. 2nd London Infy Bde on the 29th inst so struck of the Coys strength. WEATHER FINE)	WRR

WRRobinson. Captain.
O.C. No 3 Coy London Divisional Train

Army Form C. 2118.

WAR DIARY
or
INTELLIGENCE SUMMARY.
(Erase heading not required.)

Place	Date	Hour	Summary of Events and Information	Remarks and references to Appendices
HEUMAR. GERMANY.	JUNE 1	18	Supplies drawn from HEUMAR Railhead at 9.45 and Conveyed to Refilling Point. Refill 10.30 and Rations of the 2/4 Batth. 10th Batth. 11th Batth. The Queens R.W. Surrey Regt. & H.Q. 2/London Infy Bde. Delivered to Units by Rail. WEATHER FINE	WKR
—	2"	18	Supplies as usual. Transport Details 2/Lt 2 G.S. Wagons HEUMAR Aerodrome WEATHER FINE	WKR
—	3"	18	Supplies as usual Transport Details 2/Lt 2 G.S. Wagons HEUMAR Aerodrome. 7/LIEUT B.C. RUSSELL posted to Company from M.Coy. as Transport Subaltern No 74/276103 Dr. ROWLANDS. Returned from Leave to the United Kingdom. WEATHER FINE.	WKR
—	4.	18.	Supplies as usual. Transport Details 2/Lt 2 G.S. Wagons HEUMAR Aerodrome WEATHER FINE	WKR
—	5	18	Supplies as usual. Transport Details 2/Lt 2 G.S. Wagons HEUMAR Aerodrome WEATHER FINE	WKR

Army Form C. 2118.

WAR DIARY
or
INTELLIGENCE SUMMARY.
(Erase heading not required.)

Instructions regarding War Diaries and Intelligence Summaries are contained in F. S. Regs. Part II and the Staff Manual respectively. Title pages will be prepared in manuscript.

Place	Date	Hour	Summary of Events and Information	Remarks and references to Appendices
HEUMAR COLOGNE	6	18	Supplies as usual. Transport Details 2Pr. 2 S.S. Wagons HEUMAR Aerodrome T.4/248315 Pt CALLAGHAN W. Returned from Rhine Army Field Punishment Corps. WEATHER FINE	WRR
"	7	18	Supplies as usual. Transport Details 2Pr 2 S.S. Wagons, HEUMAR Aerodrome. T.4/236238/Cpl. JOHNSON L. Returned from Leave to the United Kingdom. WEATHER FINE	WRR
"	8	18	Supplies as usual. Capt W.R Roberson (M.C) & S.S.M. YORK C.H. Proceeded on Leave to the United Kingdom. (WEATHER FINE.)	WRR
"	9	18	Supplies as usual. Transport Details 2Pr. 2 S.S. Wagons HEUMAR Aerodrome. T.S./0390 Sgt. WATSON A. transferred from No. 1 Coy to No. 3 Coy with effect from the 16 inst. No. 122816 Pt WALLIS. J. & No. 49332 Pt WALKER J. Joined Company from No. 23 S. Emp C. WEATHER FINE	WRR
"	10	18	Supplies as usual. Transport Details 2Pr. 2 S.S. Wagons HEUMAR Aerodrome. S.4/043602 Cpl CALLARD H.C. Returned from Leave to the United Kingdom. (WEATHER FINE)	WRR

Army Form C. 2118.

WAR DIARY
or
INTELLIGENCE SUMMARY.
(Erase heading not required.)

Instructions regarding War Diaries and Intelligence Summaries are contained in F.S. Regs., Part II. and the Staff Manual respectively. Title pages will be prepared in manuscript.

Place	Date	Hour	Summary of Events and Information	Remarks and references to Appendices
HEUMAR. GERMANY	11	18	Supplies as usual. Transport details 2 Lr. 2 G.S. Wagons HEUMAR Aerodrome (WEATHER FINE)	WKR
~	12	18	Supplies as usual. Transport Details 2 Lr. 2 G.S. Wagons HEUMAR Aerodrome. WEATHER FINK.	WKR
~	13	18	Supplies as usual. Transport Details 2Lr. 2GS Wagons HEUMAR Aerodrome. The following having proceeded for demobilization this day arrived at the strength S/9369 Spr Cpl Carks R.L. T/363 Dvr Agr Pollard G. S/25406 Pte Buckland T. T/1444 Pte Goodall J. T/35626 Dvr Taylor R.E. T/34006 Dvr Fletcher. T/3/030224 Dvr Errard G. WEATHER FINE	WKR
~	14.	18.	Supplies as usual. Transport Details 2Lr. 2 G.S. Wagons HEUMAR Aerodrome. 7 2 S.R. OSOD Brigade ? Returned from Leave to the United Kingdom. WEATHER FINE	WKR

Army Form C. 2118.

WAR DIARY
or
INTELLIGENCE SUMMARY.
(Erase heading not required.)

Instructions regarding War Diaries and Intelligence Summaries are contained in F. S. Regs., Part II. and the Staff Manual respectively. Title pages will be prepared in manuscript.

Place	Date	Hour	Summary of Events and Information	Remarks and references to Appendices
HEUMAR. GERMANY.	15.	18	Supplies as usual. Weather Fine.	WFR
—	16	18.	Supplies as usual. Transport Details 2 Ptes 2 G.S. Wagons Heumar Aerodrome Weather Fine.	OFR
—	17	18	Supplies as usual. (Weather Fine)	WFR
ENGELSKIRCHEN.	18.	21.	Supplies as usual. Company Moved from HEUMAR at 12 hours. Arrived at ENGELSKIRCHEN. at 21 hrs. Weather Fine.	WFR
—	19	18	Supplies Refill 13:30 hr. Delivered Rations to Units. Rations Conveyed from HEUMAR Railhead to Refilling Point by (M.T.) (Weather Fine)	OFR
—	20	18	Supplies Refill 14:30 hr. Delivered Rations to Units. Rations Conveyed from HEUMAR Railhead to Refilling Point by (M.T.) (Weather Showery)	WFR

Army Form C. 2118.

WAR DIARY
or
INTELLIGENCE SUMMARY.
(Erase heading not required.)

Instructions regarding War Diaries and Intelligence Summaries are contained in F. S. Regs., Part II. and the Staff Manual respectively. Title pages will be prepared in manuscript.

Place	Date	Hour	Summary of Events and Information	Remarks and references to Appendices
ENGELSKIRCHEN	21	18	Supplies Refill 14:00 hrs. Delivered Rations to Units. Rations Conveyed from HEUMAR Railhead to Refilling Point by (M.T.) (WEATHER FINE)	WAR
"	22	18	Supplies Refill 14:00 hrs. Delivered Rations to Units. Rations Conveyed from HEUMAR Railhead to Refilling Point by (M.T.) Re Hark (No258 Employed) Company Proceeded on leave to the United Kingdom. (WEATHER FINE)	WAR
"	23	18	Supplies Refill 14:00 hrs. Delivered Rations to Units. Rations Conveyed from HEUMAR Railhead to Refilling Point by (M.T.) St. Laurence 10 2/4 Airmen Proceeded on Leave to the United Kingdom. (WEATHER SHOWERY)	WAR
"	24	18	Supplies Refill 13:00 hrs. Delivered Rations to Units. Rations Conveyed from HEUMAR Railhead to Refilling Point by (M.T.) (WEATHER SHOWERY)	WAR

Army Form C. 2118.

WAR DIARY
or
INTELLIGENCE SUMMARY.
(Erase heading not required.)

Instructions regarding War Diaries and Intelligence Summaries are contained in F. S. Regs., Part II. and the Staff Manual respectively. Title pages will be prepared in manuscript.

Place	Date	Hour	Summary of Events and Information	Remarks and references to Appendices
ENGELSKIRCHEN	25	18	Supplies Refill 14.00 hrs + Delivered Rations to Units. Rations conveyed from HEUMAR Railhead to Refilling Point by M.T. - No. 175543 T/S/M York C.H. Returned from leave to the United Kingdom - No. 161677 Pte Joyce attached from 2/3rd Batt Middlesex Regt. proceeded on leave to the United Kingdom - Captain to S. ROBERSON returned from leave U.K. (WEATHER SHOWERY)	WR
"	26	18	Supplies Refill 14.00 hrs + Delivered Rations to Units. Rations conveyed from HEUMAR Railhead to Refilling Point by M.T. (WEATHER SHOWERY) 13/024084 CQMS Johnson to J. Proceeded on leave to the U.K. - Cpl Graff proceeded for Demobilisation	WR
"	27	18	Supplies Refill 14.00 hrs + Delivered Rations to Units. Rations conveyed from HEUMAR Railhead to Refilling Point by M.T. (WEATHER SHOWERY)	WR
"	28	18	Supplies Refill 14.00 hrs + Delivered Rations to Units. Rations conveyed from HEUMAR Railhead to Refilling Point by M.T. (WEATHER SHOWERY)	WR
"	29	18	Supplies Refill 14.00 hrs + Delivered Rations to Units. Rations conveyed from HEUMAR Railhead to Refilling Point by M.T. - Company moved back to HEUMAR to Quarters previously occupied. WEATHER DULL	WR

Army Form C. 2118.

WAR DIARY
or
INTELLIGENCE SUMMARY.
(Erase heading not required.)

Instructions regarding War Diaries and Intelligence Summaries are contained in F. S. Regs., Part II. and the Staff Manual respectively. Title pages will be prepared in manuscript.

Place	Date	Hour	Summary of Events and Information	Remarks and references to Appendices
HEUMAR	30	18.	Supplies as usual from Railhead by M.T. — Weather Windy & Dull.	CKK

JJRogerson Capt.
O.C. No 3 Coy London Dist. Train

Army Form C. 2118.

WAR DIARY
or
INTELLIGENCE SUMMARY.
(Erase heading not required.)

Instructions regarding War Diaries and Intelligence Summaries are contained in F. S. Regs., Part II. and the Staff Manual respectively. Title pages will be prepared in manuscript.

Place	Date	Hour	Summary of Events and Information	Remarks and references to Appendices
HEUMAR COLOGNE	JULY 1st	18	Supplies drawn from Railhead at 9.45. Convoyed to Refilling Point Refill 10.30 hrs & delivered to Units. WEATHER DULL.	WAR
"	2	18	Supplies as usual. WEATHER DULL.	WAR
"	3	18	Supplies as usual. WEATHER DULL.	WAR
"	4	18	Supplies as usual. WEATHER DULL.	WAR
	5	18	Supplies as usual. TS/7618 WHLR S.Sgt. SHUTTLEWORTH. H. T2/014266 Sgt. PATTERSON. TS/8970 Sadd Cpl. LAWSON. J.E. TS/1723 Whl. D. LOCKYER WF Proceeded to England for Demobilization. WEATHER SHOWERY.	WAR
	6	18	Supplies as usual. WEATHER SHOWERY.	WAR
	7	18	Supplies as usual. WEATHER DULL.	WAR
	8	18	Supplies as usual. WEATHER SHOWERY.	WAR
	9	18	Supplies as usual No 105039 Pte RUSSELL. H.R. 81436 Pte. VINTON. W.R. 105344 Pte SARGENT. H Proceeded on Leave to the United Kingdom. WEATHER SHOWERY.	WAR
	10	18	Supplies as usual S9/018023 SSgt LEACH. T.W transferred to M.Coy. WEATHER DULL.	WAR WAR
	11	18	Supplies as usual. WEATHER DULL.	WAR
	12	18	Supplies as usual. WEATHER DULL.	WAR

Army Form C. 2118.

WAR DIARY
or
INTELLIGENCE SUMMARY.

(Erase heading not required.)

Instructions regarding War Diaries and Intelligence Summaries are contained in F. S. Regs., Part II. and the Staff Manual respectively. Title pages will be prepared in manuscript.

Place	Date	Hour	Summary of Events and Information	Remarks and references to Appendices
HEUMAR COLOGNE	13	18	Supplies as usual. 73/024084 C.Q.M.S. JOHNSON W.J. returned from leave to the United Kingdom. WEATHER SHOWERY.	WAR
"	14	18	Supplies as usual. No 133952 Pte NEWBY J. proceeded on leave to the United Kingdom. WEATHER SHOWERY.	WAR
"	15	18	Supplies as usual. WEATHER SHOWERY.	WAR
"	16	18	Supplies as usual. WEATHER DULL.	WAR
"	17	18	Supplies as usual. No T4/065289 Dvr. HOOPER A.H. proceeded on leave to the United Kingdom. WEATHER SHOWERY.	WAR
"	18	18	Supplies as usual. 21539 Pte. GRUBB, F.C. proceeded on leave to the United Kingdom. WEATHER SHOWERY.	WAR
"	19	18	Supplies as usual. WEATHER DULL.	WAR
"	20	18	Supplies as usual. T3/SR.01005 C.S.M. WIGSTON, T. posted for duty to 139 F.A. WEATHER SHOWERY.	WAR
"	21	18	Supplies as usual. WEATHER DULL.	WAR
"	22	18	Supplies as usual. Lt. B.C. Russell proceeded on leave to the United Kingdom. WEATHER SHOWERY.	WAR
"	23	18	Supplies as usual. WEATHER SHOWERY.	WAR

Army Form C. 2118.

WAR DIARY
or
INTELLIGENCE SUMMARY.
(Erase heading not required.)

Place	Date	Hour	Summary of Events and Information	Remarks and references to Appendices
HEUMAR COLOGNE	24	18	Supplies as usual No. T/23354 S/SSM. ANKCORN. A.E. & T/026995. SGT. HAGGARD W.H. Having proceeded for Demobilization on the 21st not on strength from this date. WEATHER. DULL.	WBR
"	25	18	Supplies as usual. WEATHER DULL	WBR
"	26	18	Supplies as usual No. 105059 Pte RUSSELL H.R. 81236 Pte VINTON W.R. T/105247 Pte SARGENT. A. Returned from leave to the United Kingdom. WEATHER DULL	WBR
"	27	18	Supplies as usual. WEATHER SHOWERY.	WBR
"	28	18	Supplies as usual. WEATHER SHOWERY.	WBR
"	29	18	Supplies as usual. WEATHER DULL.	WBR
"	30	18	Supplies as usual No. 201576 Pte CASSIDY. J. Proceeded on leave to the United Kingdom. WEATHER DULL	WBR
"	31	18	Supplies as usual No. 133952 Pte NEWBY. J. Returned from leave to the United Kingdom. Horses Reclassified by Board of Officers at 15th MTRs. WEATHER FINE	WBR

W.R.R.Watson. Captain
O.C. No 3 Coy London Divisional Train

Army Form C. 2118.

WAR DIARY
or
INTELLIGENCE SUMMARY.
(Erase heading not required)

Instructions regarding War Diaries and Intelligence Summaries are contained in F. S. Regs., Part II. and the Staff Manual respectively. Title pages will be prepared in manuscript.

Place	Date	Hour	Summary of Events and Information	Remarks and references to Appendices
HEUMAR COLOGNE	Aug 1 10th 18		Supplies drawn from Railhead at 9.45 am Convoyed to Repking Point. Left 10.30 am Delivered to Units. The following having been transferred from their respective Units are taken on W.T. 16 Units. Company strength to 133952 Head N°7.453464 R° newly from N°238 Employment Company to 20167 Head 7/453465 Pte McDonnell E. from N°238 Employment Coy. to 80099 Head 7/453466 Pte Johnson G. from 23. Batt R. Fusiliers. Rgt Co. 105059 Reed 7/453464 Pte Russell W.R. 23 Middlesex Rgt.	
			G. 105118 Reed 7/453468 Pte Ashby W.S. from 23 Middlesex Rgt to 105247 Reed 7/453469 Pte Sargent S.E. 23 Middlesex Rgt.	
			G. 105339 " 7/453470 " Massino H. " " 54600 " 7/453471 " Kealey W. " "	
			— 61677 " 7/453462 " Fryer W.H.C " " 34546 " 7/453508 " Osbourne F. " Queens R.W. Surrey Rgt	
			72574 " 7/453472 " Lawrence W.G. " 2/4th Queens Rw Sry 42596 " 7/453473 " Waters S.H. " 2/4 Queens RW Surry Rgt	
			85244 " 7/453483 " Bennett W.P. " " 70331 " 7/453484 " Randall R.C " "	
			85765 " 7/453485 " Taylor G. " " 72546 " 7/453486 " Thorne E. " "	
			84996 " 7/453506 Pte Winding J. " " 70350 " 7/453509 " Waite J. " "	
			6060 " 7/453510 Pte Simpson G.R " " 85580 " 7/453511 " Gray J. " "	
			85424 " 7/453512 " Tabram E. " " 85597 " 7/453513 " Doddy " " "	
			83315 " 7/453475 Q Penfold 5-10" 82477 " 7/453498 " Lemman J. 5-10"	
			82243 " 7/453480 " Warner J.P " 83039 " 7/453499 " Collard R.L " "	
			83657 " 7/453489 " Turner J.R.O. " 82242 " 7/453481 " Harris " "	
			82982 " 7/453489 " Surry G.A " 83222 " 7/453488 " Smith Q " "	
			685764 " 7/453500 " Brotherhood P " 30784 " 7/453490 " Miles W.H.G " "	
			82205 " 7/453502 " Church G. " 83289 " 7/453501 " Cadey A " "	
			83294 " 7/453504 " Hyatt J " " 83079 " 7/453505 " Naylor W. " "	
			81860 " 7/453476 " Petrie E. 6-11" 68914 " 7/453475 " Bird J 5-9 1/2"	
			25139 " 7/453492 " Smith J " " 81846 " 7/453491 " Sandberg G.O. 5-11"	
			84044 " 7/453496 " Hill R.G. " " 83810 " 7/453493 " Goodall W.J " "	
			84367 " 7/453496 " Lewis W.F " " 84059 " 7/453495 " Goodall W.J " "	
			25446 " 7/453498 " South W. J " " 81926 " 7/453494 " Phelan S " "	
			84077 " 7/453503 " McFadden J " " 81436 " 7/453499 " Vinton W " "	
				21424 " 7/453504 " Butcher B " "	

WEATHER DULL

Army Form C. 2118.

WAR DIARY
or
INTELLIGENCE SUMMARY.
(Erase heading not required.)

Instructions regarding War Diaries and Intelligence Summaries are contained in F. S. Regs., Part II. and the Staff Manual respectively. Title pages will be prepared in manuscript.

Place	Date	Hour	Summary of Events and Information	Remarks and references to Appendices
HEUMAR COLOGNE	Augt 2	18	Supplies as usual. No T/4/083289 O. Hooper, A.H. Returned from Leave to the United Kingdom. WEATHER Showery.	BCR
-	3	18	Supplies as usual. No. 105534 Pte Yabsley. E.T/453468 D. Ashby. & S. C/105369 Pte Starling A.J. Proceeded on Leave to the United Kingdom. D. Smith Returned from Leave to U.K. WEATHER FINE	BCR
-	4	18	Supplies as usual. N° T/4053492 D. Smith N.H. Proceeded for Duty to HQ 2nd and 2 H. Bn. WEATHER DULL	BCR
-	5	18	Supplies as usual. Lieut. B.C. Russell returned from Leave to the United Kingdom. WEATHER FROZE FINE	BCR
-	6	18	Supplies as usual. N° T/453488 D. Smith, S. Admitted to 140. Field Amb. WEATHER FINE	BCR
-	7	18	Supplies as usual. N° T/185528 Cpl Munro W.J. T/486501 Cpl Moore E.& T/3884809 D. Churchward. T. Proceeded on Leave to the U.K. WEATHER DULL	BCR
-	8	18	Supplies as usual. T/386757 D. Hardesty Jn. T/144646 D. Sharp. H.C. Proceeded on Leave to the U.K. T/453470 D. Meacons Returned from Leave to U.K. WEATHER FINE	BCR

Army Form C. 2118.

WAR DIARY
or
INTELLIGENCE SUMMARY.
(Erase heading not required.)

Instructions regarding War Diaries and Intelligence Summaries are contained in F. S. Regs., Part II. and the Staff Manual respectively. Title pages will be prepared in manuscript.

Place	Date	Hour	Summary of Events and Information	Remarks and references to Appendices
HEUMAR. COLOGNE	9th	18	Supplies as usual. No 7/260073 L/Cpl Pocock MW. T/453 489 Dr Leavy LSV T/364471 Dr Lukyn L. Proceeded on leave to the U.K. WEATHER FINE	BCR
"	10	18	Supplies as usual. No 7/463503 Dr McFadden Yr T/453 501 Dr Carle Q. M/57251 Pte Harvey S S/23 YU Pte Vine JCO Proceeded on leave to the United Kingdom. WEATHER FINE	BCR
"	11	18	Supplies as usual. Sergt WR Robinson MC having proceeded to England for demobilization this day is struck off the Corps strength. WEATHER FINE	BCR
"	12	18	Supplies as usual. T/453 447 Dr Killythorne T/453 502 Dr Church Proceeded on leave to the U.K. Lieut G.S. Shepherd Returned from Leave. WEATHER FINE	BCR
"	13	18	Supplies as usual. T/453 498 Dr Lammin Proceeded on Leave to the United Kingdom. WEATHER FINE	BCR
"	14	18	Supplies as usual. M/8/453,503 Pte Mayhoe W. Proceeded on Leave to the United Kingdom. WEATHER FINE	BCR
"	15	18	Supplies as usual. No T/453 487 Dr Turner R6. Proceeded on Leave to the United Kingdom. WEATHER FINE	BCR
"	16	18	Supplies as usual No T/453 481 Dr Harmer HJ. Proceeded on Leave to the United Kingdom. WEATHER FINE	BCR

Army Form C. 2118.

WAR DIARY
or
INTELLIGENCE SUMMARY.
(Erase heading not required.)

Place	Date	Hour	Summary of Events and Information	Remarks and references to Appendices
HEIJMAR	17	18	Supplies as usual. N° 735R0406. Coml Wegola transferred to N°4 Coy London R/t with effect from 16.15 inst. N°T/453510 Dr Simpson C&R having proceeded to Esplanade Demobilization on 4th 15th inst on struck of the Strgth of that Det. N°T/453480 Pt Norman proceeded on Leave to the U.K. N°201676 Pte Bradshaff M338 Employment Coy Returned from Leave to the United Kingdom. (WEATHER FINE)	BCR
—	18	18	Supplies as usual. N°T/453494 Dr Ranfold J Proceeded on Leave to the United Kingdom. WEATHER FINE.	BCR
—	19	18	Supplies as usual. N°T/453498 Dr South W Proceeded on Leave to the United Kingdom. N°T/453468 Dr Ashly MT T/453381 D Starling + N°105534 Pte Galaghy Returned from Leave to the United Kingdom. (WEATHER FINE.)	BCR
—	20	18	Supplies as usual. Pte Rogers Returned to N°1 Coy. WEATHER FINE	BCR
—	21	18	Supplies as usual. 105307 Pte Middlewood Returned from Leave to the U.K. Dr Winston attached from N°1 Coy. WEATHER FINE	BCR
—	22	18	Supplies as usual. T/453479 Dr Collard A.R. Proceeded on Leave to the U.K. N°T/453494 Dr Hill BS. Proceeded on Leave to the U.K. WEATHER FINE.	BCR

Army Form C. 2118.

WAR DIARY
or
INTELLIGENCE SUMMARY.
(Erase heading not required.)

Instructions regarding War Diaries and Intelligence Summaries are contained in F. S. Regs., Part II. and the Staff Manual respectively. Title pages will be prepared in manuscript.

Place	Date	Hour	Summary of Events and Information	Remarks and references to Appendices
HELMAR	23	18	Supplies as usual. No 7/453495 Pte Knowles J. Proceeded on Leave to the UK.	BCR
	24	18	Supplies as usual. 7/453466 Pte McDonnell B returned from Leave to the UK. WEATHER FINE	BCR
			No 7/165325 Cpl Munro W. 7/165501 Lan Cpl Moore. 7/384809. Dr Churchward T. 7/384751 Dr Hardy J. 7/414646 Dr Sharp J. returned from leave to the UK. WEATHER FINE	
	25	18	Supplies as usual. No 7/260093 La Cpl Moore returned from Leave to the UK. No 7/289981 Pte Bryant. Proceeded on Leave to the UK No 158635 Pte Yeoman. E. returned from Leave to the UK WEATHER FINE	BCR
	26		Supplies as usual No 1271344 Pte Venn J.Cl. 1151251 Pte Harvey G.A. No 7453501 Pte Cade A. 7/364491 Dr Lukyn L. 7/453503 Dr little Saxton F. N7/453489 Dr Surry. returned from Leave to the UK. WEATHER FINE	BCR
	27		Supplies as usual No 7/293505 Pte Bramm. E. Proceeded on Leave to the UK. Lieut R.J. Hicks Proceeded on Leave to the UK. WEATHER FINE	BCR

Army Form C. 2118.

WAR DIARY
or
INTELLIGENCE SUMMARY.

(Erase heading not required.)

Instructions regarding War Diaries and Intelligence Summaries are contained in F. S. Regs., Part II. and the Staff Manual respectively. Title pages will be prepared in manuscript.

Place	Date	Hour	Summary of Events and Information	Remarks and references to Appendices
HEUMAR	28	18	Supplies as usual. N° T/453502 Dr Church C	BCR
	29	18	Supplies as usual N° T/4/05 & N° Bolzell A. T/453340 & Luck Bd WT/453488 Dr Smith GP Admitted to 140 Field Ambulance	BCR
	30	18	Supplies as usual. WEATHER FINE	BCR
	31	18	Supplies as usual WEATHER FINE	BCR

OCwell
Lieut.
OC N° 3 Coy London Div¹ Train

WAR DIARY

INTELLIGENCE SUMMARY

Army Form C. 2118.

Place	Date	Hour	Summary of Events and Information	Remarks and references to Appendices
SIEGBURG	SEPT 1st	18.	Company moved from HEUMAR at 9am & arrived at SIEGBURG at 1.15pm. Supplies Refill 2.15pm. & Delived to Units. Dr Turner P.T.O. Harmer & Haynes Returned from Leave to the United Kingdom	BCR BCR
—	2	18	Supplies Refill 1pm & Delivered to Units. WEATHER FINE	BCR
—	3	18	Supplies as usual. N⁰ 7/M 53496 Dr Douglas Returned from Leave to the United Kingdom. WEATHER FINE	BCR
—	4	18	Supplies as usual. N⁰ T/4 53498 Dr Scott W. T/45-3498 Dr Lamonin Returned from Leave to the United Kingdom. N⁰ T/05 4413 Dr Lovell T/4 53488 Dr Smith S.R.V/457340 Dr Knox G.D. Returned to Duty from Hospital. WEATHER FINE	BCR
—	5	18	Supplies as usual. Pte. Wesley J.R. Fowler, Scott, Wallis Proceed to No 238 Employment Coy for Demobilization. WEATHER FINE	BCR

Army Form C. 2118.

WAR DIARY

INTELLIGENCE SUMMARY.

(Erase heading not required.)

Instructions regarding War Diaries and Intelligence Summaries are contained in F. S. Regs., Part II. and the Staff Manual respectively. Title pages will be prepared in manuscript.

Place	Date	Hour	Summary of Events and Information	Remarks and references to Appendices
SIEGBURG	6	18	Supplies as usual. No 7/4534/79 Pte Collard A.R. returned from leave to the U.K. No 83995 Pte Cole A.M. Returned from leave to the U.K. WEATHER FINE	B.O.R
"	7	18	Supplies as usual. No 7/4534/94 Pte Hill W.S. Returned from leave to the U.K. WEATHER FINE	B.O.R
"	8	19	Supplies as usual. No 7/364682 Pte Jewell A. Proceeded on leave to the U.K. WEATHER FINE	B.O.R
"	9	18	Supplies as usual. No 7/4534/86 Pte Vears Proceeded on leave to the U.K. WEATHER FINE	B.O.R
"	10	18	Supplies as usual. No 7/4534/94 Pte Pearford 97/4534/97 Pte Rhodes S. 7/453488 Pte Smart B. 7/453485 Pte Taylor Pte. Transferred to No 2 Coy on No 7/453482 Pte Bennett W.C.7/453509 Pte Bryant. 97/453494 Pte Hill W.S. 7/453469 Pte Sangon A.D. Transferred to No 1 Coy on the 9th Inst. WEATHER FINE	B.O.R

Army Form C. 2118.

WAR DIARY

INTELLIGENCE SUMMARY

(Erase heading not required.)

Instructions regarding War Diaries and Intelligence Summaries are contained in F. S. Regs., Part II. and the Staff Manual respectively. Title pages will be prepared in manuscript.

Place	Date	Hour	Summary of Events and Information	Remarks and references to Appendices
SIEGBURG	11	18	Supplies as usual. No 7/4 6349 5 Pr Knowles G returned from leave to the U.K. on the 9th inst. 7/289981 Pte Bryant H. returned from leave to the U.K. WEATHER FINE	BCR
"	12	18	Supplies as usual. 7/453478 Pr Laverwin L. admitted to Rhine Army field Punishment Compound undergoing 14 days F.P. N° 2. WEATHER FINE	BCR
"	13	18	Supplies as usual. No 7/293565 Pr Brannon E. returned from leave to the U.K. No 7/453496 Pr Fearis W.H. Returned from leave to the U.K. WEATHER FINE	BCR
"	14	18	Supplies as usual. No 7/453477 Pr Kellythorne returned from leave from the U.K. WEATHER FINE	BCR
"	15	18	Supplies as usual. No 7/269985 Pr Hill C.D. admitted to X Rays ward. WEATHER FINE	BCR

WAR DIARY

INTELLIGENCE SUMMARY
(Erase heading not required.)

Army Form C. 2118.

Instructions regarding War Diaries and Intelligence Summaries are contained in F. S. Regs., Part II. and the Staff Manual respectively. Title pages will be prepared in manuscript.

Place	Date	Hour	Summary of Events and Information	Remarks and references to Appendices
SIEGBURG	16	18	Supplies as usual. No 7/1034401 A/Cpl O'Callahan W.T 7/4/33509 Pt Watts Y. Reverted to No 4 Y. Coy on Home Leave. Lieut R.G. Hair returned from leave to the United Kingdom. WEATHER. FINE	BCR
"	17	18	Supplies as usual. WEATHER. FINE	BCR
"	18	18	Supplies as usual. 7/4/21194 Sgt Denny DCM Joined Coy from No 4 Coy. WEATHER. FINE	BCR
"	19	18	Supplies as usual. WEATHER. DULL	BCR
"	20	18	Supplies as usual. 7/4/33509 Pt Watts Y returned from 4 Bn? Leave. WEATHER. DULL	BCR
"	21	18	Supplies as usual. WEATHER. DULL/COLD	BCR

Army Form C. 2118.

WAR DIARY
or
INTELLIGENCE SUMMARY.

(Erase heading not required.)

Instructions regarding War Diaries and Intelligence Summaries are contained in F. S. Regs., Part II. and the Staff Manual respectively. Title pages will be prepared in manuscript.

Place	Date	Hour	Summary of Events and Information	Remarks and references to Appendices
SIEGSBURG	22	18	Supplies as usual. 7/453496 Pte Kerr with proceeded for duty to H.Q. 2 London Inf. Bde. 7/45349 Pte Pocock N.H. returned from H.Q. 2 London Inf. Bde.	BCR
"	23	18	Supplies as usual. 7/260985 Pte McCabe returned from 26 C.C.S. WEATHER DULL	BCR
"	24	18	Supplies as usual. No 7/2117354 Sgt Darby R.M. proceeded on leave to U.K. from Kulonuen to 6 Bn 6 P.S. reported to 2/L? Leconie Regt to convey stores to SIEGBURG. WEATHER DULL	BCR
	25	18	Supplies as usual. No 7/266073 A/L Cpl Pocock usd. Pte Waarong G. 7/453472 Pt Laurence G. proceeded 76 No.UK. for demobilisation WEATHER DULL	BCR
	26	18	Supplies as usual. 11° 7/453486 Pt Morre C. returned then leave to the U.K. 5/355373 Pte Waarong G. 7/453472 Pt Laurence W.G. returned from Camp owing to Railway Strike in ENGLAND WEATHER DULL	BCR
	27	18	Supplies as usual 7/266073 A/L Cpl Pocock usd. 74/232210 Sergeant W.	BCR
	28	18	Supplies as usual	WEATHER SHOWERY BCR

Army Form C. 2118.

WAR DIARY
INTELLIGENCE SUMMARY.
(Erase heading not required.)

Instructions regarding War Diaries and Intelligence Summaries are contained in F. S. Regs., Part II. and the Staff Manual respectively. Title pages will be prepared in manuscript.

Place	Date	Hour	Summary of Events and Information	Remarks and references to Appendices
SIEGBURG	29	18	Supplies on hand	BCR
	30	18	Supplies on hand	BCR

W.C. Russell Lieut.
O.C. No. 3. Coy.
London Div: Train

Army Form C. 2118.

WAR DIARY
or
INTELLIGENCE SUMMARY.
(Erase heading not required.)

Instructions regarding War Diaries and Intelligence Summaries are contained in F. S. Regs., Part II. and the Staff Manual respectively. Title pages will be prepared in manuscript.

Place	Date	Hour	Summary of Events and Information	Remarks and references to Appendices
SIEGBURG	Oct 1st	18	Supplies drawn from HEUMAR Railhead & Convoyed to Refilling Point at SIEGBURG by (M.T.) Refill 11 Joram. Delivered to Units by Horse transport. 76/7744.53466 Dvr Johnson G. returned to duty from 4th Ent. Hosp.	BCR
	2nd	18	Supplies as usual	BCR
	3rd	18	Supplies as usual	BCR
	4th	18	Supplies as usual WEATHER DULL	BCR
	5th	18	Supplies as usual WEATHER FINE	BCR
	6th	18	Supplies as usual WEATHER DULL	BCR
	7th	18	Supplies as usual WEATHER FINE	BCR
	8th	18	Supplies as usual WEATHER DULL COLD	BCR

WEATHER SHOWERY.
WEATHER FINE
WEATHER FINE

Army Form C. 2118.

WAR DIARY

INTELLIGENCE SUMMARY

(Erase heading not required.)

Instructions regarding War Diaries and Intelligence Summaries are contained in F. S. Regs., Part II. and the Staff Manual respectively. Title pages will be prepared in manuscript.

Place	Date	Hour	Summary of Events and Information	Remarks and references to Appendices
SIEGBURG	9	18	Supplies as usual	WEATHER FINE BCR
"	10	18	Supplies as usual	WEATHER DULL BCR
"	11	18	Supplies as usual. 40/726043 A/Cpl Power A.W. T728210 Pte Cooper C.A. T/355 5/3 Pte Mooring G. proceeded to England for Demobilization. T/453513 Pte Woodly admitted to 29 C.C.S. 84108 Pte Sammells J.E. Reported to Coy.	BCR BCR BCR BCR
"	12	18	Supplies as usual	WEATHER FINE BCR
"	13	18	Supplies as usual	WEATHER SHOWERY BCR
"	14	18	Supplies as usual T/201506 A/Cpl Bassey J. rejoined T/288 Employees T/453491 Pte Loading C.W. T/453472 Pte Bavercy W.G. proceeded to England for Demobilization BCR. Lieut G.G. Stephens R.A.S.C. proceeded on leave to the United Kingdom. Lieut. J.B. Cranfield R.A.S.C. joined Coy. from 51 Q London Divisional Train 16/07/45/323 Sergt. A/C/Sgt 601 Coy R.A.S.C. admitted to 91 Field Amb.	BCR BCR BCR WEATHER FINE

WAR DIARY

INTELLIGENCE SUMMARY

Army Form C. 2118.

(Erase heading not required.)

Instructions regarding War Diaries and Intelligence Summaries are contained in F. S. Regs., Part II. and the Staff Manual respectively. Title pages will be prepared in manuscript.

Place	Date	Hour	Summary of Events and Information	Remarks and references to Appendices
SIEGBURG	15.	18	Supplies as usual. 76/4593/40 Dr. Beck E.D. proceeded on leave to the U.K. 76/746103 Gr. Rowland A.C. 76/745350 & Gr. Busher C. Proceeded to England for Demobilization	BOR
"	16	18	WEATHER SHOWERY. Supplies as usual 76/3454488 Pte Coombes J.A. proceeded on leave to the United Kingdom. 13 Horses Classified (E) admitted to the Vet Hospital Cologne	BOR
"	17	18	WEATHER SHOWERY & Cold. Supplies as usual 76/345305 Pte Waylor J. admitted to 4 Y War troops 76/405 6413 Dr Lovell A. proceeded on Leave to United Kingdom	BOR
"	18	18	WEATHER SHOWERY. Supplies as usual 76/345 7489 Pte Meuse R.W. proceeded on Leave to the United Kingdom 76/745 3513 Gr Boddy W. returned to duty from 2.9. C.C.S. 76/34087 Pte Balday B. 23 Middlesex Regt returned to duty from Convalescent Camp	BOR

WEATHER SHOWERY.

WAR DIARY

INTELLIGENCE SUMMARY

Army Form C. 2118.

(Erase heading not required.)

Place	Date	Hour	Summary of Events and Information	Remarks and references to Appendices
SIEGBURG	19	18	Supplies as usual 4/049332 Pte Walker J. rejoined 4/7238 Employment Coy	BCR
"	20	18	Supplies as usual. T/05/45/4484 Pte Taylor S.E. proceeded on leave to the United Kingdom	BCR
"	21	18	Supplies as usual T/6Th 53486 Pte Horne admitted to the 47 General Hospital. No. T/238.238 Q.M.S. Sgt. Johnson returned from leave to the United Kingdom	BCR
"	22	18	Supplies as usual EN/4 53477 Pte Feverstone returned from 47 Gen.	BCR
"	23	18	Supplies as usual EN/49332 Pte Walker J. Returned to 238 Employment Coy for Demobilization	BCR

WEATHER FINE
WEATHER FINE
WEATHER FINE
WEATHER DULL
WEATHER DULL

WAR DIARY
INTELLIGENCE SUMMARY

Army Form C. 2118.

Place	Date	Hour	Summary of Events and Information	Remarks and references to Appendices
SIEGBURG	24	18	Supplies as usual. WEATHER FINE	BOR
"	25	18	Supplies as usual. WEATHER FINE	BOR
"	26	18	Supplies as usual. 7453464 L/Cpl Newby J.S. 7493565 Pte Brammer F. Proceeded to England for Demobilization. 7453512 Pte Tatum Proceeded on Leave to the United Kingdom	BOR
"	27	18	Supplies as usual. 7453475 Pte Bird H.J. 7384809 Pte 7453492 Pte Grub A. 7390520 Pte Hornday J. 7386751 Pte Handley J.W. 760985 A/Cpl A.D. 7453660 Pte Jemson G. S/453465 Pte a/c Bonnell C. S/307256 Pte Jefferey J. 7453490 Pte McIlles W.H.S. 7364682 Pte Newell P. 7453508 Pte 7453471 Pte Peaby P. 7453498 Pte Smith H. 7462754 Pte Peace R. Proceeded to Eng for Demobilization. WEATHER SHOWERY. WEATHER SHOWERY	BOR

WAR DIARY
or
INTELLIGENCE SUMMARY.
(Erase heading not required.)

Army Form C. 2118.

Place	Date	Hour	Summary of Events and Information	Remarks and references to Appendices
SIEGBURG	28th	18	Supplies as usual. The following were transferred from N° 299 Coy R.A.S.C. on date as stated T/454.052 Dr Longrish. Cpl T/254/04/05 CSM Wright. Dr T/060 408 Cpl Swann. W. T/454.90 Cpl Piatt. W/46 T/454 041 Dr Evans. P. T/454.046 Dr Cooper R.E. T/453.417 Dr Bewick N. T/453.4211 Dr Sada. Lcp. 10 T/453.432 Dr Downey. J.B. T/453.110 Dr Manley. H. T/382.592 Dr Maple. A.B. T/454. 0898 Smith. Ls T/454.060 Dr Waltonen. J. T/454.044 Dr Wilkinson. Jas T/426.3.924 Dr Brown. AW T/454.344 Dr Clark.J S/2/010.023 S/Sgt Lack. J.W. S/4254.049 Dte Hughes. R.S. S/453.448 Pte Floyd. El S/457.486 Pte Mead. LRJ S/454.038 Pte Barker. H. on the 26 inst. The following proceeded for Demobilization S/453.448 Pte Floyd. S/457.486 Pte Mead. LRJ. (WEATHER COLD)	B.C.R
"	29th	18	Supplies as usual. The following R.A.S.C. Personnel on Command 139" Fld Amb were transferred to the 146th Fld Amb on the 23 inst. T/459.302 Dr Crippa. S. T/457.303 Dr Osborne. E. T/457.304 Dr Handera. W. T/457.305 Dr Clynes. C. T/457.306 Dr Walton. L. T/457.307 Dr Brooks. J. T/457.308 Dr Samplin. L.C. T/457.309 Dr Hopto. W/S T/457.310 Dr French. E. T/457.311 Dr Bacon. W. T/457.316 Dr Constable. W/S T/457.313 Dr Draper. J. W. T/453.513 Dr Wordly. AW. Proceed on Leave to the United Kingdom. (WEATHER COLD)	B.C.R
"	30.	18	Supplies as usual. Capt Logan Bell R.A.S.C. transferred from T/84 Coy & assumes command as from the 24 inst. T/057.496 CSM Kelly N.S. 139 Fld Amb transferred to N° 2 Coy Train. N° T/9.044 654 CSM Mulcahy. H. transferred from N°2 Coy Train. The following are transferred from N° 236 Employment Coy S/44.835 Pte Proctor. J. L. + 236/052 Pte Wilson J. (WEATHER COLD)	A.B

Army Form C. 2118.

WAR DIARY
or
INTELLIGENCE SUMMARY.
(Erase heading not required.)

Instructions regarding War Diaries and Intelligence Summaries are contained in F. S. Regs., Part II. and the Staff Manual respectively. Title pages will be prepared in manuscript.

Place	Date	Hour	Summary of Events and Information	Remarks and references to Appendices
SIEGBURG.	31	18.	Supplies as usual. Lieut. E.S. Stephen returned from leave to the United Kingdom. (WEATHER FINLY COLD)	6/11/18

J. van Bell Captain
OC N°3 Coy London Divisional Train

www.ingramcontent.com/pod-product-compliance
Lightning Source LLC
Chambersburg PA
CBHW082008220426
43670CB00014B/2580